# *"Our passport to Kauai!"* – LB, Durango, CO

**San Francisco Chronicle:**
"An incredible source of information about . . . what tourist traps to avoid and where to find the best values."

**Los Angeles Times:**
". . . filled with information on beaches, restaurants and things to do and see. Lenore Horowitz's love for Kauai comes through in her writing."

**Vancouver Courier:**
"A little gem of a book that each and every traveler should have in hand."

**Travel-Age West:**
"A downhome commentary on the best beaches, restaurants, and activities..."

"...It's like having our own tour guide!"– JH, Hartford, CT

"The best investment I made!"
– GM, Freeport, TX

**Los Angeles Times:**
"Our vacation became an adventure the day we discovered the *Kauai Underground Guide!*"

**Seattle Post Intelligencer:**
"I can't imagine riding around the island without this book resting on the dash of my rental car."

**San Francisco Chronicle:**
"Our constant companion! This book opened our eyes to delights we would otherwise have missed."

"A fabulous book! We saw places we've ignored because we didn't know they existed."
– EW, Milwaukie, OR

"I found beautiful beaches that showed me what Hawaii was like years ago."– DC, Coos Bay, OR

"You've been our valued companion, through your book, on all our trips since 1988."
– TM, El Cerito, CA

'the bible!' — *Travel & Leisure*

'Everything you need to know' — *Hawaii Magazine*

'Distinctive, thorough, & helpful!'
— Jeff Phillips, Senior Travel Writer, *Sunset Magazine*

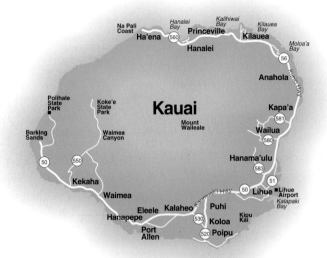

Na Pali Coast
Hanalei Bay
Kalihiwai Bay
Kilauea Bay

Ha'ena
Princeville
Kilauea

560
Hanalei
Moloa'a Bay

56
Anahola

Kamo Hwy

Polihale State Park
Koke'e State Park
**Kauai**
Kapa'a

581

Mount Waialeale
Wailua

580
Barking Sands
Waimea Canyon
Hanama'ulu

583

50
550
Lihue
Lihue Airport

51
Kalapaki Bay

Kekaha
Kaumualii Hwy
50
Lihue

Waimea
Puhi
Kipu Kai

Eleele
Kalaheo

Hanapepe
530
Koloa

Port Allen
520
Poipu

Ni'ihau
**Kauai**

**Oahu**
**Molokai**

Lanai
**Maui**

Kahoolawe

**Hawaii**

# Kauai Underground Guide

*Lenore W. Horowitz*

*16th Edition*

*Papaloa Press*

| First edition: | 1980 |
| Second edition: | 1981 |
| Third Edition: | 1982 |
| Fourth edition: | 1983 |
| Fifth edition: | 1984 |
| Sixth edition: | 1985 |
| Seventh edition: | 1986 |
| Eighth edition: | 1987 |
| Ninth edition: | 1988 |
| Tenth edition: | 1989 |
| Eleventh edition: | 1990 |
| Twelfth edition: | 1992 |
| Thirteenth edition: | 1995 |
| Fourteenth edition: | 1996 |
| 2nd printing | 1997 |
| Fifteenth edition: | 1998 |
| Sixteenth edition | 2000 |

ISBN 0-9615498-9-0
ISSN 1045-1358
Library of Congress Catalog card 82-643643

Original Line Drawings by Pat Bergeron
& Lauren, Mirah, Jeremy & Mike Horowitz, Devon Davey & Tara French
Historic Petroglyph Drawings by Likeke R. McBride
Petroglyph art by Lauren Horowitz
Photographs by Lenore W. Horowitz

*Special thanks to Mirah, Jeremy, Mike, Lauren,
& Larry Horowitz
for their invaluable help with the research, writing,
illustration, and design of this sixteenth edition
& mahalo nui loa to
Keali'i & Fred
& special thanks to David Kendall, Erv Klein, & Marvis*

# Contents

## Planning Ahead

## Beach Adventures

## Activities & Discoveries

## Adventures

## Restaurants

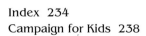

# Preface

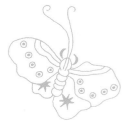

Kauai at the millennium is a very different island than the one we wrote about in our first edition of the *Kauai Underground Guide* in 1980, when sixteen typewritten pages were enough to give advice on what to do and see. Today, you can still enjoy the Hanama'ulu Tea House, Barbecue Inn, Hanalei Dolphin, Kountry Kitchen, Bull Shed, Beach House—but the island has also changed dramatically. And so has our Guide, growing to 240 pages, turning into many colors, spanning the desktop revolution in computer technology, and moving onto the internet!

To celebrate this millennium milestone, we've arranged for a special Hawaiian Music CD Sampler featuring songs by Keali'i Reichel, whose first album *Kawaipunahele* took the music world by storm in 1994 and is now the bestselling album of Hawaiian music —of all time! Keali'i joins us in doing something special for Kauai. We've created the *Kauai Underground Guide 'Campaign for Kids'* to raise money from our book sales and to encourage additional donations from our 'community partners,' to help non-profit agencies benefiting Kauai's children—for health and welfare, literacy and the arts (p. 238).

We've been writing *The Kauai Underground Guide* for more than twenty years and through two hurricanes, stopping the presses in 1982 to cover Hurricane 'Iwa, and chronicling the recovery from Hurricane Iniki ten years later. Today, Kauai faces even more profound changes, with the end of sugar as a main support of the island's economy. The closing of the MacBryde sugar company and cutbacks in Grove Farm, Lihue Plantation, and other sugar companies signal an end to an important phase in the island's history. New uses for the island's fertile land mean changes in its economy and appearance: fields of sugar cane are disappearing, replaced by fields of coffee and macadamia nuts, even housing developments. Kauai is in transition, as the new millennium begins.

This is the Kauai we will try to describe to you in our *Guide* —not what you would see from a tour bus, but the rare and special place we have discovered during more than twenty years as vacationers and homeowners. We want to share with you our favorite adventures —at the beaches, in restaurants, on tours and expeditions. We do not describe every restaurant and shop, only those we have visited, and our opinions are shaped by our preference for peace and quiet, privacy and natural beauty.

In many ways our *Guide* is unique. As a family of six, we can offer advice on beaches and activities based on having taken children to Kauai at all ages! For adults with that enviable freedom to go off by themselves, we describe in detail what one can expect to find in many island restaurants. Even a single year brings dramatic change to this island, and our working vacations keep us busy tracking what's new, what's different, and what's still as lovely as ever. You may find that in some cases prices, policies, even managements may be changed, so do your research carefully when making decisions and keep us posted about what you find out! It's been great fun hearing from people all over the country who have explored Kauai with our *Guide,* and want to help update the next one.

So as we go to press with this 16th edition, we want to thank all the readers who have helped make our *Guide* a storybook success. Who would have thought that our first edition would grow into a book which has sold more than 150,000 copies! Or that our oldest child, Mirah, would arrange such a spectacular send-off by handing our first edition to a friend she made on the beach. He turned out to be Chandler Forman of the *Chicago Sun-Times*, and when his story about Kauai—and our book— was syndicated nationwide, more than 700 letters arrived at our door, and we had to rush to press with a new edition!

When she arranged this PR spectacular, Mirah was a gregarious six-year-old with two baby brothers. Today, we have only one teenager left in our family, 16 year-old Lauren, and Mirah at 24 has become an attorney. Our boys are changing too, their love for sandcrabs and rainbow shells giving way to a passion for surf. When they were small, we hoped one day to escape from all their clutter. Today, toy cars and crayons are off the floor at last, but now our kids each bring friends, and each of the friends is bigger! We seem to be spending quite a bit of time at the airport picking up arriving friends or sending suntanned friends back home!

Watching our children change so dramatically over twenty years helps put the development of Kauai in perspective. With children and with islands, change brings the excitement of new opportunities and at the same time the loss of what was precious. The roads we travel today are certainly more congested, but our destinations seem far more interesting. Once perfect for our family with small children, Kauai is also perfect for a family with young adults, with definite and sometimes contradictory interests. And as we explore their newest horizons, we see this wonderful island unfold in fascinating new possibilities.

Like an old friend, Kauai gets better with each visit. New adventures take us to new places, and at the same time we rediscover with deeper affection what we have loved in the past. We hope you will feel the same way about this special place and return again soon!

*www.explorekauai.com*

*Lumahai Beach on the spectacular north shore*

# Exploring Kauai

Kauai is like an America in miniature, with rolling hills and valleys to the east and majestic mountains to the west. On the eastern shore, sand as fine as sugar rings half-moon bays fringed with stately ironwood trees. These are the best beaches for walking and hunting for shells and drift-wood. On the south shore, the island's flat, leeward side offers protected swimming almost all year round under sunny skies and gentle breezes. We love the north shore, where magnificent cliffs reach to touch the sky, and the foaming, churning surf crashes against the rocks. Here, rain showers freshen the air, dance among the flowers, and make the coastline sparkle. Or go west to Kekaha, for great walking beaches, or all the way to the end of the road, to Polihale Beach, with cliffs like the exotic towers of some lost civilization, and golden sand stretching as far as the eye can see. Kauai will never bore you, because a half–hour drive, at the most, can take you to a beach that almost seems to belong to another island.

Almost circular in shape, Kauai has three main tourist areas: Princeville & Hanalei to the north, Poipu to the south, and the 'Coconut Coast' between Lihue and Kapa'a to the east. Each has its own character, and all are wonderful.

## North Shore

By far the most spectacular, the north shore combines rugged mountains with beautiful beaches and green vistas — the Kauai of postcards. As the windward shore, the north also gets the most rainfall, particularly in winter months, when surf at the beaches is also stronger and more unpredictable. No matter the season, many people love the north shore for its rural tranquility and magnificent beauty, and come here to 'get away from it all,' to wind down to 'island time' in an area made remote by one lane bridges occasionally washed out in winter storms.

The major resort is on the north shore is *Princeville*, perched high on an ocean bluff overlooking Hanalei Bay. Princeville includes private homes and condos, two championship golf courses, and the *Princeville Hotel*, with elegant rooms and service, gourmet dining, and a magnificent cliffside setting. A small beach at the base of the cliff, which you reach by elevator, offers marvelous views and, when seas are calm, swimming and snorkeling. (from $300/nite. 800-826-4400 www.princeville.com for photos of rooms, facilities, activities, and rates.). Nearby, the *Hanalei Bay Resort* combines the conveniences of a condominium with hotel amenities (from $165/nite. 800-827-4427 www.hanaleibayresort.com). Reserve on the web site and earn a discount.

*Spectacular Hanalei Bay in summer, the view from the Princeville Resort. In winter, surf can reach twenty feet, and boats take shelter in the south.*

*Princeville Resort overlooks Hanalei Bay*

You don't have to stay at a hotel! Surrounding Princeville's golf courses are a host of condos and private homes offering astonishing ocean views, particularly at sunset, though getting to the beach may be difficult for most people, requiring a hike down the cliff to one of the small beaches (unlike hotel guests who have elevator privileges!)

Outside of Princeville, you can get closer to the ocean, for example in the town of Hanalei, near one of Kauai's finest beaches. You'll also find privacy on or near the beach in the lovely residential areas of Kalihiwai, Anini, Wainiha, and Ha'ena. The *Hanalei Colony Resort* in Ha'ena offers condos on a beachfront location (800-628-3004 www.hcr.com).

## South Shore

The south shore, at Poipu, on the island's leeward side, has drier weather and generally calmer swimming conditions year round. It's also flatter, with vegetation more dry. For swimming, there is wonderful Poipu Beach, and for sheer beauty, spectacular Maha'ulepu.

You have many choices for lodgings, including two resort hotels— the *Hyatt Regency* and the *Sheraton Kauai*. The *Hyatt Regency* offers spacious rooms and elegant dining in an architecturally beautiful resort. The beach is beautiful, but has strong surf and intimidating currents. Instead, the 600 room Hyatt offers guests an elaborate swimming water-

*At the Hyatt Regency in Poipu, a popular waterway complex features a salt water lagoon and a 150-ft waterslide.*

way, with riverpools, waterfalls, and 150 foot waterslide, as well as a 5 acre meandering saltwater lagoon with islands. From $300 (800-233-1234 www.kauai-hyatt.com). Nearby, the *Sheraton Poipu Beach* has 615 comfortable and spacious rooms, and is located right on beautiful Poipu Beach, great for swimming in all seasons. From about $200 (800-782-9488 www.sheraton-kauai.com).

*Poipu Beach*

Poipu's condominium resorts offer the convenience and space of an apartment along with many hotel amenities. The best location on Poipu Beach is at *Kiahuna* which is managed by 3 competing companies. Outrigger's *Kiahuna Plantation* has 115 units from $155/nite. (800-688-7444 www.outrigger.com). Castle Resorts has 95 units from $175/nite (800-937-6642 www.castle-group.com). *Kiahuna Beachfront* has selected beachfront units from $270/nite (800-937-6642 www.kiahuna.com). *Poipu Kai*, set back from the beach, is managed by Aston (800-922-7866) and Suite Paradise (800-367-8020). The *Embassy Resort* has the most luxurious suites, but fronts a beach too rough for easy swimming. From $275/nite. (800-535-0085 www.marcresorts.com).

Choose from many condos and charming B&B's, many within walking distance of Poipu Beach Park, with excellent protected swimming and snorkeling all year round. Check the *Kauai Vacation Planner* or the Poipu Beach Organization (808-742-7444 www.poipu-beach.org).

# Westside

Largely undeveloped, the west side is still 'local' Kauai. The weather is sunny, dry, even arid, which you'll appreciate when other parts of the

*Kauai Marriott—great location on Kalapaki Beach*

island have rain. Just west of Poipu and Koloa, you'll come to the town of Hanapepe and Salt Pond Beach Park, a beautiful spot enjoyed primarily by local people. The Green Garden Restaurant and a host of art galleries make the nearby town of Hanapepe fun to explore. Further west, you'll love the long, sandy beach at Kekaha, great for swimming, surfing, and beachwalking. Beyond that is the awesome expanse of sand and cliffs at Polihale. Choose from vacation homes, apartments, and B & B's in the towns of Kekaha and Waimea. *Waimea Plantation Cottages*, the only condo hotel on the westside, offers oldstyle charm in vintage plantation cottage accommodations (800-922-7866 www.waimea-plantation.com). The best swimming beach, however, is at Kekaha.

## Eastern Shore

The eastern shore, from Lihue (where the airport is located) to Wailua and Kapa'a—the "Coconut Coast"— has location as its main advantage. It's about midway between Poipu and Hanalei and about a half-hour drive from each, so you can explore the island in either direction, depending on the weather and your inclinations.

You'll find hotels, condos and B & B's, many of which can accurately be described as 'beachfront.' You should ask careful questions, however, because eastern shore beaches can have tricky currents, and

*The Kauai Marriott pool, one of the largest resort pools anywhere, features an island and four jaccuzzis.*

swimmers must be very cautious. Beachfront at its best? The *Kauai Marriott* fronts the magnificent sandy swimming beach at Kalapaki Bay in Lihue, a spectacular hotel with more than 880 acres of golf courses and waterways. Rooms may be smaller than the Hyatt's, but you can't beat the beach or the hotel's giant circular pool ringed by jaccuzzis, one of the state's largest. From $270 (800-220-2925 www.marriott.com/marriott/lihhi).

The Coconut Coast near Wailua offers a variety of moderately priced hotels as well as condo resorts and B & B's. Some excellent beachfront condos include *Lae Nani (800-688-7444), Wailua Bay View (800-882-9007), Lanikai (808-822-7700), Kapa'a Sands (800-222-4901) Kapa'a Shores (808-822-3055).* The *Holiday Inn Sunspree Resort* is great for families with children, close to Lydgate Park's rock rimmed pools and wonderful playground. Rates from $120/nite; check family specials (888-823-5111 www.holidayinn-kauai.com). For modest rates, try *Islander on the Beach* (800-847-7417 islander-kauai.com), *Kauai Beachboy, Coconut Beach Resort* (800-222-5642 www.hawaiihotels.com), and an island bargain, *Hotel Coral Reef* (800-843-4659 www.hshawaii.com/kvp/coral).

## Before You Go

* **Call the Kauai Visitor's Bureau** (800-262-1400) and request the *Kauai Vacation Planner,* which includes a descriptive directory of hotels, condos, B & B's, and activities. Ask for a free map.

* **Contact Resort Associations** on Kauai. The *Poipu Beach Resort Association* represents south shore accommodations and activities: PO Box 730 Koloa, HI 96756 (808-742-7444 www.poipu-beach.org). For Princeville information on the north shore, contact *Princeville Resort*, PO

Box 3069, Princeville HI 96722 (800- 826-4400) www.princeville.com
   * **Order a catalog of books** from *Island Bookshelf* (800-967-5944).
   * **Go surfing!** The internet changes faster than the weather, but here
are some sites for a virtual 'overview' and links. Listen to Hawaiian
music, learn about the island, and plan your trip! View the interiors of
actual hotel rooms, condos, homes, B & B's. Compare beach locations,
pools, and facilities; plan activities and adventures; shop for rates, check
availability, and make reservations at an internet discount. At
www.gohawaii.about.com you can order a newsletter and join forums.

## Virtual Kauai ~ links

| | |
|---|---|
| Kauai Vacations | www.travel-kauai.com |
| | www.kauaivacation.com |
| Ecotourism | www.alternative-hawaii.com |
| Discover Kauai | www.kauai-hawaii.com |
| Facts, Information, & Links | www.gohawaii.about.com |
| Kauai Vacation Planner | www.bestplaceshawaii.com/kauai |
| Hawaii Online Magazine | www.aloha-hawaii.com |
| Poipu Beach Association | www.poipu-beach.org |
| B & B's, condo rentals | www.vacationspot.com |
| Hawaiian music | www.tropicaldisc.com |
| Hawaiian music postcard | www.nadobra.com/postcards |
| Keali'i Reichel MP3s | www.worldsound.net/keali/ |
| Hawaiian culture, language | |
| | www.geocities.com/TheTropics/Shores/6794/ |
| Leis | www.aloha-hawaii.com/hawaii_magazine/flower_leis |
| Hawaii search | www.search-hawaii.com |
| Surf report | www.holoholo.com |
| | www.brenneckes.com (with music!) |

## Renting a Private Home or Condo

   *The Kauai Vacation Planner* lists vacation condos and homes (800-
262-1400 www.bestplaceshawaii.com), or you can check ads in publica-
tions like *Hawaii Magazine* or *Sunset Magazine*. Some internet sites offer
an accommodation overview, with links to individual owners:
www.travel-kauai.com, www.kauaivacation.com, www.alternative-
hawaii.com, www.poipu-beach.org, and www.vacationspot.com.

Contact island rental agencies: *Kauai Vacation Rentals* (800-367-5025 www.KauaiVacationRentals.com), *Garden Island Properties* (800-801-0378), *Prosser Realty* (800-767-4707 www.prosser-realty.com). Some agencies specialize. For the **south shore**, contact the *Poipu Beach Association* for a detailed member list (P.O. Box 730, Koloa, HI 96756 or 808-742-7444) and visit www.poipu-beach.org for links to properties. Agencies: *Grantham Resorts* (800-325-5701 www.grantham-resorts.com), *R & R Realty* (800-367-8022), *Poipu Connection* (800-742-2260), *Poipu Beach Travel* (800-3-ALOHA-3), *Garden Island Rentals* (800-247-5599), *Suite Paradise* (800-367-8020).

**North shore** agencies include: *Na Pali Properties* (800-715-7273 www.napaliprop.com), *North Shore Properties* (800-488-3336 www.kauai-vacation-rentals.com), *Harrington's Paradise Properties* (808-826-6114), *Blue Water Rentals* (800-628-5533), *Hanalei Aloha Management* (800-487-9833), *Oceanfront Realty* (800-222-5541), or Nancy A. Lindman (nal@aloha.net). Expect to pay at least $100 per night ($150 for a condo at or near a swimming beach). Advance deposits and one week minimum stays are usual. For popular months (December—March; August), call well in advance and check cancellation policies.

## Bed & Breakfasts

B & B's are plentiful on Kauai and come in all prices (from $45, with $60 as the average) and types, from a beachfront cottage to the spare room-with-bath in a home with gregarious host, even a river estate (808-826-6411 www.riverestate.com). Individual owners are listed in the *Kauai Vacation Planner*. Many, like www.beautifulkauai.com, have web sites and link to larger sites like www.kauaivacation.com or travel-kauai.com or www.poipu-beach.org or www.vacationspot.com.

Two agencies on Kauai represent many individual owners, as well as small hotels, inns and condos. *Bed & Breakfast Hawaii* (800-733-1632 www.bandb.com) has listings on all the islands, and *Bed & Breakfast Kauai* (800-822-1176) has an exclusive focus on Kauai. Disabled or single travelers receive special consideration from both agencies, and can also call Edee Seymour of *Victoria's Place* in Lawai for practical advice (808-332-9465). Women travelers can contact *Mahina's Guest House* (808-823-9364 www.mahinas.com). Questions to ask: What's for breakfast (continental, full meal, or stocked kitchen?) What kind of beds (length, width, etc.?) What degree of interaction with host and other guests? Most require a deposit and a minimum stay. Ask about cancellation policy. Many are booked 2 to 3 months in advance, so plan ahead!

## Rustic Retreats

If you like hiking and camping (yet amid relative comfort), you can rent cabins in some of Kauai's loveliest wilderness areas. In the beautiful Koke'e forest region, you can rent a cabin with stove, refrigerator, hot shower, cooking and eating utensils, linens, bedding, and wood burning stove at bargain rates, only $35-$45/night (maximum stay of 5 nights during a 30 day period). Contact *Koke'e Lodge,* Box 819, Waimea HI 96796 (808-335-6061). Also in Koke'e, *YWCA Camp Sloggett* offers hostel accommodations ($20/pp) and platforms for tent camping ($10/pp). Reserve in advance: YWCA Kauai, 3094 Elua St., Lihue HI 96766 (808-245-5959). Closer to civilization and conveniently located between Lihue and Koloa, *Kahili Mountain Park* has rustic cabins ($50 for two; $60 for four) and even more rustic one room 'cabinettes' ($28-$37 for two) in a serene meadow setting backed by mountains with a view of the sea. Contact Kahili Mountain Park, Box 298, Koloa HI 96756 (808-742-9921 www.kahilipark.com) Map 3.

Near road's end on the north shore, *YMCA Camp Naue* in Ha'ena offers beachfront camping in bunk houses (or your own tent) $12/nite. Contact YMCA of Kauai, Box 1786, Lihue HI 96766 (808-246-9090). Kapa'a has an *International Hostel* (808-823-6142). Rate: $16/nite/bunk.

## Beachfront & Oceanfront

As you investigate accommodations, become a connoisseur of words, especially if you want to be located on or close to a swimming beach. 'Ocean front' probably means a rocky place, or at least marginal swimming, but even 'beachfront' can be a misleading term. The so-called 'beach' could be rocky or unswimmable due to dangerous currents and strong surf. A property as a whole may be accurately described as 'beachfront,' but actually be shaped like a pie wedge, with the tip on the beach and the wide end (where *you* may end up being situated!) back on the road. Or it may be technically adjacent to a beach, but with a building, a swimming pool (or even a road!) in between.

Ask two key questions: What will I see when I open up my sliding glass door? How far do I have to walk (or drive) to get to the nearest sandy swimming beach? If you have children, ask about the closest 'child-friendly' swimming beach. Inquire about the swimming pool, as pools vary in size and location, and yours may end up being a tiny kidney next to the parking lot! Ask how far you have to walk to reach it, a key question if you have toddlers and all their paraphernalia to carry.

## What to Pack

When two suitcases disappeared during our flight home in 1982, we learned some lessons the hard way about packing. Now we pack a change of clothes, bathing suit, and toilet articles for each family member, as well as any prescription drugs, in a carry-on bag just in case someone's suitcase is lost temporarily. We also distribute everybody's belongings in every suitcase, so that no one person is left without clothes if a suitcase is lost permanently. And we label each bag clearly *inside* where the label can't be accidentally detached. A replacement-cost rider on our Homeowner's insurance policy turned out to be a wise investment, for the airline's insurance limit is $1,850 per passenger. Airlines typically subtract 10% of the purchase price for each year you have owned an item, exclude cameras and jewelry, and may take up to six months to process a claim. If your luggage is missing or damaged, save all baggage-claim stubs, boarding passes, and tickets, and be sure to fill out an official claim form at the baggage supervisor's office *before* you leave the airport. Most clearly tagged luggage makes its way to the owner within 24 hours (and they deliver). Call daily for an update.

Vacation days are too precious to spend on line in stores. We try to cut down on clothes (except for swim suits and T-shirts) and use space for other essentials— beach sandals, walking shoes, snorkel gear (that fits!), extra film, sunscreen, hat with brim, sunglasses, beach bag or back pack, tennis ball or beach ball, frisbee. Island restaurants are informal—no tie or jacket. A sweater in winter is a good idea.

## Flying to Kauai

The typical travel plan involves a flight first to Honolulu International Airport on Oahu and then a connecting flight to Kauai's Lihue Airport. This can turn into a full day of travel, particularly on the return trip to the mainland, when the clock moves ahead of you. You can gain back some vacation time on that return trip if you take the latest evening flight out of Honolulu, leaving Kauai around dinner time to make the connection. Or take United's non-stop flight between Lihue and Los Angeles, or between Lihue and San Francisco (limited schedule). Charter companies offering discount fares may save you money, but occasionally cost you time — if there's a problem with your flight, for example, you'll have no way to change carriers. Major airlines with frequent daily flights give you more options in case someone gets sick, for example, or you need to go home earlier, or (even better) later! Check airline internet sites for fare offers.

After you land in Honolulu, you will take a connecting flight on Hawaiian or Aloha Airlines for your twenty-minute flight to Kauai. Airline regulations require a minimum 70 minute layover in Honolulu to allow passengers and baggage to be transferred to inter-island connecting flights. However, you can beat the system and minimize time wasted in the airport. After landing in Honolulu, proceed directly to the Inter-island Terminal, a ten-minute walk or short bus ride. Go to your airline's ticket counter, and try to get on an earlier flight to Lihue, even as a stand-by (The computer data is often wrong, and stand-bys can usually get seats). Your luggage will remain on your originally scheduled flight, but you will be in Lihue with a head start— to fill out forms for your rental car while waiting for the baggage. On long travel days, especially with children, this saved time can be a lifesaver!

On your inter-island flight, you may be asked to check your carry-on luggage because of size, as some inter-island aircraft have very small overhead bins. Keep your jewelry, camera, prescription drugs, and favorite stuffed animals in a small bag inside your larger one, just in case.

| | | | |
|---|---|---|---|
| Hawaiian Airlines | 800-367-5320 | www.hawaiianair.com | 835-3700 |
| Aloha Airlines | 800-367-5250 | www.alohaair.com | 484-1111 |

## Traveling with Children

If you are traveling with babies or toddlers, you can request bulkhead seating (but not exit rows, which can be assigned only to adults) in advance. Be sure to get an assigned seat in the computer in advance too, so that your seats have priority if the flight is overbooked. Enroll in the airline's Frequent Flyer Program—the kids too. You should bring along your child's car seat, which can go into the baggage compartment with your luggage, as Hawaii state law requires them for children under three. Airlines now permit use of the child's restraint seat on board the aircraft, but that requires the child to have a paid seat on crowded flights.

Families who fly to Kauai from the east coast might consider staying overnight in California to help children make the difficult time adjustment in stages, particularly on the long trip home. After flying from Kauai to California, the kids can run around in the hotel, have some ice cream, and stay up as late as possible in order to push their body clocks ahead three hours while they sleep. If you book a late morning flight out of California the next day, the kids can sleep late in the morning, and if you're lucky, they will wake up fresh for the second day's flight and be ready to adjust their body clocks another three hours. Traveling through two time zones is no snap, but this plan can make it a bit easier.

On that journey home, bad weather might delay your connecting flight from Lihue to Honolulu, and so you might consider taking a flight earlier in the day, before the inter-island flights get backed up. In fact, it's a good idea to see if you can get on as a stand-by on *any* earlier flight to Honolulu once you're in the Lihue airport. This plan is well worth it if you are traveling with young children, and can't afford to miss your mainland connection!

*Kite flying at Hanalei Bay*

To amuse little ones during the long flight, pack lots of small toys, crayons, books, paper dolls, and an "airplane present" to be unwrapped when the seatbelt sign goes off. Ask the cabin attendants for "kiddie packs" or cards right away as supplies are often limited. Pack a secret snack or toy for those awful moments when one child spills coke on another. Keep chewing gum handy to help children relieve the ear-clogging which can be so uncomfortable, even painful, during the last twenty minutes of the descent when cabin pressure changes. Sucking on a bottle will help a baby or toddler.

To save shopping time, we used to stuff as many beach and swimming toys into suitcase corners as possible. 'Swimmies' (arm floats) are great for small children to use in the pool, as are goggles and masks, toy trucks for sand-dozing, frisbees, inflatable beach balls, and floats. Boogie boards, by far the best swimming toy, can be brought home in the baggage compartment after your vacation (packed in a pillowcase!). Best choices are at the M. Miura store (Kapaʻa), Progressive Expressions (Koloa), or even K-Mart and Wal-Mart. Boogie boards are better balanced than the cheaper imitations. Caution: they can be hazardous in a pool; a small child who tips over in deep water can be trapped underneath.

Rent children's equipment at *Ready Rentals* (823-8008 or 800-599 8008 readyrentals@aloha.net*)*. Free delivery. Or call *Baby's Away* (245-6259 or 800-571-0077). To protect a baby's delicate skin, bring a hat with a large brim, socks for feet, and a strong, waterproof sunblock (re-apply frequently).

## Weathering Kauai

If you dial 245-6001 for the weather report on Kauai, you will probably hear this 'forecast': "Mostly fair today, with occasional windward and mauka (mountain) showers. Tonight, mostly fair, with showers varying from time to time and from place to place." Except for storms, Kauai's normal weather pattern is mostly sunny, with showers passing over the ocean, crossing the coastline and backing up against the island's mountainous interior. Like all the Hawaiian islands, Kauai's sunny side varies with the winds. Normal trade winds blow from the north and northeast, bringing rainfall to these 'windward' shores and creating the 'lee' of the island in the south, at Poipu, and west, at Kekaha and Polihale. When the clouds back up against the mountains and bring showers to the north shore beaches, Poipu and Salt Pond may have sunny skies! However, sometimes the winds blow from the south and west, and these 'Kona winds' create the lee in the north and northeast. The north shore may be spectacular on a day when the eastside and south shores have rain.

Careful planning can make the most of any weather, however, since Kauai has 'micro climates' and a 20 minute drive can take you from rain to sun. On Kauai, no matter where you stay, be prepared to drive to the sun—all the way west to Polihale if necessary! Plan your adventures with an eye to the weather. If it's clear up north, visit the north shore, for these beaches are by far the most spectacular and if your stay is only for a few days, you may not get another chance! Rain outside? Drive south to Poipu or west to Salt Pond or Kekaha, where it's usually drier. With heavy rain, Polihale might be your best—even your only—dry option!

Only an island-wide storm should send you indoors to rent a movie, so check the weather and surf report before deciding whether to go north to Hanalei, south to Poipu, or west to Kekaha. Double check with a phone call. These merchants have agreed to be your weather tipsters: *Nukumoi Beach Center,* Poipu (742-8019*)*. *Wrangler's Steak House*, Waimea (328-1218). *Pedal 'n Paddle*, Hanalei (826-9069).

Weather patterns vary with the seasons. Showers are more frequent in winter and spring, while summer months are warmer and more humid, fall months clearer and more dry. Temperatures range between 60's at night & mid-80's most days, and in summer can reach the 90's. The beaches also change their moods with the seasons. In summer, the water may be so calm and clear that bubbles on the surface cast shadows on the sandy bottom, but winter surf at the same beach can foam and crash like thunder. Some north shore beaches disappear entirely under winter surf, and may even be officially closed for safety reasons.

## Driving on Kauai

No matter where you decide to stay, you can easily explore the rest of the island by car. Except for the wilderness area in the northwest quadrant, Kauai is nearly encircled by a main two-lane highway, with sequentially numbered 'mile markers' to make tracking easy. You can drive from Lihue to Kapa'a in about 10 minutes, from Kapa'a to Hanalei in about 30 minutes, or from Lihue to Poipu in about 20 minutes, and from Poipu to Polihale in about 35 minutes.

Kauai is still rural as far as the infrastructure goes—just two-lanes, around the island! Increasing traffic has prompted the creation of 'bypass roads.' You'll see the first one as you leave the airport; it merges with Rt.56 or Kuhio Highway, the island's main two-lane road, just north of Hanama'ulu. Traffic moves easily as you continue north — until you reach the town of Wailua, where three little traffic lights can cause unbelievable congestion during rush hour. A bypass road behind Wailua winds through cane fields, then comes out near the center of Kapa'a, offering you a view of sugar cane rather than the rear bumper of the car in front of you! You'll see the turnoff on the left, just north of the traffic light at Wailua Family Restaurant and just south of the Coconut Plantation Marketplace. It brings you to the center of Kapa'a about two blocks behind the ABC Store. Sometimes, however, the sugar harvest closes the road, and traffic on Rt. 56 reverts to a crawl! At those times, polish your left hand turn skills, try not to drive between 4 and 6:30, and be patient. Remember, you're on vacation!

A third bypass road connects the center of Koloa with eastern Poipu and the Hyatt Regency Hotel. Turn left off Maluhia Road at the center of Koloa, then take the first right onto Weliweli, and follow the signs to Poipu. On the newest bypass road, you can take a scenic route between Nawiliwili Harbor and Puhi, avoiding the center of Lihue. In Nawiliwili, near the small boat harbor, take Niumali Road to Halemalu Road, and follow it past the Menehune Fishpond to Puhi Road which reconnects with Rt. 50, and from there you can continue on to Koloa and Poipu.

While driving your rental car on Kauai, keep this in mind: speed limits are strictly enforced, especially in residential and business areas. It's illegal to make a U-turn in a "business district," even if it doesn't look like much of a business district. On 'Wacky Wednesday' or 'Super Saturday' or 'Aloha Friday' (which vary on different parts of the island) gas prices are cut by 4 cents.

The best places to explore on Kauai are accessible by either paved roads or established dirt roads in the cane fields which are maintained as 'rights of way' to the beaches. So pack a picnic lunch and some beach mats, sunscreen and your book, and explore some of the island's most beautiful hidden beaches! Plan your adventures according to the weather and the season. In winter, the surf is more unpredictable and dangerous on the beaches to the north and northeast, while the best and safest swimming is on the south shore. In summer, the surf may be up on the south and west, with north shore beaches beautiful for swimming. Whatever the season, follow this simple rule for swimming safety: don't swim alone or too far out at any beach whose currents are unfamiliar to you. Read **'Beach Safety'** carefully (p. 77). When you park, be sure to lock up and store your valuables in the trunk!

## 800 Kauai Treats

*Papayas*        Akana Farms      800-572-7292
10 pounds of Kilauea sunrise papayas shipped overnight (about $45)  page 93

*Flowers*        Kauai Tropicals  800-303-4385
A box of beautiful ginger, heliconia, anthurium, shipped overnight (from $48)  page 91

*Aloha Angels*    Uncle Eddie's Aloha Angels
800-538-6514  www.aloha-angels.com

*Kauia Kookies*   Tasty cookies in tropical flavors
800-361-1126

*Online*   www.shopping-hawaii.com    www.hawaiibooks.com

# Beach Adventures

*Kalapaki Beach, a family favorite for swimming & playing — and
exploring the Marriott Hotel afterwards. Page 30.*

# *Eastern Shore Best Bets*

## Beaches

Ninini Beach 31
Kalapaki Beach 30
Hanama'ulu 31
Lydgate Park 32
Wailua Bay 34
Kealia Beach 34
Donkey Beach 36
Anahola Beach 36

## Hotels

A  Coconut Beach Resort
B  Islander on the Beach
C  Kauai Sands
D  Holiday Inn Sunspree
E  Outrigger Hotel
F  Marriott, Kauai Lagoons

## Shopping

Lihue, Wailua 37
Kapa'a 38

Anahola Bay for great beachwalks and family fun

For island tastes, visit Farmer's Markets in Lihue and Kapa'a (p.88)

Free hula shows at Coconut Plantation Marketplace (p.86)

Wailua River, Kauai's only navigable water-way. Great for kayak explorations, (p.128) or water-skiing (p.115)

Long beachwalks along Wailua Beach south of Lydgate Park

Lydgate Park has snorkeling and rafting for the whole family!

**Kauai's main traveled roads**: Rt. 56 (Kuhio Hwy) travels north from Lihue to Wailua, Kapa'a and Anahola. Rt. 56 curves to the west towards Kilauea and then Princeville, Hanalei & Ha'ena. Rt. 50 connects in Lihue and goes south to Poipu and west to Waimea.

Hule'ia River and Alakoko (Menehune) fish pond (p.128)

Kalapaki Beach

# Eastern Shore Funfinder

## Activities

Water ski on the Wailua River 115
Hike Sleeping Giant Mountain 101
Horseback Riding 102
Golf
  Grove Farm Golf Course  99
  Wailua Golf Course  97
Windsurf, catamaran, kayak,
  snorkel, body board
  rental  109
Sport fishing 109
Snorkel & Scuba 106-7
Surfing 112

## Tours

Helicopter tours 118
Boat tours 127
Kayak tours
  Wailua River to Fern
    Grotto 127
  Hule'ia River 128
  Sea kayak 129
Grove Farm Plantation Tour 130
Kauai Museum 131

## Family Fun

Lydgate Park  32
Kalapaki Beach 30
  Body board & kayak rental 109
Free hula show 104

## Shopping  37

## Farmers' Markets  88

## Restaurants  137

### Kilauea
1   Lighthouse Bistro 196
    Kilauea Bakery 195
    Pau Hana Pizza 195
2   Roadrunner Cafe 198

### Anahola
3   Duane's Ono Burger 170

### Kapa'a
4   Kapa'a Fish & Chowder 158
5   Kountry Kitchen 163
    Masa's 166
6   Rocco's 175
    Norberto's El Cafe 168
    Ono Family Restaurant 170
7   Sukothai 176

### Wailua
8   King & I 160
9   A Pacific Cafe 171
    Panda Garden 173
    Papaya's Garden Cafe 173
    Pony Island Cantina 174
10  Waipouli Deli 180
11  Margarita's 164
12  Bull Shed 144
13  Kintaro 162
    Mema 167
    Caffe Coco 145
    Wah Kung 179
14  Flying Lobster 150
    Eggbert's 149
    Palm Tree Terrace 172
    Al & Don's 142
15  Wailua Marina 179

### Hanama'ulu
16  Hanama'ulu Tea House 154
    JR's Plantation 156

### Lihue
17  Okazu Hale 169
18  Duke's 148, 149
    JJ's Broiler 155
    Cafe Portofino 146
    Tokyo Lobby 178
    Kauai Chop Suey 159
    Whaler's Brew Pub 181
19  Barbecue Inn 143
    Ma's Family, Inc. 165
    Hamura's Saimin 152
    La Bamba 164
    Garden Island BBQ 150
    Kiibo 160
20  Oki Diner 169
21  Joni Hana 184
22  Gaylord's at Kilohana 151

*The beautiful Wailua coastline along the 'coconut coast'*

# Favorite Beaches

\* Our favorite swimming beach is **Kalapaki Beach**, above, wonderful for swimming, skim boarding, and when the surf is right, boogie boards. The sand is perfect for playing ball or frisbee, running, or simply sunning. Rent a catamaran or kayak, if surf conditions are calm.

\* **Lydgate Park** in Wailua is perfect for families — an enormous lava rock-rimmed pool offers wonderful swimming and snorkeling, with a smaller rock-rimmed pool just right for toddlers. Beyond the pools, the beach is great for long walks. Lydgate also offers the best playground on Kauai, the Kamalani playground for the climbing and swinging set, and the beach is a great spot to watch glorious golden sunrises.

\* For water activities, try **Wailua**. Wailua Beach is popular with local surfers, and on the Wailua River, you can water ski, or kayak and explore upstream towards the Fern Grotto.

\* Surfers will love **Kealia Beach**, where wonderful, even rollers can give great rides when conditions are right.

\* For picnics and beach walks, visit beautiful **Anahola Bay.**

\* Hungry? For inexpensive lunch in Lihue, try Hamura's Saimin, Barbecue Inn, Kalapaki Beach Broiler. Spend a bit more and enjoy Duke's Barefoot Bar, Gaylord's or Whaler's Micro Brewery.

## Great Days on the Eastern Shore

Day 1 (Wailua/Kapa`a). Breakfast at Kountry Kitchen (p. 164). Morning: water-ski or kayak on the Wailua River (p. 128), or hike Sleeping Giant Mountain (p.101). Lunch: Palm Tree Terrace (p. 172). Afternoon at Lydgate Park, great for kids or long beachwalks (p. 32). Dinner: Mema's (p. 137) or Kintaro (p.134).

Day 2. (Lihue) Breakfast at Tip Top (p. 177). Morning: kayak trip up the Hule'ia River (p. 128) or tour Grove Farm Planation (p. 130). Lunch at Kalapaki Beach Hut (p. 157) or Whaler's Brew Pub (p. 180). Afternoon: relax or sail at Kalapaki Beach. Dinner: Cafe Portofino (p. 146) or Duke's Canoe Club (p. 147).

## Kalapaki Beach

Kalapaki Bay is unforgettably beautiful. Almost enclosed by craggy green hillsides, this natural harbor has a wide sugar sand beach with some of the best swimming on the island. The waves roll to shore in long, even swells and break in shining white crests which are usually great for swimming and rafting. At times, surf is very rough, but even if you can't swim, you can enjoy beautiful views. On one side, the green ridges of the mountains have the contours of a giant animal sleeping in the sun, while on the opposite side, houses on stilts perch so precariously on the side of a

*Sail a catamaran on Kalapaki Bay*

sheer cliff that you wonder what combination of faith and hope keeps them standing.

Fronting this beach is the spectacular Marriott Resort at Kauai Lagoons, a headline-maker from the time it opened in the late '80's as a Westin Hotel because of its lavish design and elaborate collections of far eastern art and tropical birds and animals. Here you'll find Kauai's largest swimming pool, its tallest high-rise, its only two-story escalator.

Kalapaki Beach is a favorite family spot. The firm sand is perfect for games and hard running, and the waves can at times break perfectly for boogie boards. Build sandcastles, play beach volleyball, rent a kayak or catamaran, or try your hand at windsurfing. Heed any high surf warnings, however, for at certain times, particularly in winter months, the waves can break straight down with enormous force, and every so often a really big wave seems to come up out of nowhere to smash unwary swimmers.

*Directions*: Take Rice St. through Lihue, and turn left into the main entrance of the Kauai Marriott. Pass the main lobby, and turn right at the first street, follow it down the hill to the beach access parking lot. Map 1

## Ninini Beach

The drive to this tiny beach, "Running Waters," is more interesting than the destination. You wind along a cane road right next to the airport runway, so close, actually, that the jets taking off and landing almost make you want to duck! Turn off Kapule Rd. just south of the Lihue airport at the marble gates (once the limo entrance to the old Westin) and follow it through brush and rustling grasses, then through the hotel grounds, always bearing towards the water, until you reach the lighthouse at Ninini Point. From the picnic table near the lighthouse you'll have a gorgeous view of the coastline, a great spot for lunch. Surf crashes on the rocks, and the beach is not safe for swimming. Come instead for the view and the seclusion. Map 1

## Hanama'ulu Beach

A perfect crescent of soft shining sand, the beach at Hanama'ulu Bay is perfect for building sandcastles and hunting sunrise shells. In summer, the waves are gentle enough for children to enjoy. Rolling to shore in long, even swells only about a foot or two high, they break into miniature crests which turn to layers of white foam flecked with sandy gold, like the lacy borders of a lovely shawl. Even the occasional "wipe-outs" were not

*Hanamaʻulu Beach*

serious because the sandy bottom slopes very gradually.

Kids can chase lots of tiny sandcrabs, and there is plenty of shade for babies beneath the tall ironwood trees which fringe the sand. Behind the beach, the Hanamaʻulu Stream forms shallow pools as it winds toward the bay, and they can hunt for tiny crayfish and other creatures with nets. The deep gold of the river is shaded by trees so tall and dense you can hardly see the sky, and the dark green leaves trail into the water behind stalks of lavender water hyacinths, their petals streaked with the colors of peacock feathers. A picnic pavilion faces the river, and other tables look out over the beautiful curve of the bay. Everything is uncrowded, as this beach is frequented by few tourists. Unfortunately, it is also in the path sometimes used by helicopters returning to the airport from their scenic tours. Try to ignore the noisy choppers, and plan your visit for the morning, as the mosquitoes get hungry about 4 pm!

*Directions*: Turn off Rt. 56 towards the sea at Hanamaʻulu, between the 7-Eleven and the school. Bear right at the fork which has a sign to the Beach Park. The road ends at the park. Map 1

## Lydgate Beach Park

Lydgate Park just south of the Wailua River is a favorite spot for families. A rock-rimmed pool provides safe swimming for babies and toddlers, even in winter months. Adjacent is an enormous rock-rimmed pool which breaks the surf into rolling swells excellent for swimming, rafting, and floats of all kinds. The pool is one of the best year–round snorkeling spots on the island, for families of brightly colored fish feed along the rocky perimeter, so tame they almost swim into your hands.

The rocky wall protects snorkelers and swimmers from surf and dangerous currents. You can also fly a kite, play frisbee on the wide, sandy beach, and collect shells and driftwood. There's a lifeguard, and also showers for rinsing off sand and salt.

Kids will love the Kamalani Playground, 16,000 square feet of funland, with mirror mazes, a suspension bridge, lava tubes and circular slide. The beach south of the lava rock pools is ideal for long walks, very beautiful and almost deserted. Continue past the rocky point in front of Kaha Lani Condominiums, and you can walk along the section of beachfront called Nukoli'i, in front of the Outrigger Hotel. The sand is firm and fine, perfect for walking, and you'll have spectacular views of the coastline, particularly beautiful when sunrise or sunset paints the sky with gold and orange, and deepens the blues of the ocean, bright with shining

*Lydgate's rock rimmed pools*

foam. The patterns of foam crossing the sand are the most lovely we have ever seen. You'll probably find only one or two people, probably fishermen checking their lines. Swim with caution, however, for the surf is rough and currents powerful; Lydgate's pools are much safer.

*Directions*: If you are driving north on Rt. 56, turn right onto Leho Rd. just past the Wailua Golf Course. The right turnoff to the park is clearly marked. Follow this road to the Park and the rock pools. If you are driving south on Rt. 56, you must turn left onto the Leho Road just across the bridge over the Wailua River, at the Holiday Inn Sunspree. Map 1

## Wailua Bay

Wailua Bay's long, curve of golden sand is perfect for walking. In the middle is the mouth of the Wailua River, sometimes shallow enough to ford, but at other times deep and treacherous. Swimming in the brackish, calm water of the river can be fun, although parents of young children should not let them stray from the edges because the water can become deep very quickly. Swimming where the river empties into the bay is not recommended because currents can be dangerous and unpredictable. South of the river, local kids congregate at one of the best spots for surfing and boogie boards on Kauai, particular in summer! A lifeguard is usually on duty.

The Wailua River offers many activities – water skiing, kayaking, or touring Fern Grotto with Smith's Boat Tours (822-4111).

*Directions:* On Rt. 56, just north of the bridge over the Wailua River.

## Kapa'a Beaches

A white sandy beach, which runs almost the length of Kapa'a town, offers relatively safe swimming and fun for families with small children. An offshore reef breaks the surf and wind chop, creating a quiet lagoon, except in winter months when an eastern swell can make a strong current flow out of the channel. Usually, however, the water is calm, filled with children splashing while babies play in the shaded sand.

*Directions:* Take Rt. 56 through Kapa'a. Turn towards the water at Niu St. by Kapa'a ballpark. Map 1

## Kealia Beach

North of Kapa'a on Rt. 56 and just past a scenic overlook turnout, you will see spectacular Kealia Beach, a long, wide curve of golden sand ending in a rocky point. When the surf is up, lots of surfers ride the long, even rollers. During summer months, the waves can be gentle enough for children at the far end of the beach where lava rocks extending into the sea create a cove where the water is quieter. Kealia has long been one of Jeremy's and Mikey's favorite beaches for surfing and body boarding. The sandy bottom slopes so gradually that you can walk out to catch some wonderful long rides, though at times the waves can be too powerful for children (even adults). Exercise caution, particularly in winter. Surf near the boogie boarders, and not the hard board surfers who are looking for

*Body board fun for kids at Kalapaki, Kealia, Anahola, Lydgate, and Hanama'ulu.*

the bigger thrill. Watch out for the small, blue 'men o' war' jellyfish, which wash ashore, in certain seasons, after high surf. If you see them on the sand, they are probably also floating in the water! They pack a nasty sting, so go to another beach for the day. Firm, level sand makes this a perfect walking beach, and children will enjoy playing in shallow pools behind the beach where a stream flows into the ocean. Strong rip currents near the river mouth, however, can make ocean swimming hazardous.

*Directions:* Drive north of Kapa'a on Rt. 56. Between mile markers 10 and 11, turn off to the right where you see all the cars parked. Map 1

## Donkey Beach

Donkey Beach is a lovely and peaceful spot, a long curve of sand which ends in piles of rock on both sides. Surf and currents are strong, even in summer, making swimming risky and only for experts. Waves rise slowly; curl in long, even swells; crest with gleaming foam, and break straight down with thunderous explosions of spray. The rhythm is hypnotic—you could watch them form and crash for hours. We saw no one in the water, though—our first hint that Donkey Beach was for sun-worshipers rather than swimmers. In fact, it has for years been a place where nude sunbathing was the rule. Times are changing, however, as the land once devoted to sugar is developed into homesites. Now plans to develop the area mean security patrols, and people are asked to cover up! So you won't feel out of place if you hang onto your suit.

*Directions:* For years, access to Donkey Beach from Rt. 56 has been informal, crossing the cane field on foot. Now, developer Kealia Plantation plans a scenic public bike and walking preserve along the cane road from Kealia Beach leading to Donkey Beach.

## Anahola Bay

The beach at Anahola Bay is so long that to walk from one end to the other may take you nearly an hour. The colors are magnificent, particularly as the sun is rising, or in late afternoon as it moves to the west over the dark green mountains, deepening the blue of the water and the gold of the sand while brightening the tall white puff clouds until they glow with light.

While the walking is spectacular, swimming can be risky, for the surf near the center of the bay can be strong and currents powerful most of the year. The southern end of the bay is more sheltered, and local families come for snorkeling and picnicking at the park near the end of Anahola Road. You can also drive to the northern end of the bay, where the Anahola stream flows into the sea. Children will love playing in the large shallow pools formed by the stream as it winds toward the bay, which is sometimes filled with tadpoles just slow enough to be netted by the younger set. The tiny river fish were harder to catch but fun in the trying, as were the small shrimp we discovered hiding by the grasses near the bank. The children also enjoyed making voyages of discovery on their boogie boards where the stream is deeper.

Anahola Bay is a favorite place for the whole family, and a good choice on weekends when other, more well-known beaches become crowded. Watch out for the small, blue 'men o' war' jellyfish which are sometimes washed ashore after a storm. If you see them on the sand, go to another beach for the day, for they're probably in the water too, and the sting can be very painful. A short drive (or long walk) north of the river will take you to Aliomanu Beach, popular with local families because its extensive offshore reef is terrific for fishing and seaweed harvesting. Snorkeling is for experts only, who should venture out if tradewinds are light and the current from the river is not strong. It's a great spot for a picnic, with little sandy 'nooks' along the road perfect for two. You can walk a long way along the sand, climbing some rocks, passing homes that peek out from the vegetation, listening to the sound of waves. Phone in a picnic order to Duane's Ono Burger (next to Anahola Store) for great burgers (with sprouts, avocado, bacon, cheese, tomatoes, pineapple - you name it! 822-9181)

*Directions*: Turn off Rt. 56 at the Aliomanu Road just north of Duane's Ono Burger and the Anahola Store and follow it to the mouth of the stream. To get to the beach park at the southern end of Anahola Beach, take Anahola Road (just south of Ono Burger) towards the water.  Map 1

## Eastern Shore Shopping Stops

At KILOHANA about a mile west of Kukui Grove on Rt. 50, you can visit a historic sugar plantation homestead and browse shops from the elegant to the cute. *Kahn Galleries* has works by respected Hawaiian artists. *The Country Store* and *Hawaiian Collection Room* feature island crafts and jewelry, while *Kilohana Galleries* has work by Hawaiian artisans working in wood, glass, fabric, ceramics, and papers— beautiful batiks, porcelains, jewelry, handpainted silk scarves, needlework, water-colors and drawings, as well as fabric art by Julie Patten. Just behind the plantation house, visit *Kilohana Clothing* for beautiful designs, made by Melody, with fine fabrics and careful finishing. Her aloha shirts are a family favorite! You'll love the colorful pottery at *Kilohana Clayworks.*

In LIHUE, *Kukui Grove*, Kauai's most modern shopping center, includes major department stores like *Liberty House* and *Sears*, as well as a host of specialty shops including the *Kauai Products Store*, which has original crafts, clothing, and jewelry by Kauai artists.  Near *K-Mart*, *Borders Books & Music* has Kauai's largest selection of books, tapes and CD's, and an *Espresso Cafe* offering excellent 'food for the body'—as well as the mind! Nearby, at Anchor Cove, visit *Crazy Shirts* for great tee-shirt designs, and *Island Style* for beautiful works by local artists.

In LIHUE town, the *Kauai Museum* has a wonderful shop for books, maps, as well as some crafts and memorabilia, including Ron Kent's fine, almost translucent wood bowls. You won't have to pay the museum entrance fee to visit the gift shop. Stop at *Hilo Hattie's,* at the corner of Kuhio Highway and Ahukini Road in Lihue, for aloha wear, souvenirs, and hats at factory-direct prices. Just down the street, *Wal-Mart* features island coffees, candies, nuts and gifts at excellent prices. North of Lihue, in HANAMA'ULU, don't miss *Kapaia Stitchery* for beautiful handcrafted clothing, gift items, quilts and sewing supplies, plus Hawaiian fabrics.

In **WAILUA**, *Goldsmith's Kauai* in Kinipopo Shopping Village is a must stop for original designs crafted of gold, silver, and precious gems by award-winning artists. Founder Eric Vogt has sailed off into the sunset, taking early retirement, but his goldsmith partners carry on the tradition of creating beautiful pieces to embody a client's desire. Next door, *Kinipopo Fine Art Gallery* features exhibits by artist members of the Kauai Society of Artists. Their shows have both uniqueness and professional pizzazz.

Just north of Wailua, the *Coconut Plantation Marketplace,* has lots of shops, and a free afternoon hula show (5 pm) that kids will love. At *Gecko Store,* geckos appear in  shirts, jewelry, pens and pencils, stickers, glasses, cups, even hats! At *Kauai Magic* you'll find magic tricks for magicians of any level. *Ye Olde Ship's Store* displays scrimshaw, and the *Indo European Trading Company* has a wonderful collection of clothes, furniture, scents, chimes, and boxes. *Plantation Stitchery* will solve all your crafts and fabric needs. Try *Island Surf Shop* for great fashions—including teen magic brands like Roxy and Quicksilver.  Kauai Village in Wailua has a variety of clothing and souvenir shops, including *Wyland Galleries* marine life paintings. Kids can watch the tropical fish and spotted eel in the 2,300 gallon aquarium. *Waldenbooks* is a friendly spot for browsing. *Kauai Heritage Center* has an interesting exhibits of historical artifact!

In **KAPA'A**, a family favorite is *M. Miura Store*, for the latest surfing-shirts, shorts, and aloha shirts, even boogie boards. Visit *Jim Saylor* and see his jewelry designs with precious stones— lovely rings, necklaces, and bracelets.  Jim loves designing, sketching deftly as he talks enthusiastically about a unique ring or pendant just for you!  *At Kela's,* Larry Barton displays contemporary glass art by more than 35 artists, including beautiful shell designs, elegant vases, colorful fish (822-4527 www.glass-art.com).  Next door at *Kebanu,* you'll find fountain art, photographs, and other treasures, while *Hula Girl* has a great selection of aloha style shirts, dresses, and clothing and gift items with hula motifs.  Across the street, *Island Hemp and Cotton* features comfortable beach clothes. On the north end of town*, Two Frogs Hugging* features unusual pottery, far eastern imports, boxes, and collectibles with – frogs!

Forget something? Shop from home!  www.shopping-hawaii.com

# North Shore Beaches

*Kilauea Lighthouse has a bird's
eye view of Secret Beach.*

# North Shore
# Map 2

North Shore
Kauai

Ke'e Beach

Ha'ena Beach Park

Tunnels Beach

Kepuhi Beach

560 **❶**C

Hanakapiai Beach

Kalalau Trail

Wet Caves

**Ha'ena**

Wainiha Beach

Lumahai Beach

Hanalei Bay

Pali Ke Kua ("Hideaways") **❼**

Pu'u Poa Beach **❻** Honoiki Rd **A ❺**

Hanalei Pier

Waikoko Beach

Limahuli Stream

Manoa Stream

Wainiha Powerhouse Rd

Wainiha River

Lumahai Stream

Kuhio Hwy

Wai'oli Beach Park

Ching Young Village

Weke

Aku

Hanalei Center **❷**

Wai'oli Stream

**Hanalei**

Hanakapiai Stream

Limahuli Falls

Hanakapiai Falls

## Hotels

A  Princeville Hotel
B  Hanalei Bay Resort
C  Hanalei Colony Resort

*Waioli Hui'ia Church, Hanalei*

*Lumahai Beach*

*Princeville Hotel*

Kauai's main traveled roads:  Rt. 56 (Kuhio Hwy.) travels north from Lihue, becomes Rt. 560 at Princeville, continues west to road's end at Ke'e Beach.

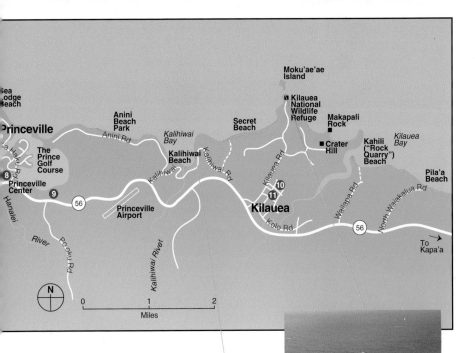

## Beaches

*Kilauea Lighthouse*

## Restaurants

*Sharing the wave at Kalihiwai. Page 49.*

*Kalihiwai Bay, a jewel on the North Shore*

## *Favorite Beaches*

* Spectacular **Hanalei Bay**, an unforgettable image of Kauai for those rainy evenings back home! Great for swimming and surfing, and for running and walking (p. 53). Start with breakfast at *Cafe Hanalei* in the Princeville Hotel (p. 189). The view is incredible!

* Our favorite family beach is **Kalihiwai,** which combines spectacular beauty with wonderful summertime swimming, as well as firm golden sand, perfect for running. In winter, surf is up, to the delight of our boys, and even spectators can have fun watching the surfers catch spectacular rides. Kids will love the brackish pools behind the beach for fishing, swimming, and playing with a rope swing (p. 51).

* **Anini Beach** is gentle enough for children, and a popular spot for snorkeling and windsurfing (p. 51).

* For long, solitary beachwalks, try **Larsen's Beach** (p .45) or **Moloa'a Bay** (p. 43).

* Adventurers love hiking to **Secret Beach**, both secluded and spectacular, with magnificent views of the northern coast (p. 48).

* The best snorkeling, when surf is calm, is at **Tunnels Beach** (p. 57) In summer months, **Ke'e Beach** (p. 58) has excellent snorkeling as well.

\* From Keʻe Beach, you can hike the cliffside trail through the Na Pali wilderness to **Hanakapiaʻi Beach** (p. 100), magnificently beautiful, though too dangerous for swimming. Try the first quarter-mile climb to a spectacular point overlooking Keʻe Beach and the Haʻena reefs (p. 99). For sunset watching, don't miss the view from the *Princeville Hotel*, or from **Tunnels Beach, Keʻe Beach** or, in summer months, **Anini Beach** (p. 110).

## *Great Days on the North Shore*

Day 1: Breakfast at Cafe Hanalei or Postcards Cafe, morning at Hanalei Bay (p. 53). Relax on the beach, or rent a kayak and explore the Hanalei River (p. 129). Afternoon picnic on Kalihawai Beach (p. 51), with sandwiches from Kilauea Farmer's Market. Watch the sunset, to Hawaiian music, at Sheraton Princeville Hotel's 'Living Room.' Dinner at Neidie's Salsa and Samba (p. 196).

Day 2: Breakfast at Zelo's or Hanalei Wake Up Cafe. Drive to the end of the road to Keʻe Beach (p. 58). Hike the cliff trail to the Keʻe Beach overlook (p. 99), or on to Hanakapia'i Beach. Or, instead, visit lovely Limahuli Gardens (p. 133). Enjoy a beach picnic, and spend the afternoon snorkeling at Keʻe Beach or Tunnels (p. 57). Sunset watching and dinner at Bali Hai Restaurant (p. 187).

Day 3. Breakfast at Kilauea Bakery or Roadrunner (pp. 193;198). Hike to Secret Beach (summer) or trail ride (p.102). Lunch at the Princeville Golf Course (p. 198). Lazy afternoon beach walk at Larsen's Beach or Moloaʻa Bay. Dinner at Postcard's Cafe (p. 197).

## Moloaʻa Bay

At the end of a well-graded, semi-paved road winding for several miles through the lush green countryside, Moloaʻa Bay's lovely curve of sandy beach is discovered by few tourists. As you follow the road through this quiet, rural landscape, you can hear wonderful sounds—the breeze rustling in the leaves, the chirping of insects, the snorting of horses grazing in tree-shaded meadows. At road's end, you will find a gate attached to an unfriendly looking fence intended to discourage parking along the shoulder of the road. Walk through the gate and cross a shallow stream, where our children often discovered tadpoles apparently not informed that frog's eggs had hatched a month earlier everywhere else.

At this point the bay, hidden by the half dozen homes which ring the beach, suddenly comes into view—an almost dazzling half-moon of shining golden sand and turquoise water. The long, wide beach ends in grassy hills and piles of lava rocks on the left, and a sheer cliff on the right. To the left, the rocks are fun to climb and search for shells and trapped fish, although this windward side of the bay is usually too rough for swimming, and the bottom is very rocky. To the right of the stream, the bay is more sheltered, the water gentler and the bottom more sandy. In summer, snorkelers can swim out through the sandy corridor to the rockier part of the bay, or float in the shallow water close to shore and dig in the sandy bottom for shells. In times of heavy surf, however, this bay, like all windward beaches, can have dangerous currents. During these times, Moloa'a Bay is a beautiful place for walking. The peaceful solitude is filled with the sound of waves. The crystal blue water, traced with the shadowy patterns of the rocks below, stretches out to the distant horizon where pale clouds fade into a limitless sky. At 5 pm you might see a dozen horses, wandering home after another difficult day of grazing, stop at the stream for a drink or a roll in the shallows—a spectacular sight with the light glistening on the water and the horses darkening slowly to silhouettes.

*Directions*: Take Rt. 56 to Kuamo'o Road, a half-mile north of the mile

*Moloa'a Bay*

16 marker. Turn right at Moloaʻa Road and follow it to the end. About 16 miles north of Lihue; 30 miles from Poipu; 6 miles from Kapaʻa.

## Larsen's Beach

*Road to Larsen's Beach*

Getting to Larsen's Beach is half the fun. A right-of-way-to-beach road wanders through pastureland, where horses grazing peacefully seem sketched into a landscape portrait of silvery green meadows with waving dark green grasses, trees and mountains, and masses of white, shining clouds. At the end of the well-graded, sandy road is a small parking area and a gate leading to the top of the cliff, where the beach below seems a slender ribbon of white against the dark blue water. Although a second, smaller gate seems to direct you to the right, walking through it takes you to a steep path ending in rocks.

Instead, walk down the hillside to the left on a well worn path with a gentle slope. Even when our children were small, they had little difficulty managing the descent or the climb back up. A five-minute walk down the slope brings you to a long, lovely beach curving along the coastline and disappearing around a distant bend—perfect for lazy afternoons of beachcombing and exploring. Although a rocky reef extending about 70 yards offshore seems to invite snorkeling, Larsen's Beach is one of the most dangerous on the island.

Before you begin the hike down, observe the ocean carefully and locate the channel through the reef, just to the left of the rocky point where you are standing. The churning water caused by the swift current makes the channel easiest to see from this height, and once noted, it can be recognized at sea level. Once you see this channel, you can also pick out the smaller channels which cut through the reef at several other points. Swimmers and snorkelers should avoid going near any of these channels, particularly the large one, because currents can be dangerously strong and even turn into a whirlpool when the tide is going out. Remember, Larsen's Beach has no lifeguard, and help is not close by. Currents can be exceptionally treacherous at *any* time, but particularly in winter months, and four years ago two experienced local fishermen drowned here. The watchword is caution: swim in pairs, never go out beyond the reef, try to

*Larsen's Beach, a great spot for beachwalking and shell collecting, even if winter surf is too strong for safe swimming.*

stay within easy distance of the shore, and examine the surface of the water carefully to avoid swimming near a channel. If you snorkel, don't get so absorbed in looking at the fish that you lose track of where you are, and don't go out at all if surf conditions don't seem right to you.

A trip to Larsen's Beach does not require swimming or snorkeling. If you bring reef-walking sneakers to protect your feet, you can walk around in the shallow water and watch colorful fish who don't seem afraid of people. Or walk for miles along the magnificent coastline of this picture-perfect beach. Hunt for shells, or simply lose yourself in the spectacle of nature's beauty. You will probably encounter only another person or two. The drive back is wonderful, with spectacular views of the rolling hills, lined by fences and stands of trees, and beyond them the dark and majestic mountains reaching to touch the clouds.

*Directions:* From Kapa'a, turn right off Rt. 56 onto Kuamo'o Road just a half-mile past the mile 16 marker (If you pass the dairy farm, you've missed the turn). Bear left at the Moloa'a Road turnoff, go about 1.1 miles and look for a dirt road on the right. The right turn marked 'beach access' will be very sharp and angled up an incline. Then another beach access sign will mark the left turn onto the long, straight road to the beach. From Hanalei, turn left off Rt. 56 at the mile 20 marker, and look for the beach access road on your left. Drive to the end of the beach access road, park, lock up, walk towards the cliff, and down the trail on the left. About 7 miles east of Princeville; 20 miles north of Lihue; 10 miles north of Kapa'a. Map 2.

# Kilauea Bay

If you've ever had the fantasy of searching through the jungle to find a remote and hidden paradise, Kahili Beach at Kilauea Bay should be your destination. The road to this unspoiled beach tests the mettle of both car and driver with challenges at practically every turn. Deeply rutted, even gouged in places by ditches and holes, it can turn into a quagmire in rain, but in dry weather, it can be navigated without too much difficulty by a careful driver even in a rented subcompact. Pick a dry day, and the road will add the zest of adventure and heighten the excitement of discovering, just down the hill from the parking area at road's end, a bay shaped like a perfect half-moon, the deep blue water sparkling with light, and the golden sand outstretched between two rocky bluffs like a tawny cat sleeping in the sun.

At the northern end is the Kilauea stream. One year it may be shallow enough for small children at low tide; the next, too deep. The width can vary from a few yards to fifty. To the left of the stream, the beach ends abruptly in an old rock quarry, a great spot for pole fishing. To the right of the stream, the sandy beach extends a long way before ending in piles of lava rocks which children will enjoy climbing and exploring for tidal pools. Chances are you'll encounter only another person or two and can watch in solitude as the waves roll towards the beach in long, even swells, break into dazzling white crests, and rush to shore in layers of gold and white foam.

Surf can be dangerously strong and the currents treacherous at certain times, particularly in winter when the beach may almost disappear beneath the crashing waves. We found the swimming safe enough in summer for our seven and ten-year-olds to surf on their boogie boards in the shallow water, although even close to shore the pull of the undertow made us watch them closely. The tiny blue Portuguese 'men o' war' are sometimes washed ashore here after a storm, so if you see any on the sand, go to another beach, for these small jellyfish pack a giant sting!

Behind the beach, the stream forms brackish pools where children can swim safely, except near the stream's entrance into the bay where the current can be swift, particularly at high tide. One August, the pools were wider than we had ever seen, like a shallow lagoon, and our family had a great time netting tadpoles. Our children loved this beach because of the variety of things they could do and the challenge of ripping the leaves off the branches that scraped the sides of the car as we maneuvered around the gullies on the way down and back. We love the beach because we have had it, sometimes, all to ourselves.

*Directions*: Just south of Kilauea, turn towards the ocean at Wailapa Road (between mile markers 21 and 22) and after .4 of a mile, turn left onto a dirt road and follow it (only in dry weather) for about a mile until you reach the beach. 25 miles north of Lihue; 39 miles from Poipu. Map 2

## Secret Beach

Secret Beach is one of those rare and special places where the world can be forgotten, where you can feel, for a few hours, as if you were alone at the beginning of time. The colors are brilliant, the breeze fresh and tangy with salt. The ocean reaches out to touch the sky at an endless horizon, and the crashing of waves is all you can hear. As you walk, you may leave the only footprints on warm, golden sand shining in the sun.

Nestled at the base of a sheer cliff just north of Kilauea, Secret Beach is well off the beaten track for good reason. You must hike down (and back up!) a rocky trail which zigzags through trees, gullies, and brush. You can drive only to the trail's beginning at the top of the cliff. From here, you can hear the waves crashing below—apparently not very far away—as you look down on a trail which seems to disappear into a tangle of jungle. The path is steep in places — sneakers are a good idea — but branches, roots, and vines offer plenty of handholds, and in a pinch, you can always resort to the seat of your pants!

The walk down will take about seven minutes, and it is pretty much straight down. As the path makes the last sharp plunge before leveling off to the sand, you can see, at last, through a screen of trees and hanging vines, a magnificent stretch of golden sand and a shining turquoise sea. In rainy times, this enormous triangle of sand may be partly covered by a lagoon fed by a stream winding down behind the beach. Towards the left, you can climb a rocky outcropping and find a small beach ending in a steep cliff. Towards the right, you can see the Kilauea lighthouse and walk a long way across the sand.

Secret Beach is not a place to come alone, for the obvious reason of its isolation. Swimming is not a good idea. The surf is rough, and the current strong and unpredictable; you'd never find a lifeguard if you were caught in a current. In fact, during the winter, this beach, enormous as it is, can disappear almost entirely under huge, crashing waves. Instead of swimming, walk along the water, hunt for shells, and forget everything but the feel of wet sand between your toes.

The walk back up the cliff will give you time to adjust to the world you left behind—just about 10 minutes of mild exertion, with the air cool under the trees and the leaves speckled with sunlight. This would not be pleasant in the mud, though, so plan your adventure with an eye to the weather and don't go after a soaking rain. By the time you reach your car and remember that you have to stop at the store for milk, the peaceful solitude you left behind will be as hard to recapture as a wave rippling on the sand. But for a few moments, you were lost to your working-day world. This may be the secret of Secret Beach, a secret worth keeping!

*Directions:* Drive north of Kilauea on Rt. 56 about a half mile. Turn right onto Kalihiwai Road. Bear left, then turn right onto a dirt road which looks like a broad red gash in the landscape. Follow towards the water till it ends. Park, lock up and walk down the trail. The rest is up to you! Note: One reader discovered another secret about this beach, when she and her family reached the bottom of the trail and ran into "a long-haired young man wearing nothing but a guitar!" So be prepared for strange music! Secret Beach is about 25 miles north of Lihue; 39 miles from Poipu; 15 miles from Kapa'a. Map 2

*Surfing at Kalihiwai on a summer day*

## Kalihiwai Bay

You'll catch your first glimpse of Kalihiwai Bay as you drive down the narrow road carved into the side of the sheer cliff which encloses it on one side. From this angle, the

## Sea changes

*Kalihiwai—our favorite family beach on the north shore. In summer, the ocean can be calm, almost like a lake (below) while in winter, thundering surf can crash onto the sand  (above).*

bay is a perfect semi-circle of blue, rimmed with shining white sand and nestled between two lava cliffs. Ironwood trees ring the beach, just about completely regrown after being sheared of their branches by Iniki's winds. A clear, freshwater stream flows into the bay near the far end, so shallow and gentle at low tide that small children can splash around safely. It becomes deep enough behind the beach for kayak adventuring up-river.

One of our favorite family beaches, Kalihiwai Bay offers wonderful summertime fun for people of all ages. Little ones will love the shallow pools behind the beach where they can fish or float on rafts, while older kids will enjoy the rope swing. Ocean swimming is terrific too! The waves rise very slowly and break in long, even crests over a sloping sandy bottom, perfect for wave jumping and boogie boarding. One summer day we watched a dozen children celebrate a birthday with a surfing party. In winter, the surf and currents in the bay can become formidable. Even experienced surfers may have difficulty managing the currents which can be particularly strong when a swell is running. Even if the surf is too rough, Kalihiwai is a lovely beach for walking or running, with firm sand and magnificent views of the cliffs.

*Directions:* A yellow siren atop a pole just south of the beach is a reminder of the *tsunami* or tidal wave of 1957 which washed away the bridge originally linking the two roads leading from Rt. 56 to the bay. Both are still marked Kalihiwai Road at their separate intersections with Rt. 56. Either one will take you to the bay, although, if you choose the Kalihiwai Road just north of the long bridge on Rt. 56, you'll have to wade across the stream's mouth in order to reach the beach. The Kalihiwai Road south of the bridge and just northwest of Kilauea is the preferable route. It winds through a rural residential area before curving down the steep cliff on the southern edge of the bay. Kalihiwai is about 25 miles north of Lihue; 39 miles from Poipu; 15 miles from Kapa'a. Map 2

## Anini Beach

At the edge of Anini Road, you will find miles of white sandy beach protected by a reef. At some places the beach road is so close to the water that you could almost jump in! A beach park offers restrooms and picnic facilities, although you can turn off the road at almost any spot, park, and find your private paradise. The reef creates a quiet lagoon, great for summertime snorkeling, and for windsurfing at any time of year. During high surf, particularly in winter, the current running parallel to the beach can become strong enough to pull an unwary swimmer out through the channel in the reef at the west end of the park. Stay inside the reef.

Across from the Beach Park, the Kauai Polo Club hosts polo matches on summer Sunday afternoons. Continue along Anini road through a quiet residential area all the way to its western end, where a  sandbar extending quite far out invites wading and fishing.  Children enjoy the quiet water and the tiny shells along the waterline, and you'll love the amazing combination of sounds— the roar of the surf breaking on the reef far offshore, and near your feet, the gentle rippling of the sea upon the sand.

In summer months, you can watch the sun set into the ocean at Anini Beach, a glorious sight which can be yours in perfect solitude.  The tall ironwood trees darken to feathery silhouettes against a pale gray and orange sky, filled with lines of puff clouds.  The water shimmers gold as the sun's dying fire fades slowly to a pearl and smoky gray, to the songs of crickets and the lapping of gentle waves.

*Directions:*  Drive north on Rt. 56, pass Kilauea, and turn towards the ocean at Kalihiwai Road (the northern one, between mile markers 25 and 26).  Bear left at the fork, following the road as it winds downhill past the park and continues to the base of the cliffs at Princeville.  Anini is about 1 mile east of Princeville.  Map 2

## Pu'u Poa Beach, Princeville

Tucked beneath the Princeville Resort Hotel's ocean bluff perch is a sandy beach set inside a reef.  When you look down from the hotel, you can see the rocky bottom that makes swimming less than perfect.  This same reef can make for good snorkeling in calm summer seas, but you must negotiate your way carefully through one of the small sandy channels into the deeper water.  In winter,  waves crash against the outer reef, and it becomes a challenging surfing spot.

Public access is available though a cement path leading from the left of the gatehouse entry to the Hotel.  Be forewarned: on the way down the cliff, you'll have to descend nearly 200 steps (and then come back *up* those same steps later on)!  You can explore the beach more easily if you visit the hotel for breakfast or lunch, both wonderful meals in a spectacular setting.  Simply take the hotel elevator down to the beach level, where lovely gardens frame the sand.  Bring a  camera!  Map 1

*Directions:*  Drive Rt.  56 north, enter Princeville at the main entrance (pick up a free map) and stay on Ka Haku Road until the end.  Park in the hotel visitor's lot if you're going to the hotel for lunch.  If not, try the small public lot just in front and to the right of the hotel entry gate.

## Pali Ke Kua or 'Hideaways' Beach

At the base of the cliff near the Pali Ke Kua Condominiums in Princeville is a lovely sandy beach set inside a reef, where you can watch the sun sparkle on the waves in near solitude.  It is a peaceful spot, secluded and beautiful, actually two beaches connected by a rocky point.  Swimming is not the best because of the coral bottom and the offshore rocks, but snorkeling can be very good in calm summer seas.  Be cautious.  As on all north shore beaches, snorkeling can be risky and is advisable only in a calm ocean; when the surf is up, currents can become dangerous.  In winter, waves can cover the beach entirely.  It's called Hideaways for good reason.  It's hard to get to, popular primarily with surfers or with people staying at Pali Ke Kua who can use the condominium's improved concrete pathway down the cliff.  The public right-of-way is much more difficult, half of it made up of steep steps with a railing, and the rest dwindling to dirt path.  It can be slippery, even treacherous, when wet.  The trek down will take about ten minutes, and the way up, as you can imagine, somewhat longer!

*Directions:*  Enter Princeville, drive to the hotel and park in the lot. The hotel staff usually doesn't mind if you take one of the back spaces nearest the cliff, where you'll see the top of the steps down to the beach. Map 2

## Hanalei Bay

A long half-moon of sandy beach carved into the base of a sheer cliff on one side and narrowing into a rocky point on the other, Hanalei Bay is simply spectacular.  You find it at the end of almost any road in Hanalei leading off Rt. 560 towards the water.  If you turn right off Rt. 560 onto Aku Road, then right onto Weke Road, you will find the Hanalei Pavilion, with showers and restrooms; at the far end of Weke is the Hanalei pier.  Several Trans-Pacific Cup Races from California to Hawaii end here, and during summer, gaily colored boats rock gently at anchor.  The boats are moved out of the bay, however, by mid-October, and by winter, twenty-foot waves are not uncommon.

Looking for surf?  You'll find the biggest breakers near the center of the curving coastline, where surfers come to hunt the perfect ride.  During winter months, when the surf can become dangerous, Hanalei Bay is still wonderful— the wide sandy beach firm and level for hard running.  Walk west to where the Wai'oli Stream, icy cold from mountain water, flows into the bay.  Sometimes it's shallow, at other times the current is formidable, but at all times it's a beautiful, peaceful spot, with waves crossing

*Hanalei can be peaceful and calm
in summer, but winter waves can
reach 20 feet, and boats move to
safer harbors on the south shore
and westside.*

from different directions in foam glistening with gold.

West of the town, you can explore almost any road turning off Route
560 towards the water. At the westernmost curve of the bay, near the mile
4 marker, you'll find a calm, protected beach where the water is relatively
quiet even when most of the north shore is too rough for safe swimming.

*Directions:* Drive Rt. 560 north, pass Princeville, and enter the town of
Hanalei (mile 3 marker). Aku Road (or any other right turn) will take you
to Weke Road, which runs along the bay from east to west. If you turn
right on Weke, the road passes public facilities and showers at Hanalei
Pavilion before it ends at Hanalei River. If you turn left onto Weke, you
can turn right onto several 'right of way to beach' streets leading to the
Bay. Showers, restrooms available at Ama'ama Rd., called 'Second
Parking Lot.' About 33 miles from Lihue, 47 miles from Poipu; 23 miles
from Kapa'a. Map 2.

*www.explorekauai.com*

# Lumahai Beach

The setting for the Bali Hai scenes in the movie *South Pacific*, Lumahai Beach is stunningly beautiful, a curve of white sand nestled at the base of a dark lava cliff, with a giant lava rock jutting out of the turquoise sea just offshore. Getting there requires a trek down from the road, possibly through slippery mud (showers are frequent on the north shore), and the trip back up is even worse, especially if you have to carry a tired child. If there are toddlers in you family, you might consider hiring a babysitter or buying a postcard!

Swimming at Lumahai Beach can be dangerous, particularly during winter months. Without a reef to offer protection from unpredictable currents and rip tides, Lumahai Beach is one of the most treacherous spots on the island. Beware of climbing that spectacular offshore rock for a photograph, as a sudden powerful wave can easily knock you off!

At the western end of Lumahai, about a mile further on Rt. 560, is a beach with wide golden sand and breakers and currents which can be big enough to make swimming dangerous. Children will love playing in the stream flowing into the sea, ice cold from mountain rainwater.

The stream meets the ocean at a huge rocky bluff, a spectacular place to sit quietly and watch the waves crash against the rocks, sending dazzling spray into the air. It is also a beautiful beach for walking, although the coarse sand is hard-going near the waterline, and you must cross a vast expanse of hot sand to get from the parking area to the sea. Bring sandals! Hunt for striped scallop shells shining in the sun, or wander all the way to the other rocky bluff that separates this part of Lumahai Beach from the part pictured in all the post-cards. Trying to cross the rocks would be hazardous, however, even at low tide,

*Lumahai Beach*

because an occasional "killer wave" can come up suddenly out of no-where and smash you into the rocks. A small cave etched into the base of the cliff with a floor of powder soft, cool sand invites daydreaming and wave-watching.

*Directions*: Pass Hanalei on Rt. 560. Look for the mile 4 marker. You'll see many cars parked on the shoulder just past a 25 m.p.h. sign. Park on the right, lock up, and begin the hike down. To get to the western end of Lumahai, drive to the mile 5 marker, look for an emergency telephone by the road. Across the street is the entrance to a sandy parking area. About 34 miles from Lihue; 49 miles from Poipu; 24 miles from Kapaʻa. Map 2

## Tunnels

Makua Beach, popularly known as Tunnels Beach, has a large lagoon perfect for swimming because it is protected by two reefs, the outer reef favored by surfers for perfect arcs, and the inner reef filled with cavities and crevices for snorkelers to explore for fish and sea life. Divers love the outer reef for its tunnels, caverns and sudden, dramatic drop off. Tunnels is about the only beach on the north shore that is usually calm enough for those trying to snorkel for the first time, although even here you may find rough surf and treacherous currents during winter months.

Listen to the surf reports, and plan any winter visits for times when surf is manageable, and preferably at low tide. In calm conditions, bring the kids and let them paddle about on boogie boards while the older ones try their luck with mask and snorkel. Bring a plastic baggy of fish food, or even a green leaf, swish it in the water and you'll be surrounded by fish! Swimming through the coral formations of the reef, which is almost like a maze of tunnels, can be great fun when the water is quiet. Enter the reef through one of the small sandy channels or the large one on the right, and dozens of fish in rainbow colors will swim right up to your mask. If the showers which frequent the north shore rain on your parade, you can take shelter under the ironwood trees—or under your boogie board! If you see a monk seal lying on the beach, give it a wide berth. It's probably exhausted, sleeping before heading out to sea. Seals don't trust humans and need privacy to rest.

Warning: Even when the area between the two reefs may look calm enough for safe swimming, watch out for these danger signs: high surf on the outer reef or fast moving ripples in the channel between the reefs. These indicate powerful, swift currents that could sweep you out through the channel into open ocean. Instead of swimming, hunt for shells on the beach, or walk around the rocks to the east, where you may find sunbathers with very dark tans in all the best places.

*The reefs at Makua Beach, or Tunnels, can be great for snorkeling.*

*Directions*: Drive west of Princeville on Rt. 560, and go 1.1 miles west of the entrance to the Hanalei Colony Resort. You will pass the mile 8 marker and the turnoff to the YMCA camp. Tunnels can get crowded, particularly in summer. Parking is difficult if not occasionally impossible because the area close to the beach is fenced off. Expect to cram your car in along the shoulder— if you can! Or in a pinch, park at Ha'ena Beach Park and walk over. No public facilities. Tunnels is about 38 miles from Lihue; 53 miles from Poipu; 28 miles from Kapa'a. Map 2

## Ha'ena Beach Park

An icy stream winds across this lovely golden sand beach curving along the coastline. The water is a dazzling blue. Reefs bordering both sides of the beach, named 'Maniniholo' after the large schools of striped convict fish feeding on the coral, provide summertime snorkeling, when the waves are gentle enough for swimming and rafting. During winter months, however, large waves can break right onto the beach, making swimming, even standing, a hazardous activity. Restrooms, showers, picnic and barbecue facilities are available, as well as camping by permit. You can walk a long way in both directions, with spectacular views of the towering cliffs and shimmering sea.

Directions: From Princeville, follow Rt. 560 west and pass the mile 8 marker. Ha'ena Beach Park will be on your right, about 40 miles from Lihue; 54 miles from Poipu; 8 miles from Princeville. Map 2

## Ke'e Beach

When you can drive no further on the main road along Kauai's north shore, you will discover a beach so beautiful you won't quite believe it to be real. The Na Pali cliffs rise like dark green towers behind the golden sand, and a reef extending out from shore creates a peaceful lagoon ideal for summertime swimming. As you walk along the shining sand, new cliffs come into view until the horizon is filled with their astonishing shapes and you begin to imagine captive princesses in enchanted castles.

Like all beaches on the north shore, the surf at Ke'e Beach varies with the seasons. Winter surf can reach 20 feet, when the ocean roars with crashing waves and churning foam with undercurrents far too strong for safe swimming. In summer, the turquoise water can be perfectly still and so clear that bubbles on the surface cast shadows on the sandy bottom.

Snorkeling can be spectacular alongside the reef, where the water,

*Ke'e Beach's lagoon (at left in this photograph) is great for summer swimming, but thunders with surf in winter.*

though warmed by the sun, will feel ice cold along the surface from rainshowers. If the tide is not too low, you can snorkel on top of the reef itself. Be careful: The coral reef may look shallow enough to walk on, but you won't want to take a chance on coral cuts. Be careful too of unpredictable currents in the channel to the left of the reef, as they can be strong enough to pull a swimmer out of this sheltered area into the open sea. A lifeguard is usually on duty to keep swimmers out of the channel.

Large trees at the beach provide shade for babies and protection from the occasional rainshowers which cool the air and make the coastline sparkle. The dark sand can be very hot, so you'll need your sandals. Small children can play and swim safely in the shallow water or climb over the rocks at low tide. Bring nets and pails for small fishermen.

Sometimes you can walk west across the rocks and around the point. From this vantage point, the Na Pali cliffs are truly magnificent —jutting into the cobalt blue ocean in vivid green ridges, the surf crashing in thundering sprays of foam. This walk can be dangerous in any but the calmest sea, and you must watch the direction of the tide carefully so that your return trip does not involve crossing slippery rocks through crashing waves. Ke'e Beach, lovely as it looks, can have treacherous currents and unpredictable surf, and so extra caution is a must. For a spectacular, bird's eye view of Ke'e Lagoon, consider climbing the first quarter-mile of the hiking trail to Hanakapia'i Beach. If possible come early and come midweek, for parking at this lovely and popular spot is hard to come by, especially in summer.

*Directions:* Follow Rt. 56 north to Princeville and then continue (The road becomes Rt. 560) to the very end. Park alongside the road, as close to the beach as you can get. Or turn right at the dirt road by the showers and restrooms, and look for a space (if you are lucky) under the trees. About 40 miles from Lihue; 54 miles from Poipu; 30 miles from Kapa'a. Map 2

# North Shore Shopping Stops

In KILAUEA, *s*top by at *Kong Lung* and explore a wonderful collection of works by local artists, as well as antiques, jewelry, souvenirs, beautiful gourmet cookware and tableware, and Hawaiian style shirts and dresses, including a special section of toys for children. Browsing is a treat! Next door is *Kilauea Bakery* and *Island Soap &Candle*. The fragrances are tantalizing, and the careful blend of oils will do wonders for your skin.

PRINCEVILLE Shopping Center has interesting shops, like *SanDudes* for beachwear and *Pretty Woman* for sophisticated clothes and jewelry, and even an internet cafe —*Akamai Computers* with DSL connection. At *Ace Hardware*, you can find beach/picnic gear. On Rt. 56 closer to Hanalei you'll find *Ola's*, where Doug and Sharon Britt display an eclectic collection of handcrafted puzzles, glass, jewelry, wooden bowls, baskets, and furniture, each piece almost a collage of extraordinary and interesting bits and pieces. In HANALEI village, island artists exhibit at *Evolve Love Gallery,* and you'll love to browse the interesting shops in the growing "downtown," like *Yellowfish Trading Co.* for vintage hula gear, postcards, and collectibles. Try *Hanalei Surf Company* and *Sand People* for wonderful beachwear, *Rainbow Ducks* for children's clothes, *Tropical Tantrum* and *Hot Rocket* for fashions. Across the street *The Back Door*, is a new shop devoted to skateboards, as well as surfing.

You may see a monk seal lying on almost any Kauai beach. Give it a wide berth — it's probably exhausted, resting before heading back out to sea. State law requires a 'safe distance' of 50 feet from the seal. If you try to get closer, you run the risk of provoking a nasty bite, or perhaps frightening the animal into the water before it has fully rested. The Hawaiian Monk Seal is on the list of endangered species.

## South Shore Beaches

*Maha'ulepu*

## Favorite Beaches

When it's raining up north, you may want to travel south (even west) to find the sun! In the island's lee, south shore beaches offer relatively calm swimming conditions all year, except during a south shore 'swell.'

\* **Poipu Beach Park** is perfect for families, the rock rimmed pool a safe place for small children, and the snorkeling at the other end of the curving beach is wonderful for older ones and their parents (p. 68).

\* Our favorite hidden beach (though increasingly popular), is **Maha'ulepu Beach** east of Poipu. Wild and beautiful (p. 65)!

\* Enjoy lunch with a slice of ocean at *Brennecke's Beach Broiler,* (p. 206) or later, dinner with the colors of sunset. Great lunches are a short drive away in Kalaheo: *Camp House Grill* and *Brick Oven Pizza* (p. 208)

## Restaurants

1   Camp House Cantina 229
2   Hanapepe Cafe 230
3   Green Garden Rest. 229
4   Camp House Grill 208
5   Brick Oven Pizza 208
6   Kalaheo Steak House 214
7   Pomodoro 220
8   Beach House Rest. 204
9   Pizzetta 185
    Tomkats Grill 226
10  Taqueria Nortenos 225
11  Keoki's Paradise 215
    Roy's Poipu Grill 222
    Pattaya 218
12  Piatti 218
    Shells 224
13  Brennecke's Broiler 206
14  House of Seafood 212

15  Hyatt Regency Hotel:
    Poipu Bay Clubhouse 220
    Tidepools 225
    Dondero's 211

## Beaches

Kipu Kai 64
Maha'ulepu 65
Shipwreck Beach 66
Brennecke's Beach 67
Poipu Beach Park 68
Salt Pond
    Beach Park 72

## Hotels

A  Kiahuna 13
    Sheraton 13
B  Poipu Kai 13
C  Embassy Resort
    at Poipu Point 13
D  Hyatt Regency 11

Rt. 50 Kaumuali'i Highway heads west from Lihue to Kalaheo, Hanapepe, Kekaha, & Waimea.
Rt. 520 connects Rt. 50 with Koloa, & from there south to Poipu.

# South Shore
## Map 3

Hanapepe River

Wainawa Stream

Olu Pua Gardens

Kalaheo  4  5

Lawai

Hailima Rd

50

Papalina Rd

Lawai Stream

Kukuiolono Park & Golf Course

6  7

To Kekaha and Waimea

Hanapepe  1 2 3

Eleele  50

Eleele Shopping Center

540

National Tropical Botanical Gardens

Lele

Halewili Rd

Port Allen

Lolokai

Salt Pond Beach Park

Hanapepe Bay

Port Allen Airport

Crop Rd

Cane Coast Rd

Wahua Rd

Allerton Gardens

Numila Sugar Mill

Nomilo Fishpond

Lawai Kai Beach

Palama Beach

Lawai' Bay

N

0    1    2
Miles

*The wild beauty of Maha'ulepu. Page 65.*

*Heliconia blooms at NTBG Gardens, Lawai. (p.133)*

*Poipu Beach Park*

Kahili
Mountain
Park

To Lihue

50

Tree
Tunnel

520

Matuna Rd

Kaumuali Hwy

Omao Rd

Koloa Rd

530

Waikomo Rd

Waita
Reservior

**Koloa**

9

Weliweli Rd

Koloa
Sugar
Mill

Kipu
Kai

Long
Beach

520

Koloa-Poipu Bypass

Camp Rd

CJM
Stables

Ha'ula
Beach

Maha'ulepu
Beaches

Kawailoa
Bay

8

Lawai Rd

Prince
Kuhio
Park

10

Kiahuna
Golf
Course

Gillin's
Beach

Poipu
Bay
Resort
Golf
Club

Kukui'ula
Small Boat
Harbor

Spouting
Horn

Lawai
Beach

Poipu Rd

Hoonani Rd

Koloa
Landing

Poipu
Shopping
Village

11

**Poipu**

A 12
13 B 14

Poipu
Beach
Park

C

Brennecke's
Beach

15 D

Keoniloa
Bay

Shipwreck
Beach

**Kauai**

South
Shore

*Great Days on the South Shore*

Day 1. Breakfast at Tomkats, Koloa (p. 226). Take a boat cruise (p. 124) along the south shore to Kipu Kai (winter) or Na Pali Coast (summer). At the end of the day, head to Maha'ulepu Beach for great walking (p. 65). Sunset dinner at Beach House (p. 205). Or watch the sky glow at sunset from Poipu Beach Park (p.68) and dine at Brennecke's (p. 206). Stroll through the beautiful Hyatt Resort after dinner (free valet parking).

Day 2. Visit Kauai's National Tropical Botanical Gardens (p.133), or bike to Maha'ulepu (p. 82) or trail ride (p. 102). Then snorkel at Poipu Beach Park. Before dinner, enjoy the Hawaiian music show at Hyatt's Seaview lounge. Dinner at Roy's. Stroll through the Kiahuna and Sheraton grounds after dinner.

# Kipu Kai

You can only get to Kipu Kai by boat, for the private road crossing the gap in the mountains between Rt. 50 and the south shore is deeply rutted and gouged, suitable only for the sturdiest 4 wheel drive vehicles. Some boat companies offer day trips to this lovely section of Kauai's coastline (p. 127).

Kipu Kai is actually three beaches which share a rocky peninsula shaped like an alligator. Long Beach is, as you would expect from the name, stretches out in a long line of fine sand in the shape of a half moon, nearly enclosed by outcroppings of rocks at each end. Set at the base of the rocky mountains behind Kipu Kai, Long Beach is special among south shore beaches, combining the favorable weather of the south with a rugged beauty more characteristic of the north shore. As if this weren't enough, the ocean is relatively gentle due to the rocky points which embrace the beach, breaking the surf and creating a protected lagoon.

A wonderful old rambling ranch house sits atop Turtle Beach, so named for its shape. The house was built in stages by the Waterhouse family using orders of wood and supplies floated ashore from cargo ships. From the veranda overlooking the bay, Jack Waterhouse used to communicate with the "rest of the world" by signals. According to his will, the Waterhouse family descendents retain use of the land until the end of the next generation, when Kipu Kai Ranch is destined to become a state park.

## Maha'ulepu

At the end of a dusty drive through winding sugar cane roads, you will find a beautiful sandy beach carved into a rocky point. This part of the south shore can be very dry and very hot — and you'll soon find a thin red film on every surface inside your car, including you! But it's worth the dust to reach a beach astonishing in its wild beauty, the surf crashing against the rocks and sand, the churning turquoise water almost glowing with sunlight. Beautiful it is, but often not safe enough for swimming. Unless surf on the whole south shore is flat, you may find the waves crashing with enough force to knock you down, and currents powerful enough to make even local people wary.

Maha'ulepu is a lovely beach for walking and exploring. On the eastern end, a lovely half-moon of golden sand nestles at the base of a rocky cliff. A long walk to the west takes you past a rocky reef which at low tide juts out of the sand in fascinating formations. As you reach the end of the curve, the tip turns out to be a point, and on the other side, you'll find another, even longer stretch of beach. Here the water ripples in toward shore, protected by an offshore reef where the waves roll in long, even swells. You might see a fisherman casting his line or even a

*Maha'ulepu*

*Solitude at Maha'ulepu*

swimmer snorkeling among the rocks if the sea is calm. When the tradewinds are strong, windsurfers splash color on the sparkling sea. At the western-most end, at Gillin's Beach, you will find a new house built on the spot where plantation manager Gillin once lived. Sunwarmed tidal pools are shallow and still, and kids can catch tiny fish in nets.

At the far eastern end of Maha'ulepu is a rocky bluff. After a moderate uphill climb, you will come to a promontory with spectacular views of the coastline. Rock formations are astonishing, and a tiny beach set into the cliffside shelters interesting pools of tiny sea life. Be careful near the rocks, as a sudden wave could knock you off.

*Directions:* Take Rt. 50 to Rt. 520 (the Koloa Road), and follow signs to Poipu. Take Poipu Road past the Hyatt Regency, continue on to the unpaved road, and pass the golf course and the quarry. When you come to a stop sign, turn right and head toward the water. This is sugar company land; you might have to stop at a gatehouse and sign a release to gain entry. At road's end, park or turn left to another lot. Map 3

## Shipwreck Beach

Shipwreck Beach along Keoniloa Bay was never much of a beach—until the hurricane blasted the south shore of Kauai and created a new coastline. What was once a thin curve of sand is now enormous, a long, golden crescent divided by lava rocks. It's called Shipwreck Beach with good reason; the surf is powerful, breaking in long, shining arcs which crest slowly, one at a time, with deceptive smoothness, and then crash in thunderous explosions of spray not far from shore. Local people warn that beyond the break point are dangerous currents and large rocks. A better place for family swimming would be Poipu Beach Park, and novice

*At Shipwreck Beach, you can walk along the rocky bluff and explore the rock formations.*

surfers would be better off at Wailua Beach, where rocks and wind are not a problem and a lifeguard is on duty.  Be particularly careful during summer months, when a south shore swell can bring big surf.

Instead of swimming, you can climb the cliff to explore strange caves and rock formations.  The colors are breathtaking—the deep blue of the water and the gold of the cliffs dazzle the eye, and the view down is a dizzying spectacle of surf crashing against the rocks.  Be careful, though.  Avoid going close to the cliff's edge, as the footing is slippery with loose sand.  It's great for photographers but not for children.

*Directions:*  Take Poipu Road past the main entrance to the Hyatt Hotel.  Turn toward the water on Ainako Road.  Park in the lot.  Public access restrooms and showers are by the parking lot.  Shipwreck is 14 miles from Lihue;  24 miles  from Kapaʻa;  44 miles from Princeville.  Map 3

## Brennecke's Beach

Legendary for years as the best beach for body surfing in Hawaii, Brennecke's Beach is finally recovering from Hurricane Iniki, which smashed giant boulders into the seawall and washed away most of the sand.  Today, as the sand is slowly coming back, the waves are gradually returning to their old pattern, breaking far out for the big kids, and then again closer to shore for younger ones to catch a swift and exciting ride.  After Hurricane Iwa caused a similar level of destruction in 1982, the return of the sandy bottom took ten years.  This time, however, the county has received funds to aid the recovery by restoring Brennecke's Beach to what it was like long ago. Following recommendations by the Army Corps of Engineers, the seawall will be removed, in order to conserve the sand. We're hoping for great things when this project is completed! — perhaps by our seventeenth or eighteenth anniversary edition. . . .

*Directions:* Take Poipu Beach Road past the Waiohai, turn right on Ho'owili Road then right at Ho'one Road and park in the lot by Brennecke's Beach Broiler. Poipu Beach Park is across the street, and Brennecke's Beach just down the road to the left. Map 3

## Poipu Beach Park

You could not imagine a more perfect beach for children than this lovely curve of soft golden sand sloping down to a gentle, friendly sea. The waves, with changing shades of turquoise sparkling with sunlight and dazzling white foam, break gently over a protective reef across the entrance to this small cove. For babies and toddlers, a ring of black lava

rocks creates a sheltered pool where the water is shallow and still. For older children, waves beyond the pool roll to shore in graceful swells perfect for rafts or body boards. Children can explore the long rocky point at the far end of the beach and find tiny fish in the tidal pools. Bring nets and pails for the hunt! You'll find a lifeguard, as well as restrooms, outdoor showers, barbecues, picnic tables, and shaded pavilions.

Just around the rocky point, in front of the old Waiohai Hotel (destined to become a time-share resort operated by the Marriott) you can enjoy some of the best snorkeling on the island. Hundreds of fish in rainbow colors feed on the coral, so tame they almost swim into your hands. Carry snorkeling fish food in a plastic bag, or even a green leaf, and they'll swim right to you! Stay inside the reef to avoid being caught in a strong current. Sometimes you may see a monk seal taking sun on the sand. It's resting, gathering strength to face another day in paradise!

*Directions:* In Poipu, take Ho'owilili Road to Ho'one Road. Park in lot.

## Poipu Beach (Kiahuna & Sheraton)

Once upon a time, you could walk all along Poipu Beach from the Beach Park to the Sheraton, but today access is blocked, so you'll need to park near the Sheraton Hotel. The beach in front of the Kiahuna and the Sheraton is great for swimming and playing in the waves, though be careful as the drop off is fairly steep, and the current can be strong. Wonderful rolling waves are great for rafting and swimming. You can also take surfing lessons from Margo Oberg's surfing school.

To park near the Kiahuna and Sheraton, turn right off Ho'owilili Rd. at the Sheraton's sign, then turn left at Hoonani Rd. and continue to end. Enter the last driveways on the left and on the right to public parking.

## South Shore Shopping Stops

In POIPU, the must stop, according to the Horowitz kids, is *Nukomoi*, next to Brennecke's Restaurant, for its terrific selection of surf wear by Roxy, Quicksilver, and fun local brands like *Chicks Who Rip* (Lauren's favorite is a tee-shirt featuring Rosie the Riveter). Owner Christine French and daughter Kelly assemble the latest greatest stuff at reasonable prices, including Billabong wallets and cool Roxy hula watches.

In KOLOA, Stop in at *Hula Moon* for jewelry and other crafts by Kauai artists. At *Kauai Fine Arts*, (also in Hanapepe) you'll find old maps, engravings, and books, with a particular focus on the exploration of Hawaii by French, Russian, English and American explorers. Poipu Shopping Village near Kiahuna has galleries, including *Ships Store Gallery*, clothing stores, collectibles, as well as *Whaler's General Store*.

In LAWAI, the *Hawaiian Trading Post* at the junction of Rt. 50 and Rt. 530 near Koloa has a wide selection of jewelry, including Ni'ihau shell leis. For bargains in souvenirs, try the daily outdoor souvenir market at Spouting Horn.

*Salt Pond Beach Park — great for families, and often a sunny spot when other parts of the island are cloudy.*

# Westside Beach Adventures

## *Favorite Beaches*

    * **Salt Pond Beach Park** offers great swimming, protected by a reef, as well as usually sunny weather. Kids love the tidal pools (p. 72).

    * At **Kekaha**, you'll find firm sand and miles of beach perfect for beachwalking and running, as well as surf for body boards (p. 74).

    * Drive all the way to the end of the road to magnificent **Polihale Beach**, the westernmost part of the island, perfect for sunsets (p. 76).

    * On your trips west, stop off at Hanapepe's **Green Garden** for inexpensive island style food — and lilikoi chiffon pie (p.229). **Wrangler's Restaurant** in Waimea makes great hamburgers and salads (p. 233), or try the new **Ono Burger** in Waimea for the burgers that made the Anahola branch famous. Afterwards sample a frostie at **Pualani's Fruit Stand** across the street.

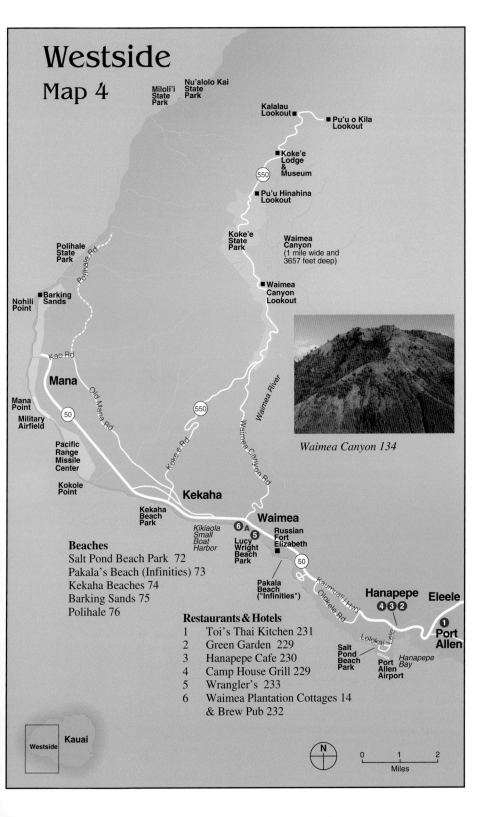

# Westside
## Map 4

Miloli'i State Park

Nu'alolo Kai State Park

Kalalau Lookout ■

■ Pu'u o Kila Lookout

■ Koke'e Lodge & Museum

550

■ Pu'u Hinahina Lookout

Koke'e State Park

Waimea Canyon (1 mile wide and 3657 feet deep)

■ Waimea Canyon Lookout

*Waimea Canyon 134*

Polihale State Park

Polihale Rd

Nohili Point

■ Barking Sands

Kao Rd

**Mana**

Old Mana Rd

550

Waimea River

Waimea Canyon Rd

Mana Point

Military Airfield

50

Pacific Range Missile Center

Kokole Point

Koke'e Rd

**Kekaha**

Kekaha Beach Park

*Kikiaola Small Boat Harbor*

**6** A
**5**

**Waimea**

Russian Fort Elizabeth ■

Lucy Wright Beach Park

50

## Beaches
Salt Pond Beach Park  72
Pakala's Beach (Infinities)  73
Kekaha Beaches  74
Barking Sands  75
Polihale  76

Pakala Beach ("Infinities")

Kaumuali'i Hwy

Olokele Rd

**Hanapepe**

**4 3 2**

**Eleele**

**1**

**Port Allen**

Salt Pond Beach Park

Port Allen Airport

Lolokai

*Hanapepe Bay*

Lele

## Restaurants & Hotels
1  Toi's Thai Kitchen 231
2  Green Garden  229
3  Hanapepe Cafe 230
4  Camp House Grill 229
5  Wrangler's 233
6  Waimea Plantation Cottages 14
   & Brew Pub 232

Kauai

Westside

N

0    1    2
Miles

## Great Days on the Westside

Day 1: Drive to Polihale Beach (p. 76) for picnic, or drive Waimea Canyon Road to Koke'e (p. 134). Stop off at Kekaha Beach if time permits. Frostie at Pualena's. Dinner at Wrangler's (p. 233).

Day 2: Tour the Na Pali Coast by boat (p. 124), or visit the quaint town of Hanapepe, test its swinging bridge, browse the art galleries and have lunch at Hanapepe Cafe (p. 230). Afternoon: Salt Pond Beach Park or Kekaha. Dinner at Toi's Thai Kitchen (p. 231).

## Salt Pond Beach Park

What is most astonishing about Salt Pond Beach Park is the intensity of the colors—the brilliant blues of the water and sky, the bright gold of the sand, the vivid greens of sugar cane fields extending in squares and rectangles up the slopes of nearby mountains—all bathed in sunshine that makes everything sparkle. The beach is a perfect semicircle, where the sand slopes downward with the lovely grace of a golden bowl to hold the sea. A reef near the mouth of this sheltered cove breaks the surf into slow, rolling swells that break again gently near the shore so that children can raft and swim safely inside this natural lagoon most of the year. At both ends of the beach, tidepools can be calm enough at low tide for babies and toddlers, and great fun for older ones when the incoming tide splashes over the rocks, making waterfalls. Kids can try their luck at catching tiny, swift fish in nets.

Walk along the beach and explore tidal pools and the ancient salt ponds where local people still harvest sea salt. The park is spectacular, especially when brightly colored windsurfers race out across the reef, and particularly favored in terms of weather. Even when clouds and rain prevail elsewhere, this little point of land seems to escape them, and in winter, the water seems a few degrees warmer and more friendly.

Showers, rest rooms, picnic tables, and barbecues make Salt Pond a popular weekend spot for local families and increasingly for tourists, although the beach never seems crowded. Be careful in periods of high surf, however, as unpredictable currents can create hazardous swimming, and stay inside the lagoon. For lunch, stop at the Hanapepe Cafe or Green Garden (fabulous coconut cream or lilikoi chiffon pies).

*Salt Pond Beach tidepool — perfect for kids!*

*Directions:* Take Rt. 50 west to Hanapepe and pass through the town. Turn left at Lele St., and take the first right onto Lokokai Rd. Continue until you see the parking area. Salt Pond Beach Park is 18 miles from Lihue; 28 miles from Kapa'a; 58 miles from Princeville. Map 4

## Pakala's Beach or 'Infinities'

On this lovely, curving beach, the sand and sea are deep gold, as if sprinkled with cinnamon, because the A'akukui stream carries red sugar cane soil to the sea. You can hear the crash of the waves as you walk across the pastureland, and by the time you pass through the trees which ring the sand, you'll feel like you're alone on a deserted island. It is a lovely spot. The waves rise gracefully in long, even lines crested with gold. Each wave breaks and rushes onto the sand in shining foam, and then it rolls back out again to meet the wave coming in, a fascinating ballet, sometimes meeting like dancers in perfect rhythm, sometimes colliding in bursts of spray. You could watch the waves for hours and never see two waves embrace in exactly the same way.

The bay is divided by a rocky point where local fishermen try for pompano. If you cross the stream and climb the rocky ledge, you come to a sandy beach dotted with shells, sea glass, and coral. Beyond the reef is a surfing spot famous for long, perfectly formed waves that surfers can ride on to "infinity." Paddling out over the shallow reef takes a long time, but the ride, according to our son Jeremy, is really special.  Be careful at low tide, when shallow water over the reef which can expose an unwary surfer to spiny sea urchins.  To the right of the rocky point, the beach stretches a long way before disappearing around a bend.  The firm golden sand is perfect for walking, and the waves can be quite gentle.  This western spot is a good place to try when other parts of the island are in rain.

*Directions:*  Drive west of Hanapepe on Rt. 50 past the mile 21 marker. Look for a low concrete bridge and a level area on the shoulder of the road for parking.  Next to the bridge over the A'akukui Stream, an overgrown path leads through a pasture to the beach.  Wear sturdy sandals and stay away from the thorny kiawe which grows near the beach.  About 1 mile further on Rt. 50 you'll find public restrooms, and just across the Waimea River, public showers.  Map 4

## Kekaha Beaches

Stretching for miles along Kauai's western coast, the Kekaha beaches combine swimming, surfing, and walking with the predominantly dry weather of the island's leeward side.  As Rt. 50 curves toward the sea at the

*Miles of golden sand at Kekaha*

small town of Kekaha, the beach is narrow, but a mile or two north, it widens and becomes more golden, with long, rolling waves breaking evenly in brilliant white crests. At times, the waves can break perfectly for surfing and body boarding, although, as everywhere on Kauai, surf and currents can be dangerous and unpredictable, and you may find high surf and rip currents. Watch where local people are swimming and follow their lead – especially if they are not going into the water!

Even if swimming is not advisable, the sand is firm and flat, one of the finest beaches on Kauai—or anywhere—for walking, running, or playing frisbee or football. We recommend driving the full length of this stretch of beach so that you can select the most favorable spot and then double back to park. Despite its clear, sunny weather, the western side of the island has not yet been developed as a tourist area, and so these beaches are frequented primarily by local residents and are not very crowded. You can walk for miles along the sand, with beautiful views of Ni'ihau, purple on the horizon. Or drive north towards Barking Sands and Polihale Beach, winding through sugar cane fields where silvery grasses wave in the breezes against the deep red-gold of cleared fields and the vivid blues of the sea and the enormous sky.

*Directions:* Drive northwest of Waimea on Rt. 50 until the road curves towards the water near the mile 25 marker. Map 4

## Barking Sands

The sandy beach from Kekaha to Polihale extends for about 15 miles, and the section off the Pacific Missile Range Facility is often available for public use. After signing in at the main gate, you can drive to a long stretch of sandy beach along Major's Bay. Like Polihale Beach, the surf here can be extremely strong, often too powerful for safe swimming. While the waves break magnificently in long, shining tunnels that look like a surfer's dream, unpredictable currents as well as a sudden drop-off make for particularly hazardous swimming conditions. You have to look carefully for channels through the coral reef fronting the beach to find sandy bottom, or you can go to the northernmost point of Major's bay where the reef ends. The wide, sandy beach is both hot and difficult to walk on, and shade is almost nonexistent. It is a spectacular place for a picnic, though, and you can see Ni'ihau, purple on the horizon, just past the golden, shining sand and glistening turquoise sea.

*Directions:* Drive northwest of Kekaha on Rt. 50 until you see the gatehouse entrance. Map 4

## Polihale Beach Park

From the time you leave paved road behind to jolt north through a maze of sugar cane fields, you know you're in for something special. Gradually, beyond the tall sugar cane rustling in the breeze, a dark ridge of jagged peaks appears on the right. As you get closer, these giant cliffs reveal splendid colors— trees and bush in vivid greens against the black rock slashed with the deep red of the volcanic soil. When you can drive no further, the beach at Polihale emerges from the base of the cliffs—an enormous stretch of brilliant white sand more immense, it seems, than the cliffs which tower above and the band of deep blue sea beyond. Only the sky seems the equal of this vast expanse of glaring sand, so wide that to walk from your car to the ocean on a sunny day will burn your feet, and so long that no single vantage point allows the eye to see its full extent. "Beautiful" is too small a word for this awesome place. Polihale—home of spirits—is more appropriate, not only because the majestic cliffs and beach dwarf anything human to insignificance, but also because here man's access to the western coast really ends. Beyond lies the Na Pali wilderness, unreachable except by boat or helicopter, or by the handful of hikers who dare to climb the narrow and dangerous trails. Polihale is the threshold between the known and the unknown, the tamed and the untamed, the familiar and the wild.

Swimming is treacherous; the rolling, pounding surf even at its most gentle is only for strong, experienced swimmers. No reefs offer protection from the powerful ocean currents. Come instead for the spectacle, to picnic and walk, to gaze at the grandeur of the cliffs above the endless sea and sand, to listen to the silence broken only by the crashing surf, to appreciate in solitude the splendor of nature's power. A feeling of awe lingers even after you return to paved road and a world of smaller proportions.

*Directions:* Just before Rt. 50 ends, a State Park sign will mark the left turn onto the dirt cane road. Follow signs for about 5 miles. Restrooms, showers, picnic tables. Be careful — don't get your car mired in muddy roads, or stuck in sandy dunes. Map 4

## Westside shopping stops

HANAPEPE, Kauai's 'biggest little town,' has a cluster of specialty shops. *Kauai Fine Arts Gallery* offers a wonderful collection of antique maps and prints, with a particularly fine selection of nautical and Pacific themes. Next door, the *Hanapepe Cafe* is a great place for lunch or a mid-afternoon coffee on a rainy day. *Uncle Eddie's Angels* is a must stop for angel-lovers!— or for anyone who appreciates the celestial in crafts. His handcrafted 'aloha angels,' sell as fast as they fly in! (800- 538-6514). *Dr. Ding* sells surf gear and surf fashions, including Lauren's favorite 'chicks who rip' shirts, and next door, *Aloha Oe* features a wonderful collection of hand sewn aloha shirts and clay art and jewelry. Explore the swinging bridge, and visit the *Taro Ka* chips factory down the street and taste a sample (or two, or three...) Stop in at *Kauai Kookie Factory* on Rt. 56 next to Camp House Grill & Cantina.

In WAIMEA, try *Liko's* for surf wear and Roxy items, as well as Liko's beautifully crafted surfboards. At *Delites*, you'll find an inexpensive selection of crack seed specialties, including favorites  like lemon peel and pickled apricots at excellent prices. Don't miss *Pualani's Fruit Stand* for terrific smoothies and wonderful fresh fruit.

## *Beach Safety*

We describe the beaches in their summer mood, when the surf and currents can be at their most gentle. From mid-October to mid-April, however, swimmers must be particularly cautious on the windward beaches to the north and northeast where the surf and currents are more unpredictable and danger-ous. On the south shore, surf is "up" in summer months, and the ocean more calm during winter. Plan your beach adventures according to surf conditions (Call 245-6001 for a report on the size of the swell and the times of high and low tides). A few simple suggestions: Don't swim alone or too far out at a beach where the currents are unfamiliar, and avoid swimming where a river flows into the sea. Never turn your back on the ocean; keep your eye on the waves. Before you swim, observe the water carefully. Look out for the fast moving water running laterally which indicates a strong current. Should you ever find yourself caught in a strong undertow or current, and if your efforts to free yourself are not successful, remember this: don't panic, conserve your energy and drift with the current until it weakens.

These currents usually weaken beyond the point where the waves break, and many are shaped like horseshoes, so that at some point you will probably be able to swim back in.

Be particularly careful when you are snorkeling, when you can easily get distracted by the fish and lose your sense of direction. Stay close enough to shore that you can swim in at any time, and remember that unfamiliar beaches will have unknown currents. You'll find the safest snorkeling in the rock-enclosed pool at Lydgate Park on the eastern shore, or at sheltered Poipu Beach to the south. Beware of walking or even standing close to the edge of cliffs or rocks to photograph the pounding surf, as waves vary in size and strength and a huge one may come up suddenly and wash your camera away—perhaps you along with it! These sudden large waves can be treacherous because they are unexpected as well as powerful, particularly on the northern and western beaches without reefs to protect against strong ocean currents. Avoid swimming in the murky water near where a stream flows into the sea.

When surfing, watch where the local surfers ride the waves. They know where to avoid strong currents, rocks, and dangerous wave breaks. They are also experienced, however, and seek a bigger thrill! Keep an eye out for that occasional oversize wave. Rather than trying to ride it (or worse, run from it), you may want to dive through or drop down under it. These big ones often come in threes, so be ready!

Portuguese 'men o' war,' tiny blue jellyfish, pack a walloping sting in their long, trailing tentacles. They sometimes dot the waterline after heavy surf. Don't step on them or pick them up. If you are stung while swimming, pull the jellyfish off carefully, trying not to touch the stinger any more than you have to, or use some sand to scrape the stinger off. Warm water helps or vinegar or meat tenderizer can be used as to help break down the poison. The best medicine, however, is prevention. If you see them on the sand, pack up and head out for another beach! An even smaller critter, the bacterium leptospirosis has been found in Kauai's rivers and streams, so avoid freshwater swimming far from the ocean's edge if you have open cuts or sores. Instead, swim in the ocean or the brackish water where a stream flows into the sea.

Your beachbag should contain some antibiotic ointment and bandaids for coral cuts, and, if possible, some vinegar in case you meet a man o' war. Keep a spare sun tan lotion in the glove compartment of the car.

On Kauai, as anywhere, follow normal rules of self-protection: Lock your car against theft as you would at home, store valuables in the trunk, and avoid walking alone at night in unlit, deserted areas—including those romantic beaches.

## Beware the Hawaiian Sun

If you lie out in the sun between 11:30 am and 2:30 pm you will fry like a pancake, even in a half hour, because Hawaii lies close to the equator and the sun is exceedingly strong. You'll need a good sunscreen, even on cloudy days, for ultraviolet rays can cause a burn. Sunscreens which contain PABA may give some people a rash. 'PABA- free' sunscreens are available and are highly effective. Read the labels carefully. The best lotions protect against both UV and UA rays. Choose 'waterproof' rather than 'water-resistant' lotions, though don't put too much faith in manufacturer's claims. Even waterproof sunscreens wash off in salt water and should be reapplied periodically, as we do every two hours in summer. We've had good luck with lotions which form a skin-like coating, like Sundown, and sticky gels like 'Bullfrog.'

Children need special care and effective lotions. Dermatologists currently recommend a lotion rated SPF 15 for kids (and everyone else). For spots which kids rub often, like right under the eyes, you can try sticky gels like 'Bullfrog' or a lotion in chapstick form. It's a good idea to make a firm rule that kids get 'greased up' in the room or parking lot before heading for the beach as they hate to stand still once the sand is in sight! Bring T–shirts (the most reliable sun-protection) for after-swimming sandcastle projects. It's a good plan to schedule family beach visits for the early morning or late afternoon, and plan meals, naps, or drives for the noonday sun hours. Sunburns are often not visible until it is too late, but you can check your child's skin by pressing it with your finger. If it blanches dramatically, get the child a shirt or consider calling it a day. Keep a spare lotion in the car, for without lotion, beaches can be hazardous to your health!

Babies need a complete sunblock and a hat to protect the scalp; use lotion even on feet. Babies should stay in the shade as much as possible, so an umbrella (K-Mart, Wal-Mart, Longs) would be a wise purchase for the beach.

# Golden Sand & Silver Screen

*Movies filmed on Kauai*

## the '30's

Cane Fire/White Heat (1933)

## the 50's

Adventures of Captain David Grief (1957)
Beachhead (1953)
Bird of Paradise (1951)
Miss Sadie Thompson (1953)
Naked Paradise/Thunder over Hawaii (1957)
Pagan Love Song (1950)
She Gods of Shark Reef (1958)
South Pacific (1958)
Sunny Travels in Hawaii (1954)
Voodoo Island (1957)

## the '60's

The Beachcomber (1960)
Blue Hawaii (1961)
Diamond Head (1962)
Donovan's Reef (1963)
Gilligan's Island (pilot episode) (1964)
Hawaii Eye (1962)
Lost Flight (1968)
Lt. Robinson Crusoe (1966)
None But The Brave (1965)
Paradise Hawaiian Style (1965)
Sangra Ari (1962)
The Seven Women from Hell (1961)
The Wackiest Ship in the Army (1961)
Yoake no Futari (Rainbow Over the Pacific, 1968)

## the '70's

Acapulco Gold (1978)
The Castaway Cowboy (1974)
Death Moon (1978)
Fantasy Island TV series (1978-84)
The Hawaiians (1970)
He's My Brother (1974)
Islands in the Stream (1975)
King Kong (1976)
Seven (1979)

## the '80's

Behold Hawaii (1983)
Body Heat (1981)
The Last Flight of Noah's Ark (1980)
Island of the Alive (1986)
Millennium (1989)
Raiders of the Lost Ark (1981)
Sesame Street goes to Kauai (1981)
The Thorn Birds (1983)
Throw Momma from the Train (1987)
Uncommon Valor (1983)

## the '90's

George of the Jungle (1997)
Flight of the Intruder (1991)
Honeymoon in Vegas (1992)
Hook (1991)
Jurassic Park (1993)
Lord of the Flies (1990)
Lost World (1997)
Mighty Joe Young (1997)
North (1994)
Outbreak (1995)
6 Days, 7 Nights (1997)

*Activities & Discoveries*

*Kahili onboard at Anini Beach*

# Artists & Artisans

For a free listing of Kauai's artists and open studios, contact Kauai Society of Artists (808-822-9304, PO 3344, Lihue HI 96766 or www.hawaiian.net/~ksa). Visit galleries featuring more than 40 KSA members at *Kinipopo Fine Art Gallery* in Wailua (822-4356) or *Evolve-Love Art Gallery* in Hanalei (826-4755) In Coconut Plantation Market-place, you'll find maritime art, maps, and antiques in *Ship Store Galleries*, and in nearby Kauai Shopping Village, seascapes at *Wyland Gallery* and Hawaiian art at *Kahn Galleries* (also in Hanalei, Kilohana, and Koloa).

You'll find the largest selection of works by island artisans at the *Kauai Products Store*, Kukui Grove Center, Lihue. Nearby, at the *Kauai Museum* shop, you'll find quilts, native wood boxes, shell leis and jewelry. At *Kilohana Plantation*, visit the pottery workshop, *Kilohana Clayworks*. At Anchor Cove Center next to the Marriott, try the small but well-stocked *Island Style*. In Kapa'a, don't miss *Kela's Glass Gallery* (822-4527 www.glass-art.com) for beautiful colors and shapes. Visit Hanapepe's colony of art shops, including *Kama'aina Koa Wood Gallery* and *Island Images*. Stop in at *Uncle Eddie's Aloha Angels*. In Waimea, *Wrangler's Steak House* has a lovely collection of local crafts. Stay for lunch!

# Athletic Clubs & Fitness Centers

*Kauai Athletic Club* next to Kukui Grove Shopping Center in Lihue offers daily and weekly visitor rates, a variety of classes and machines, and a squash court (245-5381). *Princeville Health Club*, in the Prince Golf Course clubhouse, has sweeping views of the fairways and ocean (826-5030), and visitor rates for classes, personal training, massage, and spa treatments. *Hyatt Resort* (742-1234) offers classes, first rate facilities, as well as massage and therapy. Daily, weekly rates available. A $100 massage allows you to use almost all spa facilities. You can make it an all day deal!

A 'local' style gym at modest rates: *Kauai Gym* (823-8210) – hours are limited, and not much choice in weights. Westside, *Iron Hut* (335-3383).

# Beachwalking & Running

If you can't get through your day without a run, you'll love Kauai's beaches! Our favorite running beaches, with firm sand and just the right slope, are Hanalei Bay and Kalihiwai in the north, Kalapaki on the east, and Kekaha to the west. For long meandering walks, we like Moloa'a Bay and Larsen's Beach on the north, Maha'ulepu on the south, and Anahola Beach or Lydgate Park south of the rock pools, along the Wailua Golf Course, on the east—especially beautiful at sunrise or sunset. For details about races on Kauai, call *Hawaii Visitors Bureau* (800-262-1400). For a free schedule of races, triathalons and fun-runs statewide, send a SASE to *Dept. of Parks and Recreation*, City and County of Honolulu, 650 King St., Honolulu HI 96813. Remember the sun! Fluids, sunscreen, even a hat are a must!

## Biking

Take a south shore bike tour from Kipu to hidden Maha'ulepu Beach, along the cane roads and through an old tunnel carved into the mountain leading to Koloa sugar mill. After a brief tour of the mill, continue to Maha'ulepu for a picnic, swim, and a short beach hike. It's 8 miles of great scenery, an easy grade, and frequent rest stops ($85 with *Kauai Adventure Trek* 332-8633). Eastside, explore the coastline of Kapa'a town, on a mostly level bike trail with ocean views. Call *Kauai Cycle & Tour* in Kapa'a (821-2115 www.bikehawaii.com/kauaicycle) or *Chris the Fun Lady* (822-7447 www.christhefunlady.com). On the north shore, you can rent bikes and tour Hanalei and Ha'ena. Call *Pedal & Paddle* (826-9069). Or try a 'downhill tour' along 12 miles of winding road from Waimea Canyon, at an elevation of 3,500 feet, all the way to the coast, with *Kauai Coasters* (www.aloha.net/~coast 639-2412 ) or *Outfitters Kauai* (www.outfitterskauai.com 742-9667), which also offers bicycle and kayak tours. Need bike repairs? Call *Bicycle John* (245-7579). Rent a Harley? Call *Ray's* (822-HOGG) or *Hawaiian Riders* (822-5409), which also rents mopeds & 'exotic vehicles.'

## Camping

Several state and county parks allow camping, for example Anahola, Ha'ena, Anini, Salt Pond, and Polihale Beach Parks, as well as specified areas of the Na Pali region and other wilderness preserves. For state parks, the camping limit is 5 nights in a 30 day period per campground, and less on some stopovers on the Kalalau Trail. For information, permits, and reservations contact *Department of Land and Natural Resources, Division of State Parks,* P.O. Box 1671, Lihue, HI 96766 (808-274-3444) www.hawaii.gov/dlnr/dsp/dsp.html. For Alakai Swamp or Waimea Canyon contact *Division of Forestry* at the same address (808-274-3433). For *Kauai County Parks,* camping limit is 4 days per park, or 12 nites total @ $3/nite (808-241-6670). Allow 30 days to process permits.

YWCA Camp Sloggett is set in spectacular Koke`e State Park, with access to 45 miles of hiking trails leading to the Kalalau Lookout, with views of the Waimea Canyon and Na Pali coastline. Group and hostel accommodations include tent camping and a bunkhouse with kitchenettes, shared bath facilities and hot showers (from $10/pp/nite). Reserve at least two months in advance: YWCA of Kauai, 3094 Elua St., Lihue HI 96766 (808) 245-5959 or the campground, 335-6060.

For those who want to be close to nature — and to a shower and refrigerator at the same time, *Koke'e Lodge's* cabins might be just the answer. Cabins include stove, refrigerator, hot showers, cooking and eating utensils, linens, bedding, and wood burning stoves and cost only $35-$45/night (maximum stay of 5 nights during a 30 day period). Reservations: Koke'e Lodge, Box 819, Waimea HI 96796. (808-335-6061). The Lodge serves breakfast and light lunch (9 am - 3:30 pm). Bring warm clothes for cold nights, and remember, on Kauai as elsewhere, to lock your gear in the trunk of your car before you head out. Map 4

You don't have to travel far to escape the rush! Conveniently located between Lihue and Koloa, *Kahili Mountain Park* offers reasonably priced, rustic cabins with private outdoor 'star-lit shower' ($50/two) and even more rustic one room 'cabinettes' with shared bathrooms/showers ($28/two). Newer cabinettes cost a bit more. New cabins features indoor bath and shower, or you can reserve a luxury cabin ($88/two). The setting is beautiful and serene, a meadow backed by mountains with a view of the sea. You can't beat the prices; extra persons cost only $10 a night. Linens, cookware, soap, and coffee pot are provided. Kahili Mountain Park, Box 298, Koloa HI 96756 (808-742-9921 www.kahilipark.com). Map 3

Near road's end on the north shore, *YMCA Camp Naue* in spectacular Ha'ena offers beachfront camping in bunk houses (or your own tent). It's popular with local clubs and families, but individual tourists are also welcome to stay in the bunkhouse for $12 each per night (children half price), or if you bring your own tent, it's only $10. Contact YMCA of Kauai, Box 1786, Lihue HI 96766; (808-246-9090 or 742-1200). Map 2

Rent camping equipment at *Pedal & Paddle* in Hanalei (808-826-9069 —ask about current trail conditions), *Kayak Kauai* in Hanalei (808-826-9844) and Kapa'a (808-822-9179), or *Outfitters Kauai* (808-742-9667) in

*Waioli Mission Church*

Poipu. Buy camping equipment in *Long's Drug Store, K- Mart, Wal-Mart* in Lihue, as well the small variety stores like *Waipouli Variety* (Wailua), *Discount Variety* (Koloa) *Village Variety* or *Ace Hardware* (Hanalei).

## Churches

Churches on Kauai give 'aloha' a whole new resonance. Whatever your faith, you'll feel welcome at Sunday services. The Missionary Church in Kapa'a (822-5594) welcomes visitors with a shell lei and a warm greeting. Several churches conduct services in Hawaiian language. Waioli Huia Church in Hanalei (826-6253) conducts services in Hawaiian and English, and the very friendly family atmosphere is evident in the announcement at the top of the Sunday Bulletin: "Our keikis are apt to wander during church. They do this because they feel at home in God's house. Please love them as we do." Early morning service is conducted in Hawaiian at *Waimea Hawaiian Church*, circa 1820, (338-9962). You'll pass lovely old churches in many places on Kauai, from the back roads of Koloa to the sugar cane fields of the west side. Stop and visit!

## Coffee

*Kauai Coffee* is grown near Kalaheo and Koloa, near the location of the first coffee plantation in the state, which opened in 1836. Coffee grown today on this 4,000 acre estate is free of insecticides. Stop in at the visitor's center in Lawai and sample the estate reserve coffees roasted daily (335-0813 or 800-545-8605 www.kauaicoffee.com). Some small growers are leasing land in Waimea previously devoted to sugar—try Ha'upu Growers' *Black Mountain Premium Hawaiian Coffee* (808-742-8634). Espresso cafes are springing up all over Kauai! (p. 227).

## Family Beaches

Our favorite family beaches, with something for everyone, are *Kalihiwai* (p. 49) and *Anini Beach* (p. 51) on the north shore, and *Poipu Beach Park* (p. 68) and *Salt Pond Beach Park* (p. 72) on the south shore. On the

eastern shore, the best family beaches are *Kalapaki Beach* (p. 30) and
*Lydgate Park* (p. 32) where you can snorkel safely and see whole families
of very tame, colorful fish who live in Lydgate's unique, man-made ocean
pool enclosed with lava rocks.  At Lydgate Park you'll also find the best
playground on Kauai—*Kamalani Park*—16,000 square feet of funland with
mirror mazes, a suspension bridge, lava tubes and circular slide.

With a plastic pail and an inexpensive net ($6 for an 8" net at Long's),
children can have lots of fun trying to catch fish trapped in tidal pools.  Net
fishing is fun at the rivers behind the beaches at *Anahola, Kalihiwai*, and
*Moloaʻa*, and at the tidal pools at *Salt Pond Beach Park* and *Poipu Beach
Park*.  Bring home sand, shells and driftwood for great kids' art projects.

## Family Fun

Kids will love the free hula shows at the major shopping centers:
*Coconut Plantation Marketplace* (5 pm daily  822-3641) and *Poipu
Shopping Village* (5 pm T & Th.  742-2831).  Show times may change, so
check first. Children can dress up in aloha finery for a free show, often with
local kids, at the *Hyatt,* 6 pm nightly, Seaview Terrace (742-1234).

Young artists in the family will love *Kilohana Clayworks*, where Keith
Tammarine will help them craft, paint, glaze, and fire their creations in his
working ceramics studio (246-2529).  Other fun spots: *Fernandez Fun
Factory* (in Wailua next to Foodland) is video game heaven.  In Kukui
Grove, *Wally World* offers miniature golf, a video arcade, and "splash &

bash," a motorized bumperboat ride (245-5252).

Great children's books: *Hawaii is a Rainbow* (beautiful photographs), *Peter Panini and the Search for the Menehune, Pua Pua Lena Lena, Keiki's First Books* board books. Look for them at *Borders,* where kids can enjoy *Keiki Story Time* (246-0862).

Before your trip, plan family tours and activities. A good first step is to call *Chris the Fun Lady* (808-822-7447 www.christhefunlady.com) with your family profile. For cribs and other child equipment rentals, call *Ready Rentals* (823-8008 or 800-599-8008 or readyrentals@aloha.net). Free delivery. Or try *Baby's Away* (245-6259 or 800-571-0077).

The major resort hotels (Hyatt Regency, Marriott, Princeville Hotel, Kiahuna, Sheraton) offer day camps for children of guests (about $50 per day). For example, the Sheraton Kauai Keiki Aloha Club in Poipu includes lunch, activities like kite and lei making, bamboo pole fishing, Hawaiian legends and lore, ($55/day, plus half-day and nite sessions). The family-oriented resort Holiday Inn SunSpree located near Lydgate Park, one of the best children's beaches, offers incentives like Kids Stay Free, Kids Eat Free, Kids Spree Vacation Club. For a children's day activity program, contact *Eco Tours*, which offers hikes, snorkeling, and other activities for kids ages 5-14 (822-7823 or 800-232-6699; www.ecokid.com).

## Special Mornings with Daddy

From the time they were small, each child would plan a 'Special Morning with Daddy,' a wonderfully private adventure including dining, shopping, beaching and swimming. At first, they all chose the wonderful old Kauai Surf Hotel, with ducks and a fish pond and a meandering swimming pool. Then the Surf closed, and they discovered broader horizons. And they grew up, too, during all those special mornings. They're markers in our family times, so we'd like to share the all-time favorites:

Jeremy's choice would be *Kountry Kitchen* in Kapa'a, followed by surfing at *Kalihiwai*. Lauren, the youngest, loved *Poipu Beach* — fortunately for Daddy, who has always liked it there too. Mike liked the huge breakfast buffet at the *Princeville Hotel*, then he and Daddy would head for *Hanalei Bay* to play catch and frisbee. Our oldest, Mirah, a vegetarian, on the hunt for great salads, soon decided that her special morning would be much more special at dinner!

Special Mornings With Daddy. When we first conceived the idea, we thought of how important they would be for each child in a crowded family. Over the years we've grown wiser—now we know who really found those mornings so special!

# Farmers' Markets

Farmers' Markets happen almost each day of the week—some are "official," some informal— and all are a great place to catch the flavor of the island, talk to local people, and enjoy a kaleidoscope of tastes and colors. Come early for the best selection! From truck beds, tiny stands, or the trunks of cars, local farmers will sell their fruits, vegetables, and flowers at prices more reasonable than the supermarkets. Manoa lettuce, as little as $2 for a half-dozen small heads, will be fresh from the garden and taste of Kauai's sunny skies and salt air. You'll never want iceberg again! You may find avocados at 2 for $1; fresh basil, oregano, marjoram, or chives; a shiny dark purple eggplant with just the right sound when you thump it, and bananas of all kinds—Williams, Bluefield, and the special apple-bananas. Don't be put off by the short, fat, drab-skinned exterior, for inside the fruit looks like golden sand at sunset and tastes like bananas laced with apples.

The starting time is important to know. At the Koloa market, you'll see a rope tied across the parking lot which serves as a starting line, complete with a shrill whistle, to ensure an equal chance for buyers and sellers. It drops at noon on the nose, so don't be late! At Kapaʻa market, official opening time doesn't deter buyers. They simply 'reserve' their selections,

*Shoppers wait for starting time at the farmer's market. Bananas, pineapples, papayas cost only a dollar or two, flowers just a bit more.*

permitted as long as no money changes hands. Sellers write buyers' names on bags of fruit, or on pineapple leaves, or even give out numbered tokens, like a hat check. Shopping can be accomplished in a matter of moments, but then you have to remember where everything is stashed! Sellers quickly become friends. One may offer you a slice of star fruit, or a section of honey sweet orange with deceptively green skin, or a slice of juicy pineapple topped with passion fruit. Papayas will be giants, the Sunrise variety if you're lucky, for their red-orange center rivals the color of the sun. Try fresh lime juice, or Jeremy's favorite, the juice from a passion fruit, to spark the papaya's mellow sweet flavor with tartness. Even if you aren't cooking, you'll be tempted by stringbeans as long as shoelaces, squash with squeaky skins, tomatoes still warm and fragrant, all kinds of Oriental vegetables with odd shapes, even fresh coconuts. You may even find leis of pakalana or plumeria for $3 a strand. Take home tropical flowers—bird of paradise, parrot colored heliconia blossoms, stalks of fragrant white or yellow ginger. Be ready to bargain if you are buying in quantity, and take their advice about venturing into new tastes. Most sellers price in $1 or $2 packages, so bring singles!

The largest markets are in Kapaʻa, Koloa and Lihue, and they are a little tricky to find. On Fridays, the Lihue market is in the parking lot behind the Vidhina football stadium just south of the airport. Enter off Kapule Highway (Rt. 51) at the small street leading into the stadium at its northern corner, or turn off Rice St. at Holoko Road. The Wednesday Kapaʻa market is opposite the armory; take Kukui Road off Rt. 56 and turn right at the end; then make the next right onto Kahau Road and park on your left. Or take the new bypass road from Wailua to Kapaʻa; it comes out just at the end of Kahau Road. For the Koloa market, turn left off Koloa Road just before the baseball field.

Just missed the market? You'll find roadside produce stands all over the island. Look for low acid, 'Sugar Loaf' pineapples from Kahili Farms, strawberry papayas, bananas of all kinds. Near Lihue, stop at *People's Market* on Rt. 56 in Puhi. In Waimea, visit *Pualani's Fruit Stand* for frosties made from whipped frozen Kauai fruit. Try fresh asparagus, the newest crop of the small westside growers of Black Mountain Coffee.

## Farmers' Markets

| | | |
|---|---|---|
| *Monday* | noon | **Koloa**, Ball Park on Rt. 520 next to the fire house.  Map 3 |
| *Tuesday* | 2 pm | **Hanalei**, west of town on Rt. 560.  Map 2  (until 4 pm) |
| *Tuesday* | 3:30 | **Kalaheo** Neighborhood Center, Papalina at Rt. 50.  Map 3 |
| *Wednesday* | 3 pm | **Kapa'a** behind the armory.  Map 1 (arrive 2:45) |
| *Thursday* | 3:30 | **Hanapepe**, Town Park. Map 4 |
| *Thursday* | 4:30 | **Kilauea**, Kilauea Neighborhood Ctr. |
| *Friday* | 3 pm | **Lihue**, Vidhina football stadium parking lot, near airport.  Map 1 |
| *Saturday* | 9 am | **Kekaha** Neighborhood Center, Elepaio off Rt. 50.  Map 4 |
| *Saturday* | 9 am | **Kilauea**, Christ Memorial Church. Map 2 |

## Fresh Island Fish

You can sometimes find locally-caught fresh fish at roadside stands or farmer's markets. Otherwise, try *Fish Express* in Lihue (245-9918) for filets of shibiko (baby yellow fin tuna), ono, ulua, and snappers of all hues—pink, grey, red.  Prices vary with the weather, the season, the tides, even the moon, and are generally higher in winter, when fishing boats face rougher seas.  The adventurous can try opihi (limpets) raw in the shell with seaweed, or smoked marlin.  Your fresh fish selections can be vacuum sealed for shipping (245-9918).  Also try *G's Fish Market* (246-4440) 4361 Rice St., Lihue. In Hanama'ulu, stop in at *Ara's* for homemade ahi poke and sushi platters.  In Kapa'a, try the inexpensive *Kuhio Market* on Rt. 56, one block south of the park.  You'll be surprised at the quality of the fresh ahi in, of all places, *Safeway* in Wailua.  Nearby *Cost-U-Less* sells fresh fish in larger packages—just right for a family barbecue.  On the north shore, *Hanalei Dolphin* has a fish market right behind the restaurant.

## Fresh Tropical Flowers

The exotic shapes and colors of heliconia — 'lobster claw,' 'sexy pink,' 'caribea' —the fragrance of pikaki and plumeria! At farmers' markets, you can buy armfuls of spectacular flowers for a few dollars. And for those friends back home taking care of your dog, what better way to say thank you than a bouquet? From *Kauai Tropicals,* you can order a lovely assortment of flowers for a modest price ($48) carefully boxed and shipped via Federal Express, arriving fresh and gorgeous in any mainland city— beautiful red and pink ginger, anthurium, greenery and heliconia! Some pieces will last nearly

*Bouquets of heliconia and ginger for $3.50*

two weeks. Spend $10 more, and you'll have a very special mother's day or birthday present. Or splurge on an enormous box (we call it 'Roger's Special') with blooms to fill 3 vases ($100) great for a wedding. Each box includes a ti top which will root in water (kauaitropicals@hawaiian.net 800-303-4385). Take a box home on the plane and save shipping: 742-9989.

Contact *Hawaii Tropical Flower & Foliage Association* for a free color brochure of Kauai's exotic flowers. PO Box 1067, Lawai HI 96765.

## Flower Leis

The fragrance of pikake or white ginger; the cool, silky touch of petals; the delicate yet rich colors of orchids and plumeria—even in words, flower leis conjure up moonlit nights and ocean breezes. No vacation is complete without one, especially on your last night. Many stores (even Safeway, Longs, Wal-Mart) offer ready-made leis in a refrigerated case, but these strings of imported carnations cannot compare with a local lei which reflects the traditions of the island as well as the individual artistry of the lei maker. Order a day in advance and pick it up on your way out to dinner!

The *Mauna Loa lei* ($20), is a wide woven band of small purple orchids; very handsome, it is often given to boys at graduation.  Another favorite is the lei of *white ginger,* a spectacular creation of white, or sometimes pink buds so fragrant that heads will turn as you walk by.  The tightly threaded ginger blossoms look almost like white feathers.  If the blossoms are in season, try a beautiful *ilima lei* made of papery orange-colored blossoms, very rare and difficult to string.  Or try the slender strand of fragrant green *pakalana* ($10/strand of 100 flowers).  The small, white *stephanotis,* similar in shape to a lilac blossom and even more fragrant, is threaded in single strands ($10).  *Pikake,* a tiny and delicate white flower, is the Hawaiian lei for weddings, and has a wonderful, spicy scent ($10/ strand).  *Plumeria* leis are the most common.  Usually white or yellow and sometimes pink or deep red, the large blossoms have a lovely perfume.

The best place to buy a lei is at the farmers' markets, where you can find them for $4 to $5.  At *People's Market* in Puhi (245-2210), opposite Kauai Community College, you'll find leis made fresh each morning, usually plumeria and sometimes, pikake, pakalana, or ilima.  In Anahola, you can buy plumeria leis in yellow or mixed colors from a roadside stand, or even from a truck bed parked along Rt. 56.  For something really special, order a lei from one of the island's artists.  Local people treasure leis and floral designs made by Irmalee Pomroy (822-3231) who weaves traditional

designs with her own unique and unmistakable flair.  Winnie Cummings (821-1514) in Anahola and Linda Pitman (828-1572) in Kilauea

*Lei in ti leaf wrap*

grow their own flowers and will create a lei just for you, with fragrant pakalana, ginger, or orchids, at quite reasonable prices ($10 to $15).  Ask their advice!  Watch lei makers demonstrate their techniques and designs at the annual Kauai County Fair each August.

Commercial florists include *Flowers & Joys* (Kapaʻa 821-1569) *Flowers Forever* (Lihue 245-4717).  Check  the display cases in *JC's Minimart* (Wailua 822-5961) and *Pono Market* (Kapaʻa 822-4581).

Your lei will look wonderful for only one wearing, but the fragrance lingers even when the petals turn brown.  Store your lei in a plastic bag in the refrigerator overnight so you can wear it, even though wilted, at breakfast.  Hang it to dry for a Hawaiian potpourri.  Surprisingly, you will have no trouble wearing a lei through agricultural inspection and onto the plane home, though the flowers quickly turn brown in air conditioning.  Have your lei packaged for your return trip, so it stays fresh to cheer your morning coffee back home!

## Fruits & Island Sweets

Fresh fruits can be bought all over the island, sometimes from a truck parked by the side of the road.  In Kilauea, on the road to the lighthouse, the *Martin Farm* sells papayas on the honor system.  Choose your fruits and leave your money in a box (Closed Sundays).  To taste Kauai's special sunrise papayas back home on a cold winter morning, call *John Akana* in Kalihiwai (800-572-7292), and he will ship 10 pounds by federal express for about $45.  Order before 7 am on Tuesday and the fruits will arrive on the mainland by Friday.  Great for that college student during exam week!

You'll love fruit 'frosties,' a tasty confection of frozen fruit whipped smooth.  Try combinations of mango, banana, papaya, pineapple—whatever is in season—at *Pualani's* (Waimea) & *Banana Joe's* (Kilauea). Tropical fruit 'smoothies' are made at fruit stands like *Banana Joe's* and *Mango*

*Mama's* (Kilauea), *Killer Juice Bar* (Kapa'a), *People's Market* (Puhi, opposite Kauai Community College) and *Pualani's* (Waimea).

Be sure to sample local sweets. *Pono Market* in Kapa'a is like a visit to the island's past, with ethnic favorites like coconut manju. Try the manapo, a light cookie shaped like a pretzel, at *Hamura's Saimin*. Macadamia nut cookies taste like Kauai even if you're back home. Try the traditional island favorite, *Kauai Kookie Kompany,* sold in Big Save Markets or at the factory store in Hanapepe. In the Waipouli Complex, *Po Po's* mixes macadamia nuts with chocolate chips or coconut into a confection Mrs. Fields would envy. *Kauai Tropical Fudge* comes in wonderful island flavors, including banana, macadamia nut, Kona coffee, even pina colada! Look for it in many island stores, including *Nutcracker Sweet* in Coconut Marketplace, Wailua, and the *Kauai Products Store* in Kukui Grove, Lihue.

Lilikoi chiffon pie is a Kauai tradition – a light confection of passion fruit. According to local legend, *Omoide Bakery* on Kaumuali'i Highway in Hanapepe has baked the island's best pies by secret family recipe since 1956. Pies are sold frozen (order in advance 335-5291) and so will keep for several hours in the car (best in a cooler). Sample the pies at *Hamura's Saimin* in Lihue, *Green Garden Restaurant* in Hanapepe, *Camp House Grill* in Kalaheo, and don't miss pumpkin crunch pie from *Oki Diner* in Lihue. Other local specialties include *Anahola Granola*, wonderful with apple bananas for breakfast! *Papaya seed dressing*, brewed in Kalaheo, gives salad a whole new dimension. Look for them at *Kauai Products Store* in Kukui Grove. In Hanapepe, taro chips are still made in the *Taro Ka* factory.

When taro is scarce, they make potato chips, including some flavored with Chinese spices. Ready for a new twist to your PBJs? Try *Kukui* jams like guava-strawberry, or try coconut syrup on your pancakes. Make up your own gift boxes at the factory .8 mile past the junction of Rt. 50 and Rt. 530.

To take home gift packs of pineapple (ask for sugarloaf), papaya, Maui onions, ginger, even Maui potato chips, contact Esaki's Produce (Kapaʻa 822-7722). For less than $20, you can bring home 8 Kauai pineapples (you pack & carry). Call ahead, Wed. or Sat. if possible, and specify 'mainland.'

## Gifts from Kauai

Look for special island-made gifts at the unique *Kauai Products Store* (246-6753) in Kukui Grove Center, as well as *Hilo Hattie's* in Lihue, *Kong Lung* in Kilauea, *Hula Moon* in Koloa. Soaps made by *Island Soap Co.* in Kilauea (and Koloa) are especially fragrant with coconut, pikake or plumeria. In Hanapepe, *Uncle Eddie's Aloha Angels* come in all sizes, wearing beautiful fabrics and shells of Kauai! (800-538-6541). In Anchor Cove Shopping Center, stop in at *Island Style* for crafts by local artists. For handmade clothes just a bit out of the ordinary, stop at *The Kapaia Stitchery* just north of Lihue on Rt. 56 (Don't take the bypass road, or you'll miss it).

*Papaya tree — reach up for breakfast!*

Many items are handcrafted by island seamstresses who still make quilts and dresses with the same care their own grandmothers did. Aloha shirts made by Julie's seamstresses cost less than mass-produced shirts in many stores, or you can custom order one from her cotton fabrics. Visit Melody Pigao's shop, *Kilohana Clothing* at Kilohana, for beautiful clothing designs. Each Christmas, our boys order custom aloha shirts: great fabric, perfect fit.

Going home? Call *Kauai Tropicals* (742-9989) and have a box of Kauai's gorgeous flowers waiting for you at the airport. Take home *John Akana's* delicious sunrise papayas for the 'morning after' (828-1746).

## Kauai's Golf Magic *by Robert Trent Jones, Jr.*

I have played golf all over the world, and I keep coming back to Kauai! The island has unique courses, offering both challenges and enjoyment. With the north shore's spectacular landscape to work with, I laid out the original Princeville Resort course in three distinct nines to take advantage of the dramatic cliffs and breathtaking ocean views. The Ocean nine have great vistas and the sounds of the sea off the cliffs; the Woods thread through the trees, with a wonderful Zen-influenced bunker, an idea from my many trips to Japan.

Ranked first in Hawaii by *Golf Digest*, The Prince Course is more bold and dramatic, and I designed it to retain some of the wilderness character of its site. Carved out of heavy vegetation, it meanders through valleys, with panoramic views. It's a tough course (I'm told the beverage cart driver sells more golf balls than drinks) but from the proper set of tees, I guarantee you'll enjoy this golf nature trek!

On the south shore, the Kiahuna Plantation Course is a fun, yet memorable test with rolling fairways, sweeping bunkers, and small, traditional greens. Our newest creation, Poipu Bay Resort adjacent to the Hyatt Regency, is the site of the PGA's Annual Grand Slam of Golf. The back nine border the ocean, where the almost constant yet variable wind is the challenge. You have to make precise shots, judging both distance and the wind, or it will blow the ball off the green Many holes hug the cliffs, and special attention has been given to ancient Hawaiian sacred grounds.

On the east side, the Wailua Golf Course is one of the best public courses in the country. Many holes flank the ocean and are protected by palm trees. This course is a must! I am also a fan of the Kiele Course. The finishing holes really get your attention, particularly the par-three 15th, requiring skill and a brave heart to tame.

No matter which course you choose, you really can't go wrong on Kauai. The people are friendly, temperatures comfortable, the pace slow —

and a nice surprise around each corner! There's something magical about Kauai that brings people back. I know. I'm one of them!

# Golf Courses

The *Princeville Makai Course* in Hanalei, designed by Robert Trent Jones, Jr., is a 27 hole, world-class championship course with 3 challenging nines: Lake, Woods, and Ocean, famous for spectacular views and the dramatic 141-yard seventh hole, where the ocean, foaming like a cauldron, separates tee and green. Ranked 6th in the state, and one of *Golf Digest's* top 25 resort courses for 16 years. Fees, including carts, are $115 ($85/Princeville Hotel guests; $95/Princeville Resort guests); $70 after 2 pm or $39 after 4 pm. 808-826-5070 or 800-826-1105 www.princeville.com. Enter Princeville from Rt. 56, stop at the gate house for a free map. Map 2

*The Prince Course* is Hawaii's number-one rated course according to *Golf Digest.* The 18 hole, 6521-yard course, designed by Robert Trent Jones, Jr., is spectacular, set in 390 acres of pastureland, with rolling hills, deep ravines, tropical jungle with streams and waterfalls. Fees, including carts, are $155 ($100/Princeville Hotel guests; $120/Princeville resort guests); $99 after noon. Just east of Princeville, on Rt. 56. 808-826-2727 or 800-826-4400 www.princeville.com. Map 2

*Kiahuna Golf Club,* Poipu, designed by Robert Trent Jones, Jr., is an 18 hole, par 70, links-style course, predominantly flat, with smooth, fast greens and tradewind challenges. At 6,353 yards from the tips, this course is geared for the recreational golfer. Fees: $75/18 holes or $38/9 holes or $55/after 11 am ($40 after 2 pm/weekdays), including shared cart. Weekly pass $200. 742-9595 www.hshawaii.com/kvp/kiahuna. Map 3

*Poipu Bay Resort Golf Course,* Poipu, designed by Robert Trent Jones, Jr. has been the home of the Grand Slam of Golf since 1994. Par 72 Scottish links-style course, 6845 yards from the blue tees, set in 210 acres of sugar plantation land along the ocean. Views are spectacular! With cart, $145 ($95/Hyatt guests) or $245/3 rounds. Discount times: $95 after noon; $50 after 3 pm. Inquire about discounts for guests at some hotels. 742-8711 or 800-858-6300. Adjacent to the Hyatt Regency Resort. Map 3

*Wailua Municipal Golf Course,* Wailua. *Golf Digest* ranked it in top 25 U.S. municipal courses. Popular 18 hole, 6658 yard, par 72 course is built along the ocean on rolling terrain amid ironwood trees and coconut palms. Fairways are narrow, greens smallish, grass on the tough side. Unbeatable fees: $35/weekends (it gets crowded!) $25/ weekdays (241-6666). Map 1

*Kukuiolono Golf Course,* Kalaheo. 9 holes, par 35 with spectacular views and a lovely Japanese garden. Bring your camera for the plumeria

*The Kalalau trail from Keʻe Beach to Hanakapiʻai winds along the rugged Na Pali coastline, through dense vegetation, along switchbacks and over rocks, sometimes only inches away from a sheer drop. Views are incredible! Mud from the frequent rain showers can create slippery conditions, so good footgear is a must.*

*www.explorekauai.com*

grove. Honor system: $7/green fees and $6/cart. A local favorite, a secret most don't want to share! 322-9151. Turn south off Rt. 50 in Kalaheo at Papalina Rd. (the stoplight) and drive .8 mile. Enter gate on right. Map 3

*Kauai Lagoons Golf & Racquet Club*, in the Kauai Lagoons Resort, Lihue, overlooks beautiful Kalapaki Bay. Designed by Jack Nicklaus, the 262 acre *Kiele Course* is geared for golfers with a 20-handicap or better, and was named on of the Top 100 courses in America by *Golf Digest.* The front nine are long and rugged with many mounds and swales. The back nine run out to the ocean, with spectacular views of waves crashing against the rocks, and prevailing tradewinds of up to 15 m.p.h. on the southeast corner. Fees, including cart, are $150 ($110/Marriott guests). An extra-long course (7070 yards) with 4 tees, the *Kauai Lagoons Course,* ranked by *Golf Magazine* in the top ten of "America's most playable courses," is a shotmaker's course with many bunkers and more undulating greens. 6,942 yards from the tips. Fees, including cart, are $120 ($80/Marriott guests) $95 after noon. Discounts for guests at some hotels. 241-6000 or 800-634-6400. Map 1. Ask about the *'Kauai Golf Challenge'* rate ($295 for Kiele, Princeville, and Poipu Bay courses). Map 1

*Grove Farm Golf Course* near Kukui Grove Center, Lihue, is one of *Sports Illustrated's* 'Top Ten Best Nine Hole Courses.' On 200 acres of sugar cane plantation land with views of the ocean and Hule'ia Stream. It features a unique 10th hole. 3803 yards, Par 40. $40 with cart ($65/two rounds; twilight rate $45 from 1:30 pm). Discounts for guests at some condos/hotels. 245-8756 www.golfgrovefarm.com. Map 1

# Hiking

Hiking can be a spectacular way to see Kauai, for more than half of the island's 551,000 square miles is forestland, and many of its most beautiful regions are inaccessible by car. However, hiking Kauai is not without risks. Many trails can become dangerous from washouts and mudslides, and in the Na Pali coastal region, where trails are often etched into the sides of sheer cliffs, hikers must be wary of waves crashing over the rocks without warning, as well as vegetation which masks the edge of a sheer drop. A friend, for example, broke his ankle one summer when plants gave way under his feet near the edge of a ravine.

Careful planning is a must. Before your trip, send a 10"x13" stamped, addressed envelope ($3.20 stamps) to Division of Forestry, Kauai District (3060 Eiwa St., Room 306, Lihue HI 96766-1875) for a free information packet with maps and descriptions of trails in the forest preserves. For a free packet on the Na Pali region, send another stamped, self-addressed

*The Kalalau Trail into the Na Pali wilderness begins where paved road ends, at Keʻe Beach on the north shore.*

*Reward: The view after climbing the first quarter – mile.*

large envelope to Division of State Parks at the same address (or call 808-274-3444). Visit www.hawaii.gov/dlnr/dsp/kauai.html for an overview.

Bob Smith's *Hiking Kauai* describes a variety of hikes at all levels of difficulty (www.maui.net/~hionfoot). Kathy Morey's *Kauai Trails: Walks Strolls and Treks on the Garden Island* is also a good resource, particularly for the Sleeping Giant Mountain area in Kapaʻa. Request a catalog of books and maps for hiking and camping on Kauai and other Hawaiian islands from *Hawaii Geographic Society,* PO Box 1698, Honolulu HI 96806. When you arrive on Kauai, call the Division of Forestry in Lihue (808-274-3433) for a report on current trail conditions. If you visit the office, you can pick up an excellent free topo map. You can also call the Kauai Visitor's Bureau in Lihue (245-3971) for advice and help in arranging hiking trips and guides.

The most famous trail, the *Kalalau trail,* is a spectacular but strenuous 11 mile hike through the Na Pali cliff region, though even recreational hikers can enjoy the first few miles. This subsection, the Hanakapi'ai trail, has breathtaking views of the coast along switchbacks which take you into forest and back out to the ocean. About a quarter-mile of uphill walking brings you to a magnificent view of Ke'e Beach and the Ha'ena reefs. Two more miles of rigorous up and down hiking will bring you to Hanakapi'ai Beach, nestled like a brilliant jewel in a picturesque, terraced valley (Hiking beyond this point requires a day-use permit from the Division of State Parks). Unfortunately, this beach has currents far too dangerous for swimming, and the rip currents can be so powerful that more than one unwary hiker standing in the surf at knee level has been caught up in a sudden, large wave, pulled out to sea and drowned. The Kalalau trail begins where the paved road ends on the north shore, at Ke'e Beach. Remember, it's also the last source of safe drinking water.

**Important safety information:** When it rains, this narrow trail gets muddy – and dangerously slippery, a fact we appreciated first hand when we saw a woman slip over the steep edge and disappear down into the slick vegetation. Fortunately, her quick-thinking companion had managed to grab her hand so that we could pull her back up! In many places, the trail is actually a stream bed, and fills with water after heavy rains. Essential items: shoes with good traction for slippery rocks and mud (instead of jogging shoes or flip flops), sunscreen, strong insect repellent, a hat, perhaps a nylon poncho, and even a walking stick. (Consider a telescoping stick that can double as a monopod for your camera; a great one by Cascade can be found at www.rei.com). Plan on carrying your own drinking water because the bacterium leptospirosis is found in almost all of Kauai's rivers and streams. For an update on trails and conditions in Na Pali, call *Pedal 'n Paddle* (826-9069) in Hanalei, the *Division of State Parks* (241-3446), or *Kayak Kauai Outfitters* (826-9844), which offers guided hikes of the Kalalau Trail, and ocean kayak excursions on Na Pali.

In Wailua, we like to hike *Mount Nounou Trail*, on *Sleeping Giant Mountain*. This semi-strenuous 1.75-mile hike takes you to the Ali'i Vista Hale picnic shelter on the 'chest' of the Sleeping Giant. From this vantage point, you can see the inland mountains to Mount Wai'ale'ale and the Wailua River winding to the sea. The trail head is on Halelilo Road in Wailua. From Kuhio Highway (Route 56), take Halelilo Road for 2 miles and park on the right near telephone pole #38. After a moderate ascent with some climbing over boulders, through dense guava and eucalyptus, you'll walk through switchbacks, until you come to a junction marked by multiple-rooted hala trees. The trail to the left leads to another fork, and either of these paths will lead to the shelter. Explore for the best view, though avoid trails leading south towards the giant's 'head.'

*Hanakapi'ai Beach*

The *Koke'e Forest* region is beautiful in a different way. Within this 4,345 acre wilderness preserve are 45 miles of trails, from pleasant walks to rugged hikes, as well as fresh water fishing streams, and the 20 square mile highland bog known as Alaka'i Swamp. From the Koke'e Lodge, day hikers can choose from three trails which explore the plateau and Waimea Canyon rim, ranging from the half-mile 'Black Pipe Trail' to the 1.5 mile 'Canyon Trail' along the north rim of Waimea Canyon, past upper Wa'ipo'o Falls to the Kumuwela Overlook. From this perch you can see the canyon's 3,600-foot depth and 10 mile stretch to the sea. For longer hikes, arrange for guides, and hunting and fishing licenses, at the *Koke'e Lodge* (335-6061). Visit www.geocities.com/ RainForest for a virtual tour.

The Sierra Club (www.hi.sierraclub.org/Kauai/kauai.html) sponsors 3 or 4 day hikes on Kauai each month, also offers shuttle service from the airport to Na Pali trailhead in exchange for a donation. Send sase to PO Box 3412, Lihue HI 96766. The most popular destinations: Na Pali's Kalalau Trail to Hanakapi'ai; Sleeping Giant mountain trails on the eastern shore; from Shipwreck Beach to Maha'ulepu on the south shore; and on the west, the first few miles beyond Polihale along the coast (davidht@aloha.net).

Want company? *Princeville Ranch Hiking Adventures* offers guided tours of the north shore's hidden places (826-7669 www.kauai-hiking.com). Contact *Kauai Nature Tours* (742-8305 or 888-233-8365 www.teok.com).

# Horseback Riding

Guided trail rides are a unique way to explore Kauai. On the north shore, *Princeville Ranch Stables* (formerly Po'oku Ranch) offers an hour's ride across the ranch lands, or a two–hour ride towards the mountains for views. A four–hour ride ($110) includes a hike to a waterfall for a picnic lunch and swim (808-826-6777 www.kauai.net/~kwc4). Groups of 6-8 are taught horsemanship, a unique feature of this program. While a morning ride avoids the heat of the day, wear sunglasses and perhaps a hat which won't blow off. Once you're on board, it's hard to climb down and chase it!

Closed Sundays. Silver Falls Ranch escorts groups along the beautiful Kalihiwai Ridge ($69-$99 for 1.5 to 3 hrs), with lunch and swim at a waterfall (Kilauea, 828-6712 www.hawaiian.net/~sfr). Don't trust horses but like trails? Try *Hanalei Wagon Rides* (826-1677). Map 2

On the south shore, *CJM Stables* offers one or two-hour tours near Maha'ulepu Beach for $65-$90 (Poipu, 742-6096 www.cjmstables.com). Tour guides are very friendly and provide historical information, as well as photo-opportunities. Closed Sundays. Map 3.

Eastside, call *Esprit de Corps* for trail rides in verdant Sleeping Giant Mountain area. $55-$350 (Kapa'a, 822-4688 www.kauaihorses.com) Map 1. On the westside, near Waimea, *Garden Island Ranch* offers tours of the ranch land along the ocean and lower western rim of the Waimea Canyon (limit 2 riders). 808-338-0052. Map 4

## Ice Cream & Shave Ice

Kauai has its own ice cream factory, founded by Walter Lappert who wanted to retire in paradise — and ended up in business. Demand exploded for his creamy island flavors like 'Kauai pie,' and now you can see tourists in far away Silicon Valley licking a *Lappert's* cone. Lappert's celebrates its anniversary each Dec. 21 with free ice cream (Plan your next vacation to coincide!) They're up to the 25th anniversary! The more calorie conservative can try Hawaiian *Meadow Gold* ice cream, available in Foodland and Big Save Markets. Don't miss Macadamia Nut! Shave Ice is a special island treat. Stop in at the *Wishing Well* in Hanalei (in the silver trailer by Kayak Kauai) for some of the best flavors and textures. Also try the Shave Ice stand next to Hamura's Saimin on Kress St., Lihue.

## Jewelry

*Goldsmith's Kauai* in the Kinipopo Shopping Village, Wailua is a must stop! You'll find original designs crafted of gold, silver, and precious gems by award-winning artists. Although founder Eric Vogt has 'retired' to sail around the world, his partner Dana and the other designers carry on their outstanding work. They will show you photographs of their designs, or devise something special just for you, like a gold charm in the shape of a petroglyph or one of those cute butterfly fish you saw on the reef while snorkeling. Seashell and reef fish designs in gold are lovely, and prices are reasonable. In Kapa'a, *Jim Saylor* works with fine gems. While you watch, he can sketch, with contagious delight and excitement, a special setting for a loose gemstone, or help you select from his wide collection of designs.

# Luaus

For centuries, Hawaiians have celebrated birthdays, weddings, anniversaries, and festive occasions, with a luau feast, featuring a whole pig roasted in an 'imu' or underground oven and served with a colorful array of dishes, including sweet potatoes, poi, fresh island fish, chicken cooked in coconut and taro, tropical fruits and salads. The major hotels (Hyatt, Sheraton, Marriott) all offer luau extravaganzas.

At the *Princeville Hotel* on the north shore, dancers perform by the oceanside pool; kids will love the view from the bridge! (826-9644). The show at the *Hyatt* features more contemporary music and choreography along with the traditional (742-1234). *Coconut Beach Hotel* in Wailua (822-3455 www.kcb.com) has an authentic Hawaiian hula show, and one child is free with each adult. *Smith's Tropical Paradise* (821-6895) in Wailua is an all-Polynesian gala, and you can buy a ticket to the show, presented in a natural ampitheater, without buying the family-style buffet beforehand. Go early and see the gardens! *Kilohana Plantation* offers a full Polynesian Review and buffet (www.gaylordskauai.com 245-9593). Expect to pay upwards of $50/adults and $20/children for these extravaganzas.

Some excellent local shows are free. At the *Coconut Plantation Marketplace* in Wailua, you can see a free show almost every afternoon at 5 pm (To find out who is performing, call 822-3641). Showtime at *Poipu Shopping Village* is T & Th at 5 pm (742-2831). At the *Princeville Hotel*, John Akana and Mauliola Cook enchant audiences with stories & legends of old Hawaii performed in dance and chants, in the 'Living Room' (T, Th, Sun at 6:30 pm). Bring the kids, and you'll all have fun! Enjoy a glass of wine and watch the sunset. On the south shore, *Hyatt Regency* offers a free show, great for kids, at 6 pm nightly, at Seaview Terrace (742-1234).

In summer months, O Bon dances celebrate the ancestors of the congregations of island Buddhist temples. Old and young dance together in large circles under colorful, lighted lanterns. Write Waimea Shingon Mission, 3770 Pule Rd., Waimea HI 96796 for a schedule.

## Massage, Kauai Style

For something truly special, try an unforgettable, Hawaiian *lomi lomi* massage at *Mu'olaulani* in Anahola. This special massage, developed by Angeline Locey, takes place in a unique steam room, and begins with a 'salt scrub' with sea salt to cleanse your skin in preparation for the lomi lomi, which is almost amazingly soothing. Angeline and her family and staff—Bonnie, Michael, Malia, Norma Jean — consider the lomi lomi sacred to the Hawaiian tradition of healing. This extraordinary, incredibly relaxing two-hour experience costs a reasonable $125. Since the steamer may be shared by others, specify if you prefer being with your own sex. Or you can opt for massage, without steam, in a private room. Reservations 822-3235. Mornings only.

## Music of Hawaii

Hawaiian music has taken off in popularity and a new artistic direction, thanks to artists like Keali'i Reichel and groups like Hapa who give a contemporary sound to the traditions. Keali'i Reichel's first album, *Kawaipunahele*, exploded onto the music scene in 1994 and has become the all-time bestselling album of Hawaiian music. His next two albums, *Lei Hali'a* and *E O Mai,* have quickly become classics. His newest album, *Melelana,* should be in the CD changer of your car to soothe those traffic blues! You'll also enjoy Israel Kamakawiwo'ole's albums *E Ale E,* and *Facing Forward.*

For the classics, listen to the Brothers Cazimero (*Hawaiian Paradise* and *'The Best'*), or The Makaha Sons of Ni'ihau (*Ke Alaula* or *Ho'oluana),* or Hui Ohana. 'Slack Key' guitar music brings you haunting melodies without words, and Keola Beamer is a master. Another 'must listen' is *Hahani Mai* by Kekuhi Kanehele, a superb female vocalist. At *Borders Books & Music* in Lihue, you can listen before you buy. Visit *www.tropicaldisc.com* a multimedia site with links to Hawaiian musicians' home pages. Keali'i's homepage (www.worldsound.net/keali) offers free MP3s and links to a great musical postcard site. Visit www.nahenahe.net/ kealii for sound clips from *Melelana.*

While driving, listen to KKCR (96.9), north shore public radio, which often plays Hawaiian music, and find out what's up with Maunalele's show each morning. KONG (93.5) is the popular local-style commercial station.

## Photographing Kauai

* **Shoot in early morning or late afternoon.** Strong sunlight can wash out colors and shadow your subjects' faces. Choose early morning (before 10:00) or late afternoon (after 4:00), when the light is low. Light is best if it comes from the side rather than over the photographer's shoulder.

* **Vary your composition.** For a 3-D effect, combine something in the foreground, like a palm tree, with the middle-ground and background. Try vertical shots, great for people and flowers; a vertical composition of sky, ocean, surf and sand can look like a "slice of Kauai."

* **Watch out for horizons.** They should be level, not tilting. The sea will look like it is "dumping water" to the right or left, if it's not straight. Placing the horizon across the middle of the picture cuts it in half. A higher horizon emphasizes the foreground; a lower one is a better "sky shot" for great sunsets or cloud scenes. Experiment starting with the horizon down in the lower third; then in the upper third.

* **Use ISO 200 film.** The improved faster films will allow you faster shutter speeds and sharper images. For action shots, consider ISO 400 film. A polarizing filter can enhance color and really improve the appearance of clouds, the ocean, and the surf break. Make sure you have a cap or at least a filter on your lens, as well as a zipper case, lens brush, when you are travel to the beach. Sand and salt can be disastrous.

* **Move in close for people pictures.** Fill the frame with your subject. If you are trying to show your companion as well as the location, place the person to one side, the location to the other. Watch out for the palm tree that may appear to be growing out of the subject's head.

* **Great spots for great shots:** Sunsets & rainbows from Princeville Hotel's terrace, Na Pali cliffs from Ke'e Beach (or first mile of Kalalau trail), windsurfers at Anini Beach, Maha'ulepu Beach. Allerton Gardens, Kukuiolono Park plumeria grove, farmers markets, sunrise at Lydgate Park.

## Scuba & Snuba

You can dive Kauai's reefs and play with sea turtles on the south shore near Poipu or, weather permitting, on the north shore near the Ha'ena reefs. More than a dozen companies offer introductory and refresher lessons, 3-5 day PADI certification, as well as shore and boat dives, and full or half-day charters. Contact *Seasport Divers* for a helpful island map (800- 685-5889 or 742-9303 or www.kauaiscubadiving.com), and inquire about the free hotel pool introductory lesson. The longest established dive operation on Kauai, *Ocean Odyssey* (Lihue: 245-8681 www.oceanquest.net), offers a full range of lessons, shore and boat dives, certification classes, as well as free hotel introductory lessons. You can also contact *Dive Kauai* (Kapa'a: 822-0452 or 800-828-3483 www.divekauai.com).

EASTSIDE: *SeaFun Kauai* (Lihue: 245-6400), *Sunrise Diving* (Kapa'a: 822-REEF www.sunrisediving.com), *Nitrox Tropical Dives* (800-NX5-DIVE), *Watersports Adventures* (Kapa'a: 821-1599), and *Wet-n-wonderful* (Kapa'a: 822-0211). NORTH SHORE: Try *North Shore Divers* (828-1223) or *Hanalei Water Sports* (Princeville Hotel: 826-7509). SOUTH SHORE: *Fathom Five Divers* (Poipu: 742-6991 or 800-972-3078) offers classes, certification, and dives for every level of experience, including night dives. Want to see the fish but not carry the weight of scuba gear? *Snuba of Kauai* offers reef tours with the air source provided by an attached flotation raft (823-8912 www.hshawaii.com/kvp/snuba) Lawai Beach ($55/person).

The best diving in all of the Hawaiian islands can be found off Ni'ihau , the privately owned, largely undeveloped island which has been preserved by the Robinson family as a place for Hawaiian people and culture. Some companies offer all-day boat dives to Ni'ihau, a unique opportunity for experienced divers to explore untouched reefs. Winter surf conditions are usually too rough, and even in summer, the chop and currents can be formidable. Contact *Fathom Five Divers* (742-6991), *Seasport Divers* (742-9303) and *Bubbles Below* (822-3483 http://aloha.net/~kaimanu).

# Snorkeling

On the south shore, Poipu Beach Park offers excellent and relatively safe snorkeling most of the year. Just west of the rocky point dividing the park from the new Marriott (old Waiohai), you can find brilliant yellow tang, striped manini fish, butterfly-fish, parrot fish, and silvery needle fish, all feeding on the coral. More than once, we

*Snorkeling is best at Tunnels (north), Poipu Beach Park (south), and Lydgate Park (east).*

*Fred*

have met a spotted box fish (Lauren has nicknamed him 'Fred') who seems curious enough to swim right up to our masks. When surf is strong, watch out for the current at the edge of the reef. Our family also enjoys *'Tunnels,'* on the north shore, so named (in part) for the intricate 'tunnels' along the edge of the reef where the water seems to plunge to unfathomable depths. We also like *Ke'e Beach*, where we can chase the *humu humu nuku nuku apua'a*, Hawaii's state fish, and *Lydgate Park*, where large blue fish with yellow fins swim in friendly families along the sandy bottom of the rock pool.

Plan your snorkeling with an eye to the tides, the weather, and the season. North shore is best in summer, when the ocean is relatively calm and you can even find it pancake flat. In winter, when surf is up on the north, Poipu Beach Park and Lydgate Park will probably have calmer water. If you snorkel where others are snorkeling, you can get help if you need it— so avoid snorkeling at deserted beaches. Try not to lose track of where you are when you are admiring all the fish, and don't snorkel at all if the surf looks too rough, or a rippling pattern in the waves indicates strong currents.

Feeding the fish can be lots of fun. If you use commercial snorkel fish food, however, you may have a problem when the plastic film casing begins to disintegrate in the water, bringing lots of fish, perhaps too many fish for your taste! This plastic is biodegradable, not like the tougher plastics which are dangerous to sea life. We carry fish food in a plastic zip-lock bag for more control. It really doesn't matter what you put inside the bag as long as it stimulates the fish's curiosity. (Just don't use frozen peas, which are hard for the fish to digest.) Try a green leaf or piece of seaweed inside the plastic bag — it attracts the curious, rather than the ravenous, fish. Tuck your plastic bag securely into your suit, then once you are in the ocean, let the water fill it and float your 'visual display' around. Swirl the bag gently and you'll be amazed at how much interest it creates! Be sure to take your bag back out of the water with you. In a pinch, use green leaves or seaweed.

Coral cuts can be dreadful. Keep bandaids and antibiotic ointment in your beach bag and avoid touching the coral with any body part. Don't walk on it or try to pick it up. Your fins won't completely protect your feet.

A well-fitting mask makes snorkeling more fun. To test the fit, place the mask on your face (without using the straps) and breathe in; a well-fitting mask will stay on by itself. A dilute solution of detergent and water—even spit— coats the lens to avoid fogging. Rinse after applying.

**Renting gear**: Expect to pay about $5/day or $15/week for a good quality mask, fins, snorkel, and about $5-$8/day for a body board. **Lihue**: *Kalapaki Beach Boys* at the Kauai Marriott rents surfing and snorkeling gear, kayaks & a Hobie Cat 246-9661. **Wailua**: *Chris the Fun Lady* rents, gives advice — & free coffee and cookies 822-7447. *Kauai Water Ski & Surf* 822-3574 in Wailua. *Kayak Kauai* in Coconut Plantation Marketplace 822-9179. **Hanalei**: *Pedal & Paddle* 826-9096. *Hanalei Surf Co.* 826-9000. **Poipu**: *Nukumoi Surf Co* 742-7019 www.brenneckes.com *Snorkel Bob's* 742-8322. **Snorkel Tours**: *SeaFun Kauai* 245-1113 www.alohakauaitours.com

## Sport Fishing

Kauai's warm tropical waters offer great fishing for big and medium to light tackle game fish. No fishing license is required, and you can depart from ports all over the island, depending on surf and season. The north shore is beautiful though too rough during winter months. From Port Allen on the west side, you have the advantage of being close to the spectacular Na Pali coastline and its amazing cliffs—fishing with a view! Most companies equip their boats with sonar, and help to pair you up with other anglers to share the cost. Expect to pay upwards of $100 for a half-day shared rate, or as much as $875 for the whole day exclusive.

Departing from Port Allen on the west side, *Sport Fishing Kauai* (639-0013 www.fishing-kauai-hawaii.com) operates 3 Bertram Sport Fishers: 38-ft 'Kauai Kai,' 33-ft 'Marlin,' & 28-ft 'Vida Del Mar,' for a maximum of 6 fishermen, cruising up to 5 miles offshore. The specialty: a 10 hour private charter to Ni'ihau ($1075). *Hoku Au Charters* operates a 30-ft Force Sport Fisher (332-7730 www.hawaiian.net/~otto/). Also call *Open Sea Charter* (332-8213). On the north shore, try *Anini Charters* (828-1285), *Blue Ocean Adventures* (828-1114), *Kai Bear Sportfishing* (826-7269). *McReynolds Charters* operates the 30' 'Ho'omaika'i,' for six passengers, departing from Anini Channel off the North Shore (828-1379 http://mail.aloha.net/~themcrs). In Nawiliwili, *True Blue Charters* operates the 55' Delta 'Konane Star' which can be chartered for fishing and snorkeling, or touring the Na Pali coast or Kipu Kai (245-9662 www.kauaifun.com).

Fish for Kauai's largemouth bass on the largest freshwater reservoir in the state of Hawaii. Contact Fishing in Paradise (808-245-7358 kauai_freshwater@)hotmail.com)

## Sunset Drive to Hanalei

If your accommodations are on the eastern shore, consider dinner in Hanalei, for the drive north as the sun begins to set is an experience not to be missed in summer! Check the paper for the exact time of sunset, which may be earlier than you expect because Hawaii never changes to daylight savings time. Allow an extra ten minutes to park and ready your camera.

As you begin the drive, hundreds of clouds, already tinged with peach and gold, float in an azure sky above a shimmering sea. Rt. 56 winds through the countryside and along the coast, with fields of sugar cane turning silver, and the colors of land and sky changing almost mile by mile as the declining sun deepens the greens and blues and touches everything with shades of pink and gold. At Kilauea, where the road curves to the west, a line of tall, graceful Norfolk pines stands starkly silhouetted against the blazing sky. Even the grasses, their feathery tops waving gently in evening breezes, are touched with pink, and the cattle grazing in the field seem positioned by an artist's hand. Near Princeville, the clouds, luminous with reflected golds and pinks, seem enormous, dwarfing the cliffs, whose great jagged peaks have turned an astonishing purple.

We never tire of this drive, as each sunset is different. The gleaming expanse of ocean, the sharply angled mountains, the masses of clouds are blended each night by the sun's magic into a composition of colors that will never occur again in exactly the same way. One night the sun's descent may be screened by great masses of clouds rimmed with gold and glowing tangerine against the deep purple mountains and the shimmering blue grey sea. Another time, the sun may almost blind you with its blazing, fiery gold, suffusing nearby clouds with impossible shades of orange and pink and brushing distant clouds with peach. Or, one evening, the clouds may be so thick that the setting sun is apparent only in delicate touches of apricot on the clouds hovering over the sea, muted purples on the mountains, and a silver sheen on the surface of the sea. As seasons change, so does the angle of the sun, gilding the landscape with new patterns of light and color.

A sunset in the rain is the most astonishing of all, as the mountains are shrouded with grey, yet above the sea, the sky is brilliant with color, with sunny clouds stretching along the horizon, their shapes rimmed with pink light from the setting sun. As dark showers move across the horizon like 'legs of the rain,' blurring the line between ocean and sky, the sun descends into stormy clouds moving slowly toward it, and, as the last light fades, dark clouds hovering above the cliffs slowly creep across the mountains, and the world turns slowly still and dark.

*Sunset in the rain, a spectacular view from Bali Hai Restaurant.*

If the clouds are not too thick, you can enjoy the sunset from several places in Hanalei. Less than a mile past the entrance to Princeville, you can park at a scenic overlook on Rt. 56 and see most of Hanalei's western side. But you have to contend with the distractions of traffic and car radios as well as conversations of other sunset seekers ("Ralph! I *told* you we were gong to miss it!") For a more panoramic view with greater privacy, enter Princeville and follow the signs to Pali Ke Kua, park in the lot, and enjoy the view discretely from the lawn between the buildings.

The drive home after dinner is another sensuous experience of cool evening breezes you can almost taste as well as feel. As you drive south, you can hear wonderful sounds —the chirping of crickets, the leaves rustling in the breeze—and see the different shades of darkness in the landscape, lit by the moon against an enormous star-filled sky and the shimmering waves of the wide ocean beyond.

## Sunset Watching

Watch spectacular sunsets from the 'Living Room' at the Princeville Hotel, and enjoy cocktails and music, or at the Beach House on the south shore. Or go to the beach! Bring a blanket (and possibly beach chairs, CD

*Sunset in full moon*

player with headphones, a Keali'i Reichel CD, a good book, a small ice chest with drinks and snacks). On the north shore, visit Tunnels or Ke'e, or closer to the eastern shore, Anini Beach. On the south shore, try Poipu Beach Park (you won't see the sun actually 'set' but a gorgeous 'glow'), or if you are really ambitious, drive to the westernmost beaches, Barking Sands or even Polihale Beach.

## Surfing & Body Boarding

When they were small, our children loved to take their boogie boards to Poipu Beach Park. As they grew older, they craved the bigger waves. Surfing, like everything on Kauai, depends on the tides, the winds, and the season. In summer, the surf is 'up' on the south and west, and so kids who are learning about surfing may find that northern beaches like Kalihiwai, our family's favorite, can offer just the right amount of challenge (p. 51). Hanalei (p. 53), Kalapaki (p. 30) and Kealia (p. 34) can also be good summertime choices, depending, of course, on surf conditions. Wailua Bay is a local favorite, though you must be careful of currents near the river mouth (p. 34). Westside, Kekaha can be challenging, especially during a summer swell (p. 75). Experienced surfers will like Shipwrecks (p. 67), Pakala's (or 'Infinities,' p. 73) in summer, Hanalei or Kalihiwai in winter.

In winter months, surf is 'up' on the north shore, and the waves can become more powerful and currents dangerous. Hanalei can be gentle enough for you one day and the next, a crashing, thundering caldron too tough even for experienced surfers. The same is true for Kalihiwai, and eastern shore beaches like Kealia, Kalapaki, and Wailua, where you may not be able to paddle out with your board to where the waves are breaking, even with fins, because of strong currents. As in all water sports, caution is a must. The wave pattern varies along the beach, and some spots are safer than others, so watch where the local kids are surfing and follow their lead. Don't go out alone, or take a body board to an area with hard board surfers. Observe the protocol of surfers waiting their turn out on the waves.

For surf lessons on the south shore, *Margo Oberg*, a seven time world surfing champion, operates a surf school for all skill levels (Poipu: 742-8019). Rates: $45 for 1.5 hours in groups of up to 7 (or up to 10 with 2 instructors). You'll surf the inside break in front of the Kiahuna Resort, where surf conditions are usually relatively safe— waves less than four feet and winds moderate. Instructors are knowledgable and make sure everyone gets 'up.'

Arrange lessons and surf board rentals (about $20/day) at *Nukumoi Surf Co.,* Poipu: (742-8019) where you can check out the videos of Kauai's best surfers in action,

*Sharing the wave at Kalihiwai*

*Kalihiwai – perfect for skim boards*

including the owner's daughter, A.S.P. touring pro Rochelle Ballard. Rent boards at *SeaSport Divers* in Poipu (742-9303) and at *Progressive Expressions*, which also offers lessons, in Koloa (742-6041). For surfing lessons on the north shore, call Celeste Harvel, *Windsurf Kauai* (828-6838). Skilled surfers can arrange a lesson from elite coach Russell Lewis (828-0339). Arrange rentals at *Hanalei Surf Co.*, Hanalei (826-9000), *Kayak Kauai* (826-9844) and *Kai Kane*, Hanalei (826-5594). Eastside, call *Kalapaki Beach Boys* (245-9662 www.kauaifun.com) for rentals and lessons, *Kayak Kauai* (822-9179), or Ambrose (822-7112) in Wailua.

When surf is too flat (or too rough) for body boards, our kids use skim boards to catch long, exciting rides across the shallows, or in an inch of foam along the shorebreak. Made of polished wood or resin, these boards skim along the thin layer of foam. Our kids love to skim board at Kalihiwai, where the stream flows into the ocean, Hanalei, Anahola, and Kalapaki.

## Surf Wear & Surf Gear

The magical names of Roxy, Quicksilver, Billabong! Our kids prefer *Nukomoi* in Poipu for the best array of shirts, shorts, wallets, jewelry, & stickers selected by owner Christine French and daughters Kelly and

Rochelle (Rochelle Ballard, international surfing pro). In Wailua, visit *Kauai Water Ski & Surf* next to Kinipopo Shopping Center for a great selection of surf wear and boards. In Kapa'a, the family favorite is *M. Miura*. At Kukui Grove Center, Lihue, it's *Deja Vu*. In Poipu, *Progressive Expressions* for surf boards and surf wear. In Waimea, stop in at *Liko's*, where Jeremy bought one of Liko's beautifully crafted surfboards. In Lawai, call Dave for Lauren's favorite '*Chicks Who Rip*' line of tee-shirts he designs with daughter Shauna (332-8422 www.chickswhorip.com).

## Water Skiing

The Wailua River on the eastern shore is a great spot for water skiing, wake boarding, kneeboarding, slalom, and other waters sports. For $85, you can get a driver, equipment, lessons, and the boat, and you can put the whole family in it! Call *Kauai Water Ski & Surf Company* (surfski@aloha.net 822-3574). The Wailua River is getting crowded with kayaks and water skiers, so county policies may tighten for watersports.

## Weddings on Kauai

Considering a wedding on Kauai? There are no residency, citizenship, blood test, or waiting period requirements, though bride and groom must both be at least 18 years old to marry without parental consent, and both must apply in person for a license, valid for 30 days (pay in cash: $50). For a free "Getting Married" pamphlet, contact the *State Department of Health, Marriage License Office*, 1250 Punchbowl St., Honolulu HI 96813 (808-586-4544). Island weddings have become a thriving business. For a list of companies, send $3 to the Kauai Wedding Professionals Association to order its '*Bridal Guide*' (KWPA, PO Box 761, Kapa'a HI 96746 (808-822-1477). Many wedding companies have web sites, which you can find through links on larger sites like www.kauaivacation.com or www.travel-kauai.com or www.bestplaceshawaii.com. Confused about all the choices? You can consult Liz Hey (800-822-1176 heyliz@hawaiian.net) for help in finding the best 'match.'

You can make some important arrangements yourself. Contact the *Division of State Parks* for a list of scenic wedding sites (808-274-3444).

You can even be married onboard the lovely sailing yacht, the Lady Leanne II (808-822-1422). For a reception, you can reserve a private tea room at *Hanama'ulu Tea House* (call Sally at 808-245-2511), or a private room at Kintaro (822-3341). Restaurants with elegant private dining rooms include Gaylord's (245-9593 www.gaylords.com) and Piatti (742-2116). Order spectacular tropical blooms for a reasonable price from *Kauai Tropicals* (800-303-4385), and traditional leis from *Irmalee Pomroy* (808-822-3231), Kauai's foremost artist in flowers. How about a release of colorful butterflies! (888-BUTRFLI) Music? Guitarist *Hal Kinnaman* will play beautiful Hawaiian, contemporary or classical music at your wedding (808-335-0332). Transportation? *Kauai Limo Corp.* (245-4877 or 800-764-7213).

## Windsurfing

Sheltered Anini Beach is ideal for windsurfing. An offshore reef creates a peaceful lagoon in most winds, and on most days, you can see brightly colored sails and students from two windsurf companies. At *Windsurf Kauai,* Celeste Harvel (828-6838) can teach the basics as well as a complete certification course. A gifted teacher, she has special size boards for kids, and a special dog, Kahili who actually may hop aboard and go for a ride! *Anini Beach Windsurfing* (826-9463) also uses the latest in equipment and teaches surfers at all levels. Both companies offer small group lessons ($60/pp for a 3-hour session, morning or afternoon). Drop-ins are welcome, though it's safer to reserve ahead. You can also rent equipment for $15/hr. Questions? Stop in at *Hanalei Surf Company* for advice and information. On the east side, Kalapaki Beach at the Marriott is the place! Call *Kalapaki Beach Boys* (246-9661).

# *Adventures*

## Helicoptering Kauai

Many of the most beautiful places on Kauai are inaccessible by car. For this reason, a helicopter tour is an unforgettable way to see this spectacular island. Kauai is breathtakingly beautiful from the air, almost like an America in miniature, with rolling hills and valleys on the eastern shore and majestic mountains on the west. The island has a flat, dry southland as well as a forested wilderness to the north, and, on the west coast, wide sandy beaches where the setting sun paints the sky with gold before slipping silently into the enormous sea. There is even a "Grand Canyon" on a small scale, where pink and purple cliffs, etched by centuries of wind and rain into giant towers, seem like remnants of a lost civilization. So much variety is amazing on an island only 30 miles in diameter!

And what you'll see is beyond your fantasies—a mountain goat poised for an instant in a ravine, a white bird gliding against the dark green cliffs, a sudden rainbow in the mist, incredible, tower-like mountains of pink and brown in the Waimea "Grand Canyon," a glistening waterfall hanging like a slender silver ribbon through trees and rocks, a curve of pure white sand at the base of the purple and gold Na Pali cliffs, a spray of shining white foam bursting upon the rocky coast. Then, like the unveiling of the island's final mystery, the entrance into the very center of Mt. Wai'ale'ale's crater, where in the dimly lit mists of the rainiest place on the earth, waterfalls are born from ever falling showers. You have journeyed to the very heart of the island, the place of its own birth from the volcano's eruption centuries ago. From your hotel room, you would never have believed that all this splendor existed, and your only regret will be that you didn't take more film!

It's so special, you yearn to go up again. Even the second time, the tour is exhilarating. In fact, with a better sense of the island's geography, you are more sensitive to details too easily missed when you are overcome by the majesty of the scene for the first time. You may see some of the amazing irrigation canals and tunnels carved into the mountains a century ago to bring water to the sugar cane fields below. Or, on some remote and sheer escarpment along the Na Pali coast, a terrace where taro was once

*www.explorekauai.com*

cultivated by the ancient Hawaiians. Gilded by the sun, these knife-like green ridges look like the 'skirts of Pele,' goddess of the volcano's fire.

Because of the expense of the tour, we worried about picking the "perfect day." We began on what seemed in Lihue to be only a partly sunny day, but once in the air, we realized that the clouds would be above us rather than in our way and even enhanced the island's beauty with changing

*A rare clear view of the top of Mt. Wai'ale'ale, highest elevation on Kauai & the wettest place on the earth! The rain gauge measures the almost constant rainfall.*

patterns of light.

In choosing your tour operator, we recommend interviewing several companies by asking specific questions (see 'Helicopter Tours & Safety' below). Of the many companies offering tours, *Jack Harter Helicopters* and *Will Squyres Helicopters* stand out as special, with reputations for high quality and attention to safety. Both companies were started by very special pilots. *Jack Harter* pioneered the scenic Kauai helicopter tour, and his company's unique 90-minute tour, the best value for your money, features the fascinating pilot narration which Jack developed over more than 30 years of flying. ( www.helicopters-kauai.com 808-245-3774).

*Will Squyres* has earned wide respect over the years for his good judgment and meticulous maintenance. He's a superb pilot, has scouted locations for such memorable movies as Jurassic Park and The Lost World, and his company's hour-long tour coordinates pilot commentary with dramatic stereo music on a great sound system as you fly over the island's most spectacular scenery. Like Jack Harter Helicopters, Will Squyres Helicopters has a perfect safety record. (808-245-7541 www.helicopters-hawaii.com).

Looking at our slides and videos back home almost brings back the magic of that hour, when we seemed suspended in a horizon so vast as to seem limitless, and any effort to confine it within camera range was impossible. It is always the best day of the trip!

*The beautiful eastern shore and Sleeping Giant Mountain*

## Helicopter Tours & Safety

Helicopter tours are big business, with intense competition for tourist dollars. Many people on Kauai feel that there is a wide variation in quality and safety, however. We have heard disquieting reports: some companies speed up tours in order to cut costs and squeeze as many tours into the day as possible. Some companies are plagued with high turnover in pilots who may have sufficient flying hours to be licensed but limited experience over Kauai's unique wilderness terrain. With pilots from a dozen companies crowding the skies, safety is becoming an increasingly important issue. In 1994, two accidents involving fatalities occurred on Kauai involving Papillon Hawaiian Helicopters and Inter-Island Helicopters. In 1998, an accident involving Ohana Helicopters claimed six lives.

| 1994 | Interisland Helicopters | 1 fatality |
| 1994 | Papillon Hawaiian Helicopters | 3 fatalities |
| 1998 | Ohana Helicopters | 6 fatalities |

After the 1994 incidents, the Federal Aviation Administration (FAA) issued 'Special Federal Aviation Regulations' (SFARs) in October, 1994, requiring detailed safety briefings for passengers, and emergency flotation devices onboard single-engine helicopters. The most controversial rule was the 'standoff requirement,' which prohibited flights closer than 1,500 feet to the ground or water, except during takeoff and landing. Helicopters had to fly higher and farther away from the cliffs, craters and valleys that passengers most want to see.

Since, 1994, The FAA has granted exemptions to most companies on Kauai, reducing the standoff requirement to 500 feet. This change has allowed pilots more discretion in determining safe altitude given Kauai's unique cloud layer conditions, which at times make it impossible to fly 1500 feet above the cliffs and valleys, and at the same time observe the FAA required safe distance (500 feet) below the cloud layer. On Kauai, weather conditions can change very quickly. The 1998 accident occurred when an Ohana Helicopters aircraft crashed into a mountain side shrouded in low hanging clouds.

*Na Pali's rugged coastline*

These are some key questions to ask when you are interviewing companies. First, find out whether the company is operating under a certificate issued by the FAA under Part 135 of Federal Aviation Regulations. In order to maintain a certificate of this type, the company must follow a more rigorous (thus more expensive) maintenance program, and its pilots must pass annual flight tests not required of companies operating under Part 91 of Federal Aviation Regulations. This certificate must be displayed in the company's office. Ask to see it. To verify or ask questions, call the FAA in Honolulu at (808) 836-

0615. The distinction between Part 91 and Part 135 operators can tell you about the standards a company operates under, although this information is no guarantee of performance!

Ask who will be piloting your flight, noting that an ad which hypes the number of flying hours logged by the company's owner tells you nothing about the flying experience of his pilot employees. Not every pilot employee who qualifies for a helicopter license has had extensive experience with Kauai's wilderness terrain. You also have a right to know whether the company, or *your* pilot has been involved in any accidents during the past three years. (You can check with NTSB at www.ntsb.gov). Beware of companies which are reluctant to answer, or say they "can't be sure" who will be piloting your flight. Advertisements claiming that the owner is the "operator" can be misleading. Any owner can "operate" his company without being the pilot for every flight. That may be true of some flights—from one a day to one a month—but very possibly not true of your flight! You should also ask if the company's FAA certificate has ever been revoked or suspended, and whether it is currently under FAA investigation for accidents or maintenance deficiencies, as opposed to record-keeping violations. Since each helicopter must display its individual 'certificate of airworthiness,' look for it or ask to see it.

Another important question to ask is the exact length of the tour. Actual in-flight time for the around-the-island tour should be no less than 60 minutes, or Kauai will appear to whiz past your window, limiting your opportunities to explore the more remote terrain inside the island's perimeter, or to take satisfying photographs. Ask for the daily flight schedule, subtract 5 minutes for landing and changing passengers, and draw your own conclusions! In this area, in our opinion, economy is not always the best policy. Given the high operating cost of the air tour business, cheaper tours will almost certainly be short, possibly too short, and the extra dollars you spend for a longer tour will be well worthwhile.

Also consider the type of aircraft you will be flying. We prefer the Bell Jet-Ranger, which seats one passenger in front and three in back. *Jack Harter Helicopters* has modified the passenger windows so that they can be opened —a huge plus for the photographer. The Hughes 500-D helicopter seats two passengers in the rear and two in front next to the pilot. Like a large glass bubble, it has no windows to open. In the past few years, companies have increasingly used the more economical 6-passenger ASTAR helicopter, which seats 2 passengers next to the pilot in front and 4 passengers in the rear. The ASTAR is air-conditioned, but its windows do not open, and for passengers in the center rear seats, the view can be obstructed by the passengers seated next to the windows as well as those in front. Passengers in these center rear seats may have a harder time seeing or taking photographs. Ask about the cancellation policy in case of bad weather. Even in a rainstorm, we often see the choppers flying! Find out whether you can get a refund if you're not very comfortable — or if you can't see very much — once you're in the air.

We consider helicopter tours a unique and special way to see Kauai. We wouldn't go ourselves, or let our children fly, if we thought they were unsafe. But we make careful decisions about the pilots we fly with. We think you should do your homework carefully and have all pertinent information when making your choices as well.

## Boat Tours

The spectacular cliffs of the Na Pali coast are off limits to most visitors—unless they dare to hike on narrow and slippery trails or explore these steep and jagged ridges from a helicopter. Coastal boat tours have provided an affordable way to see these amazing cliffs up close, and enjoy a sometimes rough and ready adventure at the same time. You can explore caves etched into the cliffs, watch waterfalls sparkle in the sunshine, and marvel at how tenaciously plants and trees can cling to inhospitable rock. You'll see an enormous change in the landscape, from the dark, rich green of Keʻe Beach, where rainfall measures

*Beautiful Na Pali coast, a spectacular tour by boat.*

nearly 125 inches a year, to the reds and browns of Polihale on the western-most end of the cliffs, where it measures only 20 inches.

Spectacular, yes! But Na Pali coastal tours have also become highly controversial on Kauai. Some people have opposed the tour operators as intrusive, even destructive of Kauai's wilderness environment, particularly the fragile river ecosystem at the mouth of the Hanalei River where most tours originated. Worse, in the past few years, the tour industry seemed to get out of control. Some companies operated with legal permits; others did not. The antagonism escalated until in late summer 1998, the Governor banned motorized tour boats from operating out of Hanalei Bay waters, effectively shutting down boat traffic to all but sailboats and fishing boats.

If you're returning to Kauai looking for the north shore company you toured with in the past, you're in for a big disappointment. Most boat tour companies have moved to other harbors and launching points, so you can tour Na Pali from Hanalei Bay only in a sailing vessel, and that means only in summer months, from about May until November, as winter surf can reach 20-feet in Hanalei Bay. *Blue Water Sailing* offers summertime Na Pali tours on the beautiful 42-ft sailing yacht, the Lady Leanne II (822-1142 www.sail-kauai.com). *Captain Sundown* will take up to 15 passengers in his 40-ft sailing catamaran, Ku'uipo, out along the Na Pali coast ($100/ 6hrs). In winter months, instead of Na Pali tours, he offers a whale watch-ing cruise in the opposite direction, towards Kilauea Lighthouse and the wildlife preserve ($75/4hrs) (826-5585 www.captainsundown.com).

---

### *Power Catamaran Tours*

| | | | |
|---|---|---|---|
| Hanalei Sport Fishing | 826-6114 | Kaulana Kai | 337-9309 |
| Na Pali Eco-Adventures | 826-6804 | Liko Kauai Cruises | 338-0333 |
| Paradise Adventure | 826-9999 | Holoholo Tours | 246-4656 |
| Makana Tours | 822-9187 | Kauai Sea Tours | 826-7254 |

### *Sailing Yacht Tours*

| | | | |
|---|---|---|---|
| Blue Water Sailing | 828-1142 | Captain Andy's | 335-6833 |
| Catamaran Kahanu | 335-3577 | Blue Dolphin | 742-6731 |
| Rainbow Runner | 245-9662 | | |

### *Kayak Tours*

| | | | |
|---|---|---|---|
| Outfitters Kauai | 742-9667 | Chris the Fun Lady | 822-7447 |
| Kayak Kauai Outbound | 826-9844 | Island Adventures | 245-9662 |
| | Paradise Outdoor Adventures | 822-1112 | |

For a motorized boat tour, Hanalei is off limits, and you will have to depart from the island's west side and travel north along the coast. From Kekaha, *Liko Kauai Cruises* (338-0333), owned by Liko and his Hawaiian family, operates a swift, comfortable, 26-person, 38'-ft power catamaran, 'Na Pali Kai III.' *Kaulana Kai*, offers an excellent tour on a 25-ft Bayliner, with friendly service (337-9309).

Further south in Port Allen, eight companies have permits to originate tours. *Kauai Sea Tours* offers a full-day tour with a snorkeling stop at Nualolo Kai, and because the company has a landing permit, a guided hike to the archaeological site of an ancient Hawaiian fishing village ($132.00/ pp) or a half-day trip without the stop ($108/pp) on a 16-passenger power catamaran or a 15-passenger rigid hull ocean raft (826-7254 or 800-733-7997 www.seatours.net). *Catamaran Kahanu,* owned and operated by native Hawaiians, tours Na Pali on a 36-foot catamaran, 18 feet wide with a 'flying bridge,' a great perch for watching spinning porpoises and humpback whales (about $105/pp). The crew demonstrates Hawaiian crafts (335-3577 www.catamarankahanu.com). *Blue Water Express* tours Na Pali with a comfortable 42' aluminum, Navy reconnaissance hull power boat. Tours run about 4-hours and include a short swim (weather permitting) and sometimes snorkeling (about $95.00/pp) (822-1422 www.sail-kauai.com). *Makana's Charter and Tours* takes 12 passengers on a 32-ft power catamaran (822-9187).

Sailing Tours include *Blue Dolphin Charters* (742-6731), which operates a 56-ft sailing trimaran, the 'Tropic Bird,' along the Na Pali Coast in summer, departing from Port Allen, and also from Kukui'ula Harbor in Poipu. *Captain Andy's* (335-6833 www.sailing-hawaii.com) elegant 40-ft sailing catamaran, 'Spirit of Kauai,' sails from Port Allen to Na Pali (6 hrs at $110/adult), and also offers shorter picnic and snorkel cruises, and sunset cruises, departing from Kukui'ula Harbor, Poipu. *Holoholo Tours* cruises Na Pali in a 48-ft sailing catamaran, also a 61-ft power catamaran departing from Port Allen (800-848-6130 www.holoholo-charters.com 335-0815).

Also at Port Allen are companies operating smaller power catamarans which are quick and agile enough to go into some of the caves along the coast. *Na Pali Eco Adventures,* which emphasizes environmental policies, uses no fume, bio-diesel fuel (800-659-6804 www.napali.com) and offers Na Pali tours (about $100/pp) as well as 2 hour south shore whale watching excursions ($60/pp). *Na Pali Explorer* operates a modified zodiac, replacing the rubber bottom of a zodiac with a hard, rigid hull. The result is higher speeds in rough ocean conditions, a bouncier ride which some people prefer to the more comfortable catamarans *(335-9909* www.napali-explorer.com).

During the winter months (November—March), when seas off Na Pali are too rough and currents too strong, tour operators cruise along Kauai's south shore looking for the humpback whales which frequent Hawaii's warm waters from December to April. Some, like *Kauai Sea Tours* and *Na Pali Eco Adventures*, even provide special hydrophones to listen to whale song! *Kauai Sea Tours* also offers excursions in ocean rafts, departing from Nawiliwili harbor near Lihue and touring the south shore to Kipu Kai, with a stop for lunch and snorkeling. *Rainbow Runner Sailing* (245-9662 www.kauaifun.com) operates a 40-ft trimaran out of Nawiliwili Harbor near Lihue with a variety of tours, from 1 hour to a 4 hour picnic and snorkel trip to Kipu Kai. ($45-$85/pp). *Captain Zodiac* operates rubber raft whale watching excursions and tours to beautiful Kipu Kai beach (826-9372).

Before you choose your tour, call several companies. Inquire about the expected weather and surf conditions—and the company's cancellation policy, in case you decide not to go out if ocean conditions don't seem right to you (check the weather report yourself at 245-6001). Ask about the number of passengers the company usually takes on board, keeping in mind that the more crowded the boat, the less comfortable you may be. Inquire about your captain's experience; although every captain has to be coast guard licensed, some have more experience than others. Don't be misled by discount coupons. One company, for example, published a coupon for a hefty discount off a list price of $90, although activity centers around the island routinely offered the same discount, and almost no one ever paid full price. Bring sunscreen, especially if your craft doesn't offer any shade, and perhaps a hat and sunglasses to protect against the glare. Protect your camera and film, even a dry shirt, in a plastic bag.

*Wild Kahili ginger*

## Kayaking Kauai's Rivers

Exploring Kauai's rivers by kayak can be fun, but increasingly controversial as the rivers become more crowded. The problem is most acute at the Wailua River, which as Kauai's only navigable river, offers a variety of other water sports. On a summer day, you may see powerboats zipping along towing waterskiiers, dodging the wide tour barges lumbering along in the center on their way to the Fern Grotto, while clusters of kayaks hug the banks trying to avoid the wakes! Ten kayak companies have permits to take tours of 12 persons upriver twice a day, so simple multiplication shows you the dimensions of the problem. *Chris the Fun Lady* (822-7447) offers guided kayak tours ($85/pp) upriver beyond the Fern Grotto to a waterfall and rope swing, reached by a 45 minute hike. She also rents kayaks ($25/half-day/single and $50/half-day/double) for self-guided tours. She includes river maps and a tarp to use as a sail (If the wind is right, you can 'sail' upriver), flotation cushions, complete instructions, even a cooler! You can also call *Water Ski & Surf Company* (822-3574).

For river tours of the Hule'ia River, where Indiana Jones was filmed, contact *Island Adventures* (245-9662 www.kauaifun.com). A one-way guided paddle follows the river through the Hule'ia National Wildlife Refuge and the State of Hawaii Conservation District, to the ancient Alakoko 'Menehune' Fish Pond, made, according to legend, by the 'menehune,' Kauai's magical 'little people.' After a short hike through the Hule'ia National Wildlife Refuge, where you can observe many birds, waterfowl, and beautiful exotic plants, a van takes you to your car (about $50/pp). Hule'ia River tours are also offered by *Outfitters Kauai*.

On the north shore, explore the beautiful Hanalei River. Tours are offered by *Luana of Hawaii* (826-9195), or you can rent a kayak and tour on your own. *Pedal & Paddle* rents kayaks, camping and snorkel equipment, even mopeds. Go early for the best selection! *Kayak Kauai Outbound* (800-437-3507 or 826-9844) offers tours and also rents 2-person and 1-person kayaks for a 2-hour minimum. From its convenient riverside location, you can travel upriver, or venture downriver to Hanalei Bay. In summer months, when Hanalei Bay is calm, you may be able to paddle along the bay's edge and pull up on the Princeville Hotel's sandy beach. Everything in the kayak is in danger of getting wet, so take your camera in a waterproof bag. Bring some drinks and snacks, and perhaps snorkeling equipment so that you can explore the reef. A 2-hour trip may be all you need (and all your muscles may be able to take!) You can also load your kayak on top of the car and drive it to the beach near the boat pier at Hanalei Bay, or to Anini beach or Kalihiwai Bay about 10 minutes away. In winter months, when ocean surf and currents become too strong, your best options will be the Hanalei River or the nearby Kalihiwai River, which you can explore up to some beautiful waterfalls.

Sea kayaking can be great fun, in the right surf conditions. *Kayak Kauai Outbound* (800-437-3507 or 808-826-9844 www.kayakkauai.com) offers a day-long kayak excursion between Ha'ena and Polihale State Beach on the westside. Views are spectacular, but you must be ready for a strenu-

*Alakoko 'Menehune' Fish Pond & Hule'ia River National Wildlife Refuge*

ous workout. Traversing the 16 miles of rugged coastline takes about six hours of paddling — hard work even for the athletically-advantaged! Occasional squalls and choppy water often punctuate the ride, but in your kayak you can explore sea caves, play with dolphins, and visit with turtles. When Na Pali waters become too rough, between October and April, whale-watching tours go along the south shore, stopping at lovely Kipu Kai.

On the eastern shore, *Paradise Outdoor Adventures* offers 3 hour ($80) whale-watching kayak tours from Kapa'a to Hanama'ulu near Lihue (822-1112 www.kayakers.com), rentals, and in summer months guided ocean kayak tours of the north shore. Poipu-based *Outfitters Kauai*, (808-742-9667) offers guided kayak tours and combination bike and kayak trips.

Remember the sun! A hat, sunscreen, and drinking water are a must! Bring a towel and spare shirt for an emergency cover up. If you paddle up river, don't drink the river water, and if you have an open cut you must be particularly cautious. The bacterium *leptospirosis* has been detected in all of Kauai's rivers, and can cause serious, even fatal, flu-like symptoms.

## Museums & Historical Tours

The story of Kauai is in many ways the story of the sugar plantations which shaped the island's multi-ethnic culture as much as its agriculture and economy. For this reason, a visit to the *Grove Farm Homestead* in Lihue offers a fascinating glimpse into the island's past. One of the earliest Hawaiian sugar plantations, Grove Farm was founded in 1864 by George Wilcox, the son of Protestant missionary teachers at Waioli Mission in Hanalei. Planting and harvesting Grove Farm's sugar crop, which grew from 80 acres to more than 1,000, ultimately involved a workforce of several hundred Hawaiians, Chinese, Koreans, Germans, Portuguese, and Filipino laborers, who brought to Kauai a rich heritage of ethnic cultures. A two-hour tour takes you through Grove Farm's cluster of buildings nestled amid tropical gardens, orchards, and rolling lawns, but be warned: the tour is extremely popular and you'll need to reserve a place at least a week in advance. You'll see the gracious old Wilcox home, the large rooms cooled by breezes from shaded verandas, and elegantly furnished with oriental carpets, magnificent koa wood floors and wainscotting, and hand crafted furniture of native woods. You will also tour the "board and batten" cottage of the plantation housekeeper, who came to Kauai, like many Japanese women, as a "picture bride" for a laborer too poor to travel home to select his wife in person. All buildings are covered by traditional "beach sand paint" (literally sand thrown against wet paint) to protect them against both

*Man in gourd mask by John Weber, artist on Captain Cook's third voyage*

heat and damp for as long as 20 years. The leisurely, friendly tour includes a stop in the kitchen for cookies and mint ice tea. For students and scholars, the library's extensive collection of Hawaiiana and plantation records is available by appointment. Grove Farm Tours are conducted Monday, Wednesday, and Thursday at 10 am and 1 pm. Reservations required: 808- 245-3202 or PO Box 1631, Lihue HI 96766.

Like other Hawaiian sugar plantations, Grove Farm was established at a significant point in the economic history of the islands. In the 1850's, the monarchy first began to sell land, and Hawaii entered the age of private property. Before this time, land was never sold but given in trust to subjects in pie shaped slices from the interior mountains to the sea, so that each landhold would include precious fresh water as well as coastline.

The Wilcox family, particularly two Wilcox women, made significant contributions to the development of Kauai. Elsie Wilcox, a Kauai School Commissioner, was the first woman in the territory to be elected to the State Senate; Mabel Wilcox, a public health nurse, was decorated by both France and Belgium for outstanding service in World War I. Elsie and Mabel restored *Waioli Mission House* in Hanalei (open T, Th, and Sat 9 am-3 pm), and Mabel planned *Grove Farm Homestead* in 1971 at age 89.

If the Grove Farm tour doesn't fit into your schedule, you can visit the *Kauai Museum* on Rice St. in downtown Lihue Monday-Friday 9:30 am to 4:30 pm. The Rice Building exhibits the *Story of Kauai*—the volcanic eruptions which shaped the land, the Polynesians who voyaged to the island in canoes and left behind marvelous petroglyphs, or rock pictures; the missionaries who altered its culture; and the sugar planters who, like George Wilcox, defined much of its agricultural destiny. To complement this permanent display, the monthly exhibits in the adjacent Wilcox building feature the work of local artists as well as the contributions of Kauai's different ethnic cultures. For example, one summer we saw an exhibit of Japanese, Chinese, Hawaiian, and Filipino wedding dress and traditions. Another time, we explored a marvelous retrospective on Filipinos in Kauai, from their arrival in 1906 as poorly paid laborers to present day achievements in education and social work. The Folk Arts Exhibition includes quilt and tapa making, lei making, and Hawaiian games and sports. The museum shop has an extensive collection of books and maps on Kauai and Hawaii, and several times a year sponsors a craft fair, where you can find shell jewelry, feather headbands and hatbands, koa carvings, and other local art forms. To visit the museum costs $3 for adults (If you don't finish touring by the end of the day, you can get a free pass for the next!). Gift shop is free. Call about exhibits and lectures: 245-6931.

Armchair travelers should request a catalog of books on Hawaiian history & natural history (including *Petroglyphs of Hawaii* by L. R. McBride), as well as reprints of hard-to-find titles by Hawaiian authors: Petroglyph Press, 201 Kinoole, Hilo HI 96720 (800-903-6277). An elegant new pictorial history, *Kauai The Garden Island*, by Chris Cook shows the island's evolution in vintage photographs (808-245-7363).

## Movie Tours

This guided narrated tour of Kauai's movie locations has become extremely popular, the brainchild of a local family with lots of energy. Their tiny company has expanded, and now has several small vans that tour the locations of Kauai's most famous movies (*South Pacific, Raiders of the Lost Ark, Honeymoon in Vegas*, etc.) and at the same time show the actual scenes on a TV monitor in surround sound! The real advantage may be seeing a lot of the island in a comfortable, small touring van, from Ke'e Beach on the north shore (*Thorn Birds*) to the south shore. If you don't like to drive, this may be just the ticket! 822-1192 or 800-628-8432 www.hawaiimovietour.com

## Natural History Tours

Halfway between Kapa'a and Princeville, be sure to visit the *Kilauea Lighthouse*, built in 1913, which once warned mariners away from Kauai's rugged north coast until technology replaced light flashes with radio transmissions. Come for spectacular views of the coastline and Mukuae'ae island, and if you're lucky, a glimpse of Spinner Dolphins or Humpback Whales on summer vacation in the waves. This is the northernmost point of Kauai, indeed of all the Hawaiian islands, and changes in weather are often first detected by the weather station here. Best of all, you will see a tiny part of the *Hawaiian Island National Wildlife Refuge*, which shelters more than 10 million seabirds in a chain of islands scattered over 1200 miles of ocean–like the Red-footed Booby. You will hear the amazing story of how seamen carried 4 tons of French prisms up a sheer cliff to build the giant clam shaped light. Call 808-828-1413 for the latest schedule of hours.

*Allerton Gardens National Tropical Botanical Gardens in Lawai*

Closed weekends, federal holidays. Above the lighthouse, *Crater Hill* offers a panoramic view of the north shore, a great spot for a picnic! Sometimes the new road (You'll see the security gate on the right as you drive along Kilauea Rd. towards the lighthouse) is locked; at other times, open. Hiking tours of Crater Hill: 808-828-1413. Map 2

More of Kauai's rare birds and plants can be seen at the *Koke'e Natural History Museum* in Koke'e State Park, open daily between 10 am and 4 pm (808-335-9975 www.aloha.net/~kokee). Donations welcome! Interested in birds? Go to www.birders.com for information and links. You can also arrange bird watching tours in the Alakai Swamp near Koke'e with *Terran Tours* (808-335-3313). Map 4. Curious about those bison you've seen grazing near the Hanalei River? Try a wagon tour of the pasture sponsored by Institute for Environmental Agriculture: 826-9028. Map 2

## Tropical Botanical Tours

The guided tour of *National Tropical Botanical Gardens* in Lawai is a unique opportunity to explore a 186 acre preserve of tropical fruits, spices, trees, rare plants, and flowers of astonishing variety and beauty— 50 varieties of banana and 500 species of palm. Instead of a formal garden, the plant collections are part of the natural landscape of the Lawai Valley. Park and join your group at Spouting Horn and climb aboard a vintage 1941 Dodge touring bus which takes you into Lawai Kai, the Allerton family's spectacular private gardens, a rustic paradise irrigated by an ingenious water system of fountains, streams, waterways, and rocky pools. Stroll at a leisurely pace among the shaded pathways, under spreading, giant trees, to pavilions where a statue reflects a graceful image in a pool speckled with fallen leaves. The "cutting garden" is filled with brilliantly colored heliconia. Reserve well in advance for the 2-hour, 2-mile walking tour Tues-Sat at 9am, 10am, 1pm, and 2pm ($25/pp). Bring your camera! Map 3. 808-742-2623 www.ntbg.org or write NTBG, PO Box 340, Lawai HI 96765.

On the north shore in Ha'ena, a walking tour of NTBG's *Limahuli Gardens* will lead you uphill through 17 acres of lush rain forest and gardens filled with native plants to an ocean lookout. You'll love spectacular Limahuli falls, plunging more than 800 feet, and the ancient terrace constructed for growing taro nearly a thousand years ago by the earliest Hawaiians. Formal tours ($15/pp) and self-guided strolls ($10/pp) over the 3/4 mile loop trail. Open Tues-Fri and Sundays 9:30am-4pm. Reservations: 808-826-1053. Rt. 560, 1/2 mile past mile 9 marker.

In Kilauea, at *Guava Kai Plantation* you can learn about the propagation of this wonderful fruit. Map 2. On the south shore in Kalaheo, flower photographers will love *Kukuiolono Golf Course*. The plumeria grove is a rainbow of colors in summer! Turn south on Papalina (at the traffic light), drive up the hill for .8 miles, and turn into the entrance on the right. Map 3

Above Wailua, the *Keahua Arboretum,* a 30-acre preserve of grassy meadows, trees, streams, is great for a quiet picnic. From Rt. 56, take Kuamo'o Rd. (Rt. 580) up Sleeping Giant Mountain, about 7 miles. Follow signs. Don't get discouraged when the road gets bumpy! You'll cross a stream and come to a grassy spot for a picnic surrounded by trees. Map 1

## Waimea Canyon & Koke'e State Park

The drive to the top of Waimea Canyon, the 'Grand Canyon of the Pacific,' makes a great day trip. The drive along the Koke'e Road (Rt. 550) from Rt. 50 to the end of the winding road will take about 45 minutes. As you travel along the rim of the canyon, which is ten miles long and 3,600 fee deep, you can stop at several scenic overlooks.

At *Koke'e Lodge*, stop for lunch—excellent soups and sandwiches, and visit the *Koke'e Museum* (donation) for interesting exhibits and trail maps to

the nearby trail heads. If possible, plan some time for exploring the wilderness preserve. Even a short hike shows you great views and wonderful flowers. Bring a jacket; at nearly 4,000 feet, temperatures can be very cool. Some hikes are manageable enough for families and take only a couple of hours, for example the trail to Waipo'o Falls which descends through wild ginger and orchids to a beautiful two-tiered waterfall. Mosquito spray, sun screen, a canteen, camera (wildflowers are beautiful!) and a hat are musts! For a virtual peek at the forest, visit www.geocities.com/RainForest.

*At the end of the Waimea Canyon Road, a spectacular lookout.*

Even if you don't hike, the drive takes you to a spectacular lookout, the Kalalau Lookout, with a vista of the island's west side (Parents be careful: the railing won't keep small children safe!) Rental car companies will advise you to go easy on the brakes and transmission, and use low gear as you negotiate the curving road. It's even more important on the way back down! The road is hard on cars, as we learned when our classic 1984 red Suburban made it to the top, then coughed and sputtered to a halt in front of the pay phone at the Koke'e Lodge! Your rental car will probably do just fine, but we'll never forget the trip back down, with 'Red Rover' riding in style atop the gleaming flatbed, whimsically named 'A Tow in Paradise.' Only on Kauai would the driver park his enormous rig half dozen times to share his favorite photo-stops!

Don't want to trust that rental car? *Kauai Mountain Tours* can take you on a four-wheel-drive tour of Koke'e and the Forest Reserve, with information about the native plants and birds (245-7224). The company also offers 'backroads' tours on the south shore of the Kilohana Crater and Maha'ulepu Beach, including an amazing tunnel carved through the mountain long ago to haul sugar cane. Moisture drips in the crevices, and you will marvel at the human effort required to carve a path through this sheer rock (245-8809 or 800-452-1113 www.alohakauaitours.com).

*Cafe Hanalei, Princeville Hotel*

## Eastern Shore Restaurants

### *Lihue*

| | | | page | meals | |
|---|---|---|---|---|---|
| Barbecue Inn | 245-2921 | Oriental | 143 | $$ | BLD |
| Cafe Portofino | 245-2121 | Italian | 146 | $$$ | LD |
| Dani's | 245-4991 | Island-style | 147 | $ | BL |
| Duke's Canoe Club | 246-9599 | Seafood/steak | 148 | $$$ | D |
| Duke's Barefoot Bar | 246-9599 | Burgers/sand | 149 | $$ | LD |
| Gaylord's | 245-9593 | Continental | 151 | $$$$ | LD |
| Garden Island BBQ | 245-8868 | Chinese/BBQ | 150 | $$ | LD |
| Hamura's Saimin | 245-3271 | Saimin | 152 | $ | D |
| JJ's Broiler | 246-4422 | Steak/seafood | 155 | $$$ | D |
| Kalapaki Beach Hut | 246-6330 | Burgers/sand | 157 | $ | BLD |
| Kauai Chop Suey | 245-8790 | Chinese | 159 | $$ | LD |
| Kiibo | 245-2650 | Japanese | 160 | $$ | LD |
| La Bamba | 245-5972 | Mexican | 164 | $ | LD |
| Ma's Family Inc. | 245-3142 | Island-style | 165 | $ | BL |
| Okazu Hale | 245-6554 | Island-style | 169 | $ | LD |
| Oki Diner | 245-5899 | Island-style | 169 | $ | 24 hrs |
| Paradise Seafood | 246-4700 | Fresh fish | 174 | $$$ | LD |
| Tip Top Cafe | 245-2333 | Amer/oriental | 177 | $ | BL |
| Tokyo Lobby | 245-8989 | Japanese | 178 | $$ | LD |
| Whaler's Brew Pub | 245-2000 | American | 181 | $$$ | LD |

### *Hanama'ulu*

| | | | | | |
|---|---|---|---|---|---|
| Tea House | 245-2511 | Chin/Japanese | 154 | $$ | D |
| JR's Plantation | 245-1606 | American | 156 | $$$ | D |

### *Wailua*

| | | | | | |
|---|---|---|---|---|---|
| A Pacific Cafe | 822-0013 | Pacific Rim | 171 | $$$$ | D |
| Al & Don's | 822-4221 | American | 142 | $$ | BLD |
| Bull Shed | 822-3791 | Steak/PRibs | 144 | $$$ | D |
| Caffe Coco | 822-7990 | Vegetarian | 145 | $$ | BLD |
| Camp House Grill | 822-2442 | American | 147 | $$ | BLD |
| Eggbert's | 822-3787 | American | 149 | $$ | BL |
| Flying Lobster | 822-3455 | American | 150 | $$$ | D |
| Hong Kong Cafe | 822-3288 | Chinese | 155 | $ | LD |
| King & I | 822-1642 | Thai | 160 | $$ | D |
| Kintaro | 822-3341 | Japanese | 162 | $$$ | D |

*$ under $12    $$ under $18    $$$ under $22    $$$$ under $27    $$$$$ over $27*

| | | | | |
|---|---|---|---|---|
| Margarita's | 822-1808 | Mexican | 164 | $$ | D |
| Mema's | 823-0899 | Thai/Chinese | 167 | $$ | LD |
| Palm Tree Terrace | 821-1040 | American | 172 | $$ | LD |
| Panda Garden | 822-0092 | Chinese | 173 | $$ | D |
| Papaya's | 823-0190 | Vegetarian | 173 | $ | BLD |
| Pony Island Cantina | 823-9000 | Mexican | 174 | $$ | LD |
| Wah Kung | 822-0560 | Chinese | 179 | $ | LD |
| Wailua Marina | 822-4311 | Everything | 179 | $$ | LD |
| Waipouli Deli | 822-9311 | Island-style | 180 | $ | BLD |

*Kapa'a*

| | | | | |
|---|---|---|---|---|
| Kapa'a Fish&Chowder | 822-7488 | Seafood/steak | 158 | $$$ | D |
| Kountry Kitchen | 822-3511 | American | 163 | $$ | BL |
| Masa's Sushi | 821-6933 | Japanese | 166 | $$ | LD |
| Norberto's El Cafe | 822-3362 | Mexican | 168 | $$ | BD |
| Ono Family | 822-1710 | American | 170 | $$ | BLD |
| Rocco's | 822-4422 | Italian | 175 | $$ | D |
| Sukothai | 821-1224 | Thai/etc. | 176 | $$ | D |

## North Shore Restaurants

*Kilauea*

| | | | | |
|---|---|---|---|---|
| Farmers Market Deli | 828-1512 | sandwiches | 184 | $ | L |
| Lighthouse Bistro | 828-1555 | Italian | 196 | $$$ | LD |
| Pau Hana Pizza | 828-2020 | Pizza | 193 | $ | LD |
| Roadrunner Cafe | 828-TACO | Mexican | 199 | $ | BLD |

*Princeville*

| | | | | |
|---|---|---|---|---|
| Bali Hai | 826-6522 | Steak/seafood | 187 | $$$$ | LD |
| Cafe Hanalei | 826-9644 | Pacific Rim | 189 | $$$$ | BLD |
| Chuck's Steakhouse | 826-6211 | Steak/seafood | 191 | $$$ | LD |
| La Cascata | 826-9644 | Italian | 194 | $$$$$ | D |
| Princeville Restaurant | 826-5050 | American | 199 | $$ | BL |
| Winds of Beamreach | 826-6143 | steaks/seafood | 201 | $$$ | D |

*Hanalei*

| | | | | |
|---|---|---|---|---|
| Dolphin | 826-6113 | Seafood/steak | 191 | $$$ | LD |
| Hanalei Gourmet | 826-2524 | Sandwiches | 193 | $$ | BLD |
| Neidie's | 826-1851 | Brazilian | 196 | $$ | LD |

| Postcards Cafe | 826-1191 | Seafood/vege | 197 | $$$ | BD |
| Sushi & Blues | 826-9701 | Japanese | 200 | $$ | D |
| Tahiti Nui | 826-6277 | Steak/seafood | 200 | $$$ | BLD |
| Zelo's Beach House | 826-9700 | American | 202 | $$ | BLD |

## South Shore & Westside Restaurants
### Koloa

| Pizzetta | 742-8881 | Pizza/pasta | 185 | $$ | BLD |
| Tomkats Grill | 742-8887 | American | 226 | $$ | LD |

### Poipu

| Beach House | 742-1424 | Pacific Rim | 205 | $$$$ | D |
| Brennecke's | 742-7588 | Seafood/steak | 206 | $$$ | LD |
| Case di Amici | 742-1555 | Italian | 210 | $$$ | D |
| Dondero's | 742-6260 | Italian | 211 | $$$$$ | D |
| House of Seafood | 742-6433 | fish/steak | 212 | $$$$ | D |
| Keoki's Paradise | 742-7534 | Steak/seafood | 215 | $$$ | D |
| Pattaya | 742-8818 | Thai/Chinese | 217 | $$ | LD |
| Piatti | 742-2216 | Steak/seafood | 218 | $$$ | D |
| Roy's Poipu Grill | 742-5000 | Pacific Rim | 221 | $$$$ | D |
| Naniwa | 742-1661 | Japanese | 217 | $$$ | D |
| Poipu Bay Clubhouse | 742-1515 | American | 219 | $$$ | L |
| Shells | 742-1661 | American | 224 | $$$$ | BLD |
| Taqueria Nortenos | 742-7222 | Mexican | 224 | $ | LD |
| Tidepools | 742-6260 | Seafood/steak | 225 | $$$$$ | D |

### Kalaheo

| Brick Oven Pizza | 332-8561 | Pizza | 208 | $$ | LD |
| Camp House Grill | 332-9755 | Burgers/sand | 208 | $$ | LD |
| Kalaheo Coffee Cafe | 332-5858 | Deli/coffee | 213 | $ | BL |
| Kalaheo Steakhouse | 332-9780 | Steak/PRibs | 214 | $$$ | D |
| Pomodoro | 332-5945 | Italian | 220 | $$$ | D |

### Hanapepe, Eleele & Waimea

| Green Garden | 335-5422 | Everything | 229 | $$ | LD |
| Hanapepe Cafe | 335-5011 | Vegetarian | 230 | $$ | LD |
| Camp House Cantina | 335-0006 | Mexican | 229 | $$ | LD |
| Toi's Thai Kitchen | 335-3111 | Thai | 231 | $$ | LD |
| Waimea Brew Pub | 338-9773 | American | 232 | $$$ | LD |
| Wrangler's Steakhouse | 338-1218 | Steaks/sandw | 233 | $$ | LD |

# READERS' CHOICE ...

**FOR OCEAN VIEW**
*Eastern Shore*
Bull Shed  144
Duke's Canoe Club  148
*North Shore*
Bali Hai  187
Cafe Hanalei  189
La Cascata  194
*South Shore*
Beach House  205
Shell's  224

**FOR PASTA**
*Eastern Shore*
Cafe Portofino  146
*North Shore*
La Cascata  194
*South Shore*
Casa di Amici  210
Piatti  218
Pomodoro  220

**FOR FRESH ISLAND FISH**
*Eastern Shore*
A Pacific Cafe  171
Duke's Canoe Club  148
Bull Shed  144
Palm Tree Terrace  172
*North Shore*
Cafe Hanalei  189
Hanalei Dolphin  192
Postcards Cafe  197
*South Shore*
Beach House  205
Brennecke's  206
Piatti  218
Roy's Poipu Grill  221
Tidepools  225

**FOR FAMILY FRIENDLY DINING**
*Eastern Shore*
Barbecue Inn  143
Bull Shed  144
Duke's Canoe Club  148
Hanama'ulu Tea House  154
Hong Kong Cafe  155
Kountry Kitchen  163
Norberto's El Cafe  168
Ono Family  170
*North Shore*
Postcards Cafe  194
Cafe Hanalei  189
Winds of Beamreach 200
Zelo's 201
*South & Westside*
Camp House Grill  208
Brennecke's  206
Brick Oven Pizza  208
Wranglers's  233

**FOR STEAKS & PRIME RIB**
*Eastern Shore*
Duke's Canoe Club  148
Bull Shed  144
*South Shore*
Keoki's  215
Kalaheo Steakhouse 214

**FOR ORIENTAL FOOD**
*Eastern Shore*
Hanama'ulu Tea House  154
King & I  161
Kintaro  162
Mema Thai Cuisine  167
*South Shore*
Pattaya  217
Toi's Thai Kitchen  231

# Eastern Shore Restaurants

## 'favor...eats'

The eastern shore's potpourri of dining reflects Kauai's rich multicultural heritage. **The Hanama'ulu Restaurant and Tea House** combines reasonable prices and friendly service with excellent Japanese and Chinese cuisine. In LIHUE, **Barbecue Inn's** bargain-priced lunches and dinners include soup, a beverage, fresh-baked bread, entree, even dessert! In this family-friendly restaurant, you'll find some of the tastiest food and best values on the island. Looking for local saimin? Try **Hamura's Saimin** or **Okazu Hale** for great noodles.

**Gaylord's at Kilohana** provides a romantic garden setting for lunch and dinner in an elegantly restored sugar plantation estate house. At the Kauai Marriott, **Duke's Canoe Club** offers a beautiful beachfront setting, as well as excellent food, reasonable prices, and the most sumptuous salad bar on the island. **Duke's Barefoot Bar** downstairs has well-priced burgers and sandwiches, while across the hotel's lagoon, **Whaler's Brew Pub** features a spectacular ocean view, as well as reasonably priced lunches and dinners. **Cafe Portofino** in Nawiliwili serves excellent Italian cuisine at affordable prices. Vegetable lasagne is terrific! **Kauai Chop Suey** has reasonably priced Oriental food. At **Kalapaki Beach Hut,** try a first-rate hamburger or fish sandwich!

Ten minutes north of Lihue, WAILUA is fast becoming the dining center of Kauai, with a wide range of cuisines and prices. **Mema Thai & Chinese Cuisine** and **King & I** offer truly memorable Thai food at a great price.

*A banana flower bearing fruit*

**Kintaro** prepares the best Japanese dinners, sushi and sashimi on Kauai. For imaginative Pacific Rim cuisine, particularly fresh fish, Jean Marie Josselin's **A Pacific Cafe** has earned well-deserved fame. Don't miss the **Bull Shed** for the biggest, tastiest prime rib on the island as well as steaks, chicken, and excellent fresh fish—with an ocean view— at affordable prices. Vegetarian cravings? Try **Caffe Coco** or **Papaya's**.

On a budget? Try Mexican cuisine at **Norberto's El Cafe** and tasty Chinese food at **Hong Kong Cafe**, or take-out at **Wah Kung** in Wailua. At the Coconut Plantation Marketplace, **Aloha Kauai Pizza, Fish Hut** and **Taco Dude** serve excellent take-out, and **Palm Tree Terrace** has wonderful, reasonably-priced fresh fish dinners. For breakfast, try **Kountry Kitchen** or **Ono Family Restaurant**, Kapa'a.

# Al & Don's

From roomy booths next to Al & Don's enormous windows, you can see the ocean, rimmed with ironwood trees, stretching out to the horizon. The decor, though nondescript, is pleasant, and tables are large and comfortable. Waitresses bring coffee immediately, and your order is prepared quickly and served cheerfully. Food is reasonably-priced though not memorable. Pancakes are a trifle heavy, and the corned beef hash, mediocre. Eggs are the best bet. Check out the senior's menu and nightly early-bird specials for under $10.

Al & Don's is like a 'Denny's' with a view. The chief attraction is what you see out the window, not what appears on your plate. That's why breakfast, in full daylight, maximizes its appeal. If you go for dinner, be sure to time your arrival for before sunset.

Wailua, Kauai Sands Hotel. 822-4221. Open 7 am - 10 am, and 6 pm - 8:45 pm daily. Credit cards. Map 1

*www.explorekauai.com*

# Barbecue Inn

Where do local folks go for a lunch which includes soup, a beverage, fresh bread, an entree like a teriyaki chicken sandwich, and dessert for only $6.95? In this family-owned restaurant, you'll find some of the tastiest food and one of the best food values on the island. A local favorite since 1940, Barbecue Inn is the rare kind of place with something special for everyone in the family. At dinner, more than 30 choices— fresh fish, seafood, steak, prime rib ($6.95–$14.95) include soup or fresh fruit, a salad, homemade bread, vegetable, dessert, even a beverage! At lunch, entrees cost even less, averaging $6.95 (but you don't get salad).

Kids will love the cheeseburger ($3.95), which arrives still sizzling on a toasted sesame bun, smothered with melted cheese and garnished with fresh, local manoa lettuce! For only $4.25, kids can order fried chicken, hamburger, spaghetti, or chow mein dinners, ten choices in all, including a beverage, or a grilled cheese sandwich made on delicious home-baked bread toasted crisp and golden. Grown-ups will love the teriyaki steak ($16.95), a tender rib-eye with perfectly flavored homemade sauce, or teriyaki beef kabob and shrimp tempura ($11.95), light, crisp and tasty.

You will be surprised at the high quality of the 'extras' which many restaurants pay scant attention to. Miso soup is superb. Bread is home-made — light, fragrant, and exceptionally tasty. You should also squan-der a dollar on some homemade "lavosh" which is buttery, almost like shortbread. It's so good, you will want seconds, so splurge on an extra order (or buy some for the beach). The fruit cup appetizer is so fresh— pineapple, papaya, watermelon, honeydew, and mango — that you'll almost hope your kids will refuse to eat theirs because there are no canned peaches! The green salad would win no awards for imagination, but you'd be surprised at how much fun the kids have picking out the shred-ded cabbage and homemade croutons. And everyone will devour the homemade pies—coconut, chocolate, or chocolate cream—pies so light they are almost as amazing as the price: $1.00 a slice, same price as a Coke. Buy a bag of BBQ Inn's cookies or crunchy 'cinnamon toast' to keep in the car for emergencies!

You will see a lot of working people coming off the job, and the portions are so enormous you can understand why. Waitresses are unfailingly cheerful, even when small children decorate the floor with crumbs and ice cubes. All this makes Barbecue Inn a good dinner choice for hearty eaters and hungry families, for anyone who appreciates ordi-nary food cooked extremely well, as well as some very special treats.

Lihue. 2982 Kress St. (off Rice St.). 245-2921. Closed Sundays. Breakfast 7:30 am -10:30 am. Lunch 10:30 am - 1:30 pm. Dinner 5 pm - 8:30 pm (4:30 pm - 8:45 pm F, S, Sun) Air conditioned. Non-smoking section. Credit cards. Map 1

## The Bull Shed

Since 1973, The Bull Shed has been famous on Kauai for high quality meals at unbeatable prices. Bull Shed's prime rib is truly special —a thick slice of tender beef, perfectly cooked with a tasty bone (if you ask for it), delicious *au jus* and fresh horseradish sauce— at $19.95 the best deal for the best portion on Kauai! Fresh island fish is another winner, a huge portion filleted by manager Tom Liu himself, then perfectly grilled. At Bull Shed, 'surf and turf' sets the island standard!

A glance at the menu will tell you why the Bull Shed is so popular. Prices are amazingly reasonable, entrees come with rice and the salad bar, and half cost less than $15. Combination dinners are served with a 7.5 oz. tenderloin filet instead of the usual small sirloin. Lobster tail is enormous, a full 12 oz., and perfectly cooked. The wine list is also reasonable, with more than half the primarily California selections less than $20.

The Bull Shed has become a favorite with each member of our family, in itself a small miracle. Our 6:45 pm arrival time is early enough to beat the crowds, and all four of our children eat everything that is served to them—a rare achievement. Lauren's teriyaki chicken breast ($12.95 or $6.95 child's portion) is always perfectly soft and juicy. Mike loves the teriyaki sirloin ($15.95), and Jeremy orders fresh island ahi, a huge portion for only $16.95, one of the best we have tasted, or rack of lamb ($20.95), a large portion, both tender and tasty, with a delicious teriyaki marinade. Even better, all four put away huge and healthful salads, picking their pickiest best from the salad bar ($6.95 by itself).

The Bull Shed offers one of the best food values on Kauai, in a pleasant dining room with friendly, efficient service. It's popular, so try to arrive before 7 pm, to avoid the traffic jam. Or invite some friends because 6 or more earn a reservation!

*first rate prime rib, steak & fresh fish!*

Bull Shed has not only great food and prices, but an ocean view! In fact, the restaurant is built as close to the ocean as modern technology can allow, and our favorite table, in a tiny room by itself just a few feet from the edge of a seawall, offers a spectacular view of the waves rolling towards the wall and crashing in torrents of spray.  During a storm, the waves splash right against the glass, an awesome sight!  Come on a night when the moon is full, and watch the waves send gleaming ripples through the darkness.  If it's warm, request a table by a window that opens (not all do).

Wailua, in Mokihana Resort, Kuhio Hwy.  822-3791.  Dinner 5:30 pm -10 pm nightly.  Reservations for 6 or more.  Smoking section.  Credit Cards. Children's menu (under 13).  Look for the sign (it's small) opposite McDonald's, north of Coconut Plantation Marketplace.  Turn towards the water.  Map 1

# Caffe Coco

In almost any season, you'll find something blooming or bearing fruit at Caffe Coco.  The dining room is actually a tropical grove of mango, avocado, pomolo ( a grapefruit cousin), and papaya, with 'walls' of thick, tall sugar cane.  The decor is a bower of bougainvillea, ferns, and orchids. Garden chairs surround a collection of tables beneath a honeysuckle-covered arbor.  The cuisine emphasizes the natural — local vegetables, fruits, and herbs—and everything is organic, fresh and deliciously seasoned.

Some dishes are outstanding, like local mahi mahi ($14.50) crusted with black sesame seeds and accompanied with rice and a tasty wasabi cream sauce.  Or try fresh ono with cilantro pesto, served with 'silver noodle salad' of bean threads with a delicious homemade peanut ginger dressing.  Green salads arrive with unusual dressings—creamy feta, for example — and vegetables are imaginative, like fresh corn and green beans with eggplant, or a tasty sweet potato dumpling.  Lighter choices include an ahi nori wrap, with soup and salad ($13), as well as omelets and vegetable salads.  At lunch we enjoyed homemade soup and an ahi sandwich on foccacia bread.  A spicy fish burrito contains a generous portion of ono, as well as rice and black beans.

You'll have to bring your own wine, or try non-alcoholic beverages served in blue or yellow goblets, like ginger lemonade or pomolo fizz, made when the enormous pomolo tree bears its fruit.  Desserts feature local fruits, like mango tart from the mango tree.

Near the entrance, you place your order at the counter where a refrigerated case displays the day's fresh ingredients. The staff will describe their favorites, even identify what's on a plate headed for the dining room.  Dine in the garden, or inside, in what is called with a grin, the 'Black Light Art Gallery.'  The paintings glow— you too, if you are wearing anything white!

As the lights from the kitchen cast a golden glow into the garden, this beautifully lush, tranquil setting can ease your spirit as well as your hunger.  If you like organic foods, Caffe Coco could become your favorite place.  If mosquitoes pick on you while ignoring your friends, bring some 'Off' and request a mosquito coil.  Come for lunch, and enjoy the garden in its full sunlit glory, and browse afterwards in the adjacent antique shop, Bambuli. Just turn left under the mango tree!

Wailua, across Rt. 56 from Kintaro. 822-7990. 9am - 9pm. Closed Mondays. Credit cards.

# Cafe Portofino

Cafe Portofino serves excellent Italian cuisine in an attractive, comfortable dining room across from the Kauai Marriott.  The hardworking owner, who settled from Italy via a stint in cruise ship food & beverage management, is committed to high food quality and professional service.  The dining room is bright, spacious, and cheerful, the white walls accented with honey–colored wood trim and leafy green plants.  Tables are well-spaced, covered in linen and set with shining crystal, and the softly upholstered swivel chairs are extremely comfortable.  A terrace offers informal dining, and at lunch you can catch a glimpse of Kalapaki Bay.

The menu offers an extensive list of entrees, including fresh fish, homemade pastas, chicken, veal and fish.  Portofino's Italian cuisine is light and healthful, the sauces based on vegetable flavors rather than heavy with cream.  Flavorful minestrone is served in a generous portion for a modest price ($4), and kids will love mozzarella marinara ($8).  Vegetable lasagne ($15) is as festive looking as a wrapped birthday present, and tastes just as wonderful, the flavors and textures of fresh zucchini and spinach brought together with a wonderful marinara sauce with tasty chunks of tomatoes. Fresh fish is tender and moist, served with rosemary roasted potatoes.  Other good choices are 'scampi alla limone' ($19), zesty and attractive, served with perfectly cooked broccoli, and 'chicken alla Angelo' ($14.50), tender chunks of chicken in a piquant sauce.  A dinner salad ($5) is nicely presented; goat cheese salad with fresh mixed greens is excellent.

Service is professional yet friendly.  Everyone seems to care about your dinner, and willing to fetch extra bread or answer questions.  The wine list is well selected, and if prices are on the high side, there are also some bargains, like a respectable vintage of Pinot Grigio for $20. At Cafe Portofino, you'll find an attractive setting, reasonable prices, distinctive cuisine, and friendly, professional service.

Lihue, across from Kauai Marriott. 245-2121. Credit cards. Dinner 5 - 10 pm nightly. Non-smoking section. Live music most nights. Map 1

## Camp House Grill—Wailua

The popular Camp House Grill in Kalaheo has opened a new branch in Wailua's Kauai Village Shopping Center, offering the same '3 squares' breakfast, lunch and dinner concept that has made the original so successful. Not surprisingly, this newest branch is experiencing growing pains in its staff and menu, which we discovered as soon as we strayed from the traditional menu standbys of hamburger ($4.95) and huli chicken ($7.95). The fresh fish was dry and tasteless, and to be charged $1 extra for a bun with the teriyaki chicken breast 'plate' seemed excessive. These unfriendly 'extra' charges also affected breakfast, when we were charged extra for salsa with the eggs, for coconut syrup instead of maple with pancakes. The best thing you can say about the dining room is that it is spacious, though perhaps uncrowded for the wrong reason! We hope for improvements as this version of Camp House settles in.

Wailua, Kauai Village Center on Rt. 56.. 822-2442. 6:30 am - 9 pm daily.

## Dani's

At Dani's, you won't find an orchid on your plate, but you will find hot, tasty, and filling meals, including local-style Hawaiian foods. Kona coffee comes free with breakfast, and you can choose from eggs, omelettes, pancakes, and tasty Hawaiian dishes. The ham and cheese omelette is very cheesy and stuffed with ham, though the hotcakes are on the heavy side. The lunch menu offers a wide variety of Hawaiian, American, and Japanese dishes, as well as sandwiches and hamburgers. Prices start at $4.50 and include soup or salad, roll, rice, and coffee or tea.

With prices this low, expect to sacrifice atmosphere. The color scheme is woodgrain formica accented by fluorescent lights, but on the other hand, the large dining room is bright, clean, and comfortably air-conditioned, and the service swift and efficient.

Lihue, 4201 Rice St. 5 am - 1:30 pm (1 pm on Sat). Closed Sundays. Credit cards. Smoking section. 245-4991. Map 1

## Duke's Canoe Club

*beachfront dining & great salad bar!*

One of the most popular restaurants on Kauai, Duke's offers a sumptuous salad bar, which can truly be a meal in itself, as well as high quality, reasonably-priced dinners. Duke's also offers the Polynesian glitz which has made its sister restaurants, Keoki's on Kauai, as well as Kimo's on Maui, so successful, with this additional bonus: Since Duke's is perched right on the edge of Kalapaki Bay, you can be in the real Hawaii as well as the Hollywood version.

If you enter at beach level, you will ascend a stone stairway carved into an indoor waterfall draped with ferns and trailing flowers. At the top, the dining room is cooled by delightful evening breezes, a perfect spot to look out over Kalapaki bay and watch the changing light tint the clouds and listen to wonderful Hawaiian music. Friendly performers stroll from table to table, offering to play your favorite songs (like 'Beautiful Kauai' or 'Hanalei Moon'). One night, some local guests were moved to dance a graceful hula, to everyone's delight—a magical moment!

Duke's reasonable dinner prices (from $14.95 for chicken) include a wonderful salad bar, with Caesar salad as well as an array of fresh vegetables and lettuces, fruits, pasta salads, fresh-baked banana macadamia nut muffins, and even rice—great for vegetarians ($9.95 by itself).

Choose from several fresh fish entrees ($19-$22) including tasty teriyaki broiled fresh ahi. You might find some sauces, like the orange-ginger, too strongly flavored, so it's wise to have sauce served on the side. Most fish filets (8 to 10 oz.) are pre-glazed, but we were able to convince the kitchen to find a naked moonfish and grill it plainly, with a wonderful result— the delicately flavored whitefish was soft, moist and delicious.

The prime rib ($23.95 or $16.95/smaller cut), however, stopped the flow of conversation. Nearly 22 ounces, it was so thick that you didn't know where to begin to tackle it. More like a family-size roast, it was a significant dining event, and tender as well as juicy, served underspiced rather than over-salted. Described on the menu as "while it lasts," this dinner may be sold out by the time you order, so you might reserve a portion when you arrive. Steaks are tender and moist, and the wine list offers some good values in the mid-$20 range.

Everyone in the family will enjoy Duke's. Children have four dinner choices, which include fries and the salad bar, for less than $6, and adults can order 'Lighter Fare' (pasta, pizza, or a cheeseburger) for under $10.

What comes to your table will be well-prepared, efficiently served, in a setting where you can watch the ocean and listen to wonderful Hawaiian music. An unbeatable combination (that's why you see so many local families crowding the tables), and walking around the Kauai Marriott after dinner is an extra treat. Reservations help a lot, though one section is set aside for walk-ins. Think twice about going in the rain, however, for you'll miss the view when they close the shutters!

## Duke's Barefoot Bar

Downstairs, right next to Kalapaki Beach, Duke's Barefoot Bar serves lunch, informal dinner, and munchies all day. Try excellent hamburgers ($6.95) and sandwiches ($6.95-$8.95), as well as salads and crisp, hot french fries. You'll love the fresh island fish daily dinner special (only $14.95)— one fin each night, perhaps teriyaki ahi, or grilled moonfish. Vegetable plate is fresh and colorful ($6.95), and you can visit the salad bar upstairs for $9.95.

In Lihue, on Kalapaki Beach, access through the Kauai Marriott. Free valet parking. *Duke's Canoe Club*: reserve a day in advance (246-9599). Dinner 5-10 pm nightly. Credit Cards. Non-smoking area. *Duke's Barefoot Bar* downstairs: 11:30 am to 11:30 pm. Smoking only. Map 1

## Eggbert's

Once upon a time, when eggs were king, many an enormous omelette was whipped up at Eggbert's in Lihue. Iniki changed all that. Eggbert's closed, and the world moved into synch with a different diet. Now Eggbert's has re-opened in Wailua at a time of low cholesterol chic, when people are counting calories and looking for ways to avoid fat. When you've got 'egg' all over your name these days, you take a hearty risk!

For 23 years, Eggbert's has been known for its omelettes and eggs benedict priced in various sizes (from $7.45), so you can opt for less yolk, less cost. You can also try tasty banana pancakes with coconut syrup or french toast ($5.95). Kid's breakfast special is $3.65. For lunch, you'll find tasty burgers, salads, and sandwiches ($6-$8), and dinner choices from $8.95 (children and seniors —"65 and Better"— from $6.50).

The location in the Coconut Plantation Marketplace is great for families—a bright, white dining space with windows on all sides to encourage breezes. Plastic chairs provide adequate comfort, and blue formica tables have rounded corners, safe at eye level for short persons who like to explore underneath. Service can be a bit on the slow side, but there's cappuccino and espresso while you wait.

At Eggbert's, you'll find things largely sunny side up— a good choice for people who like a hearty meal at a reasonable price.

Coconut Plantation Marketplace, Wailua 822-3787. Open daily from 7am. Smoking on lanai outside. Credit cards. Map 1

# Flying Lobster

Flying Lobster is a restaurant in search of an identity. The spacious dining room seems designed for a more elegant menu than what you will find. That's because the menu has been reduced in price and scope from what was once a more upscale restaurant. The lobsters have slipped off the dinner menu, and the salad bar, once famous on the island, is only a shadow of its former glory, with a shrinking selection of vegetables, prepared salads, fresh fruits, and soup. On Fridays, the all-you-can-eat Seafood Buffet ($21.95) harks back to the more glamorous past.

The menu features chicken, steak, and fish at prices ranging from $13.50 (ginger chicken) to $27 (NY steak) though you have to add $5 for the salad bar. Hamburgers ($6.25) and pasta ($8.25) are also available. The crab cake ($10.50) was high on bread, low on crab, almost like a ball of stuffing. The fresh fish ($14.50) didn't taste particularly fresh. The salad bar by itself ($11.75) seems the best choice.

The outdoor dining terrace is lovely in the evening shadows, although white fluorescent lighting somewhat diminishes the romantic effect of the candle lamps. You can enjoy the live music from the cocktail lounge nearby. Service is very friendly, and the wine list is reasonably priced.

Wailua, Coconut Beach Resort Hotel, Coconut Plantation Marketplace. 822-3455. Credit cards. Non-smoking section. Map 1

# Garden Island Barbecue & Chinese

Garden Island Barbecue in downtown Lihue has attracted a loyal following among local people for its generous portions and inexpensive prices. At lunch or dinner, you will probably find the rather spartan dining room filled, and a glance at what is on the tables will show you why. Platters are mounded with colorful heaps of noodles and vegetables, and the menu has four pages of choices costing as little as $5.50.

Food quality won't win any awards for inventiveness, but what the chef cooks is tasty and hot. Saimin steams in the bowl, wontons feature shrimps as well as ground meat, and vegetables are still crunchy. Lunch or dinner entrees include two scoops of rice and macaroni salad.

The dining room is clean, cooled by fans, and seems friendly from the moment you walk in. Garden Island may not be fancy, but if you're on a budget, you'll appreciate the generous portions of inexpensive, tasty food.

Lihue, 4252A Rice St. 10 am - 9 pm. Closed Sundays. 245-8868.

## Gaylord's at Kilohana

Once the heart of a 1,700 acre sugar plantation, Kilohana is a special place. Wandering through rooms with the spacious beauty of large proportions and wide verandas, you can easily imagine the gracious pace of life before airplanes and traffic lights. With the mountains behind and rolling lawns all around, you can glimpse, even if briefly, a way of life now forever lost.

Named for Gaylord Wilcox who built Kilohana, the restaurant's dining room and veranda look out over a manicured lawn and garden lush with leafy ferns and brilliant tropical flowers. In the evening, the flagstone terrace is lit with lanterns, and rattan chairs surround comfortable tables decked with white linen and pink napkins arranged like fans. Gaylord's is one of the most romantic restaurants on Kauai, with the kind of setting you'd want to star in if your life were a black and white movie. Candles on the tables flicker in gentle breezes, and from your chair beneath the roof you can peek out at stars shining in the velvet sky. As you gaze out at the gardens lit by the moon and stars, you can feel the soft tropical breezes which rustle the leaves. Waiters move discreetly, anticipating your every desire.

At Gaylord's you'll do best if you order as simply as possible, with all sauces served on the side. Sauteed fresh island onaga ($26.95) and grilled ahi were both excellent, perfectly cooked, moist and flavorful, much better without the strongly flavored sauces. Vegetable brochette, served with rice pilaf pleased our vegetarian. Prime rib ($20.95 for 14 oz.) is a good bet, served with lots of *au jus*. Entrees arrive with rice, potato, or pasta, as well as a vegetable—like still crunchy sugarpeas in the pod and sliced red peppers. Most cost more than $20, and unless you come for "light supper" (5 to 6:30 pm), your least expensive dinner choice is vegetable quiche ($15.95). If you add soup or salad ($3.95), the cost of dining goes up quickly. Gaylord's wine list is expensive, though you can find a few good choices for less than $30.

Despite occasional disappointments, the dining experience at Gaylord's can be wonderful. Waiters are polite, attentive, and professional, and in the quiet courtyard, you escape the usual noisy distractions of clattering trays and dishes. Small details get lots of attention: water is served in elegant iced glasses with tangy lemon slices, and coffee cups are watched carefully. If you like to linger after dinner, consider bringing a sweater, for temperatures can be chilly in winter months.

With such an elegant setting, Gaylord's is one of the island's special dining experiences, an image to haunt you when temperatures plunge back home. The food never quite seems to match the setting — though perhaps that's because of the setting! We have heard high praise of Gaylord's lunch, where excellent sandwiches, salads, vegetable platters, burgers and fresh seafood are reasonably-priced ($7.95-$10) and you can look out at the garden in the full splendor of sunshine.

Just west of Lihue, on Rt. 50. 245-9593. Credit cards. Lunch 11 am -3 pm. Dinner 5-10 pm daily. Sunday brunch 9:30 am -3 pm. Weekly luaus. Children's menu. Non-smoking area.

## Hamura's Saimin

According to legend, Oahu businessmen have flown to Kauai just to have lunch at Hamura Saimin. To look at the weather-beaten exterior, you'd have your doubts. The tiny building encloses—just barely—three horse-shoe shaped counters with stools. Although a recent face-lift has made the room look cleaner and more like a luncheonette, you can still watch the cook stir and chop and make things sizzle. The inevitability of change, yes, though some traditions die hard. A sign still warns: "No Gum Under the Counter." Nowadays, you occasionally catch someone peeking!

*no gum under counter!*

On this counter is served some of the finest saimin around, and you come to want to believe the legend about the Oahu businessmen and their expense account lunches. Airfare could certainly be offset with bargain food prices: for $5.25 you get the saimin special—tasty and fragrant soup

with noodles, chock full of vegetables and meats. The perfectly flavored won ton soup or won ton min is only $4. To take the saimin out costs 25 cents extra for the container, but you can escape the cramped little room and head for the beach. Perfectly spiced barbecued beef or chicken sticks ($.75) are another find. Kids love homemade manapu, a sweet cousin of the pretzel ($1.50/bag). Don't miss lilikoi chiffon pie ($1.25).

When the waitress takes your order, she passes a bowl of the appropriate size and color over the counter to the cook, who inserts the proper mix of ingredients, then covers all with ladles of steaming broth. If you visit often enough, you begin to appreciate technique, the consumer's as well as the cook's. The truly experienced diners mix hot mustard and soy sauce in their spoons, dipping the mixture into the soup as necessary, and using chopsticks to pull the noodles through.

There's not much variety, but what the cook cooks is very good indeed, and the visit is like a trip into the island's past, a time before tourism brought butcherblock tables and bentwood chairs, air-conditioning and gourmet teas — a time when sticking gum under the counter, though frowned upon, was still possible. So throw away your Bubble Yum before going inside, and try this taste of authentic Kauai!

Lihue, 2956 Kress St. Cash only. M-Sat 10 am - 10 pm. Open (and less crowded) Sundays for lunch. 245-3271. Map 1

# Hanama'ulu  Restaurant  &  Tea House

You could not select a better place to share a really special evening with friends than the Tea House, because this restaurant combines delicious food with the friendliest service on the island, and, as if that weren't enough, a Japanese garden setting to make everything seem just a bit magical. Here you can dine on soft mats at low tables next to the goldfish and water lilies. Children can wander around and count the carp (tell them to be careful; one of our two-year-olds tumbled in!). Local families have been coming to the Tea House for more than sixty-five years. Today they still appreciate superb cooking at reasonable prices, and it's a rare wedding, anniversary, welcome or farewell party that does not take place in one of the tea rooms by the garden.

The Miyake family cooks with subtlety and flair, and creates a genuinely special cuisine, with 35 Chinese and Japanese entrees at reasonable prices from $4.75-$14.75. We recommend the won ton soup ($6) as the finest anywhere, generously garnished with scallions, pork, and slices of egg foo young. Children will love the crispy fried chicken with its delicate touch of ginger ($6); the boneless pieces are just the right size for little hands.

When our party is large enough, we ask the owner to order a several course dinner, and we are always delighted with the new dishes we discover. Fresh island  tempura with fresh fish or shrimp is spectacular, served on an enormous platter, and the taste is just as wonderful ($9.75). Vegetarians will love the vegetable tempura ($6.50) or crispy tofu tempura ($4) served with teriyaki sauce and green onions. Sashimi of ahi and ono is fresh and elegantly arranged. A specialty, mushrooms stuffed with crab ($5.75), is lighter than many versions of the dish, and very tasty. Chinese chicken salad has lots of chicken, lettuce, crispy noodles, and wonderful dressing. The sushi bar features excellent salmon skin han-drolls with crispy grilled salmon ($4.25). California rolls ($4) have real crab without mayonnaise.

Reserve at least three days in advance to choose where you dine. Avoid the rather non-descript front dining room, and try the teppan yaki room and sushi bar. Our favorite, however, is the tea house by the gardens, where we can listen to crickets sing the songs of evening while stars light up the velvet sky. If mosquitoes like to pick on you while ignoring your friends, don't be

*Island style &*
*family friendly*

bashful about asking for a mosquito coil. The incense smell is great, and it keeps the bugs away!

In more than twenty years of dining, this special restaurant has never let us down. The cooking is consistently excellent, the prices remarkably reasonable, the service exceptionally friendly, and children are treated with more than usual tolerance by waitresses like Sally and Arlene who genuinely love them. Because this is a restaurant where you should sample as many dishes as possible, and because it is such a special place, we like to save the Tea House for our last night with our Kauai friends, and ask any *kapunas* who might be listening to speed our return! You shouldn't miss the Tea House either.

Hanama'ulu, Rt. 56. Reserve a tea room in advance. 245-2511. Credit cards. Full bar. Closed Mondays. Lunch 9 am - 1 pm; Dinner 4:30 pm - 9 pm. Banquet facilities. Ask Sally about special menus & wedding receptions. Map 1

## Hong Kong Cafe, Bar B Q & Noodles

Wailua's Hong Kong Cafe offers an excellent alternative to generic fast food. It looks like a luncheonette, with about nine green and black formica tables in an air conditioned dining room, where the major visual point of interest is a poster of Hong Kong's Victoria Harbor. It's often full because the menu offers many choices — roast duck, crispy chicken, lo mein and chow mein, sweet and sour as well as vegetarian dishes — almost everything costs less than $8. The emphasis is on island fresh vegetables. Choose plate lunches from $4.50 to $6.75, bento lunches or vegetarian dishes, including a delicious eggplant with tofu ($6.75). We love the wonton soup and saimin, of which there are nine varieties ($2.95 to $5.75), served in huge, steaming bowls of noodles, vegetables, and flavorful broth. Hong Kong Cafe is not pretentious, but you can enjoy reasonable food at reasonable prices. Bring your own wine or beer.

In Wailua Shopping Plaza, 4-361 Kuhio Hwy. 822-3288 (voice & FAX). 10:30 am - 9: 30 pm. (M-F); 4:30 - 9:30 pm (S &S). Delivery. Smoke-free. Credit cards. Map 1

## JJ's Broiler

More than thirty years ago, Kauai's first steak house opened in an old plantation house on the main street of Lihue, then a sleepy town with a single traffic light. JJ's achieved local fame for its specialty, "Slavonic steak," a sliced London broil marinated in garlic sauce. When anyone in JJ's was served this dish, everyone else knew it! Then JJ's opened right on Kalapaki Bay, its garish, hot pink sign issuing a neon challenge to the hotel restaurants just down the beach. Just as the contest was getting interesting, Iniki struck and blew all the dining spots out of business.

Today, JJ's food and service are disappointing. On one visit, the New York steak ($19.95 for 14 oz.) was tasteless and tough, and the prime rib

also unsatisfactory. Fresh opakapaka was well prepared, though served with a sauce so heavy, we were glad to have ordered it served on the side. Macadamia nut rack of lamb ($23.95) was tough and tasted burnt. JJ's best feature is a portable salad bar, a huge bowl of greens surrounded by vegetables and condiments in a lazy susan (by itself, $9.95). Bread is undistinguished, served without a plate to hold down the crumbs. Tables could use, for the prices, a cloth or even place mats!

JJ's multi–level design affords each table privacy as well as an ocean view. Above the polished wood tables, in the enormous space of the open beam ceiling, hang actual sailboats. JJ's costs the same or even more than other steak houses like The Bull Shed in Wailua, or Duke's Canoe Club right down the beach, where, in our opinion, portions are larger, the food tastier, and the service more skillful.

Lihue, Anchor Cove Center. 246-4422 Lunch 11am-5pm. Dinner 5 pm - 10 pm, daily. Credit cards. Non-smoking section. Map 1

## JR's Plantation Restaurant

Just a few feet off Rt. 56 in Hanama'ulu, J.R.'s Plantation Restaurant is housed in a historic plantation building cooled by ceiling fans and decorated with sugar plantation memorabilia — machinery parts and tools, horse collars and ox yokes, and even a red wagon wheel hung with lanterns and plants. Candles shine on wood plank tables colorful with tropical flowers, and at the rear, two private booths with black leatherette seats cozy up to a genuine indoor waterfall with cascading ferns.

The owners, Mylie in the dining room and JR in the kitchen, serve more than two dozen entrees, including chicken teriyaki ($12.95 ), a

'Luau platter' ($15.95), 'Hawaiian pasta' ($14.95) and prime rib, as well as vegetable lasagne ($12.95). Dinners include soup or salad, as well as rice, potato, or linguini romano. For $9.95, the under-12s can choose mahi mahi, pasta or chicken ($9.95). The boneless chicken breast seems to pass the stringent "no–yuk" test from small picky eaters.

For the first course, you get a bowl, which can be filled with either soup or salad of mixed greens. Vegetable soup is excellent, and the green salad is generous and served with tasty dressings. You also get hot french bread, toasted with or without garlic, but the absence of bread plates means that in short order you'll have crumbs skittering everywhere.

The house specialty prime rib is tasty and tender, served with good *au jus*, little fat, but no bone ($18.95/10 oz. slice). If you have your heart set on this dish, call ahead to reserve a portion, so you won't be disappointed. Fresh island ahi is moist and tender, though on the small side for the $19.95 price. The small wine list is basic Beringer, the top-priced chardonnay at $18, and, "for the driver," virgin smoothies ($3.50).

At JR's Plantation, prices are largely reasonable, the dining room pleasant, the staff friendly, though for about the same price you could have larger portions at Bull Shed.

In Hanama'ulu, Rt. 56. 245-1606. Credit cards. Dinner nightly 5 - 9:45 pm. Early-bird specials till 6:30 pm. Map 1

## Kalapaki Beach Hut

In the bright blue building right behind Kalapaki Beach, you will find one of our favorite sandwiches on Kauai—fresh ono, cleanly grilled, moist and tender, and wrapped in a soft roll with lettuce and juicy tomatoes. When fresh fish is scarce, it's made with frozen mahi mahi, but even that sandwich is tasty. You will also find some of the best hamburgers on Kauai — no surprise since the owner, Steve Gerald, originated 'Ono Burger' in Anahola more than twenty years ago. Since then, the term 'Ono Burger' has achieved near legendary status, a name spoken with reverence whenever fine hamburgers are discussed on Kauai.

Steve Gerald has flame-broiled many a burger, either beef or turkey, or even buffalo. Beef burgers are extra juicy, extra tasty, and meltingly delicious. The entry level burger costs $3.95 and comes with lettuce, tomato, and mayonnaise on a sesame bun. Buffalo burgers cost about $2 more, but then remember how much less costly they are to your arteries! Teriyaki or barbecue style will cost an additional forty cents, with cheese for sixty cents or with bacon and cheddar or mushroom melt for about $2.

Kids' burgers include fries and soft drink for $3.65. French fries are hot and tasty, and you have the choice of vinegar as well as catsup on the tables. Vegetarians can try a veggie sandwich or a salad.

It's open every day from 7 am (8 am Sundays) till 7 pm. Start your day with a 'breakfast sandwich,' or omelette, and all the coffee you can hold! You can hardly spend your food money more wisely.

Lihue, on Kalapaki Bay, 3464 Rice St. 246-6330. Cash only. Map 1

# Kapa'a Fish & Chowder

Kapa'a Fish & Chowder House announces its seafood emphasis with the fishing nets draped over its facade. The bar occupies most of the front dining room, and the 'garden room' in the rear is a peaceful oasis filled with hanging ferns and orchids. As we take our first steps into the new millennium, perhaps a sign of the changing times: a small smoking room off to the corner contains a single table.

In addition to more than a dozen seafood entrees, including jet set clams, shrimps, oysters, as well as fresh local fish, the menu offers chicken ($16.95), and a 10 oz. New York steak ($18.95) or filet ($22.95) and pasta primavera ($14.95). Entrees include rolls, salad, and a choice of steak fries, pasta, rice pilaf or steamed rice. The wine list is limited though reasonably-priced, or you can order a sensational Mai Tai.

Dinners include a small dinner salad (primarily romaine with dressing in a pill cup) so you might try the fish chowder served in a small pot ($5.95). The fresh fish has, for the last ten years of our visits, been chancy—sometimes moist and flaky, other times overcooked and dry. Most recently, the fish ($18.95-$22.75) arrived perfectly cooked and tasty, though we have learned the wisdom of asking for all sauces to be served on the side, and thus avoided ruining the dish with heavy handed seasonings. A new creation, star fruit salsa, was delicious. Children can color in their own finny friend menu and choose from chicken, pasta or fish dinners ($4.50-$7.50).

Dining at Kapa'a Fish & Chowder House means taking your chances. If you catch it right, you can enjoy a pleasant seafood dinner in the garden room, softly lit with lanterns and candles. But you'll spend top dollar for your fresh fish dinner, more than you'd pay at the nearby Bull Shed, where 'surf or turf' quality is more consistent.

Northern Kapa'a on Kuhio Hwy. (Rt. 56). Reservations 822-7488 (No reservations for 7-7:45 pm). Credit cards. Dinner from 5:30 pm daily. Request garden room. Non-smoking section. Children's menu. Map 1

# Kauai Chop Suey

Kauai Chop Suey combines unpretentious surroundings, excellent dinners, and unbeatable prices. The dining room, usually crowded with local families, is clean, bright, and cheerful, with well-spaced tables and fly fans to keep the air moving. The decor is a crisp combination of red and white, accented with red Chinese lanterns and green leafy plants.

The real attraction is the prices. A big tureen of scallop soup ($7.25) is sensational, with a subtly seasoned light broth, tender slices of pork and scallops, and an egg-drop texture. Saimin ($2.75/$4.50) is excellent. Pineapple shrimp ($6.95) is a perfect balance of sweet and sour, and the shrimps, eight large ones, arrive crisp and exceedingly tender. Special fried rice (at $7.50 one of the most expensive dishes on the large menu) is indeed special—especially tasty, especially generous, and chock full of delicious roast pork, chicken, shrimp, black mushrooms and crunchy snow peas. Kauai Chow Mein ($8.15) is a colorful blend of shrimp, chicken, steak, char sieu, broccoli, and carrots.

Your level of satisfaction, we discovered, has a lot to do with the service, which has a lot to do with the work load in the kitchen. Even if you see empty tables, the owner may tell you to come back in 15 minutes, and in this way control the pace at which the chefs have to cook. Once you are seated, you may not see your waitress for a while. That's because, as we saw on our last visit, there was only one waitress, and she was taking orders from all the tables, while two other waitresses served and a couple of busboys cleared the plates. It's not a very efficient system, and it certainly lacks the personal touch, but the prices are amazing, and you can bring along your own wine or beer to make the waiting more pleasant. Think twice about bringing the kids— unless you feed them before you come! To bring food home in a box will cost you 21 cents (tax included). You pay and you pack! Be warned: your feet must be across the threshold by 9 pm or you will be told, with great politeness, that the kitchen is closed.

Lihue, Pacific Ocean Plaza. 245-8790. No reservations. Cash only. Take-out 245-8790. Lunch 11-2 pm Tues. through Sat. Dinner 4:30-9 pm Tues. through Sun. No beer or wine, but tea is free. Map 1

*mango–sunset wrapped in fruit*

## Kiibo Restaurant & Sushi Bar

Kiibo has a pleasant, though small dining room with a clean, though utilitarian decor. Comfortable upholstered chairs surround bamboo colored tables. At one end is a low table on rice mats for patrons wishing to remove their shoes. Everything is understated, even the air-conditioning!

Order tempura a la carte and select from five different types of fresh fish, chicken, pork, beans, tofu, onion, sweet potato, carrots, even eggplant. On our most recent visit, however, what arrived at the table was more like breaded shrimp. Teriyaki chicken was a great success, sweet yet tangy, and both juicy and tender. Sukiyaki appears in a steaming iron caldron, rich and pungent with sauce and translucent noodles.

Priced from $5.50, entrees come with miso soup and rice attractively displayed on a square tray. Lunch is a better deal, however, with selections about a dollar less than the same choices on the dinner menu. Lunch is also the better meal; given the cautious size of the portions, dinner might leave you hungry. If you spend a little more, you might find a better quality dinner in more pleasant surroundings—for example, at Hanama'ulu Tea House or Kintaro.

Lihue, 2991 Umi St. 245-2650. Cash only. Lunch daily 11 am - 1:30 pm. Dinner daily 5:30 - 9 pm. Closed Sundays. Map 1

## The King & I

*The ne nè, Hawaii's state bird and an endangered species, is slowly increasing in numbers on Kauai*

The King and I is one of those wonderful restaurants you always dream of discovering tucked away in a shopping center, like your child's favorite toy under the socks in the corner of his closet. The King and I is a dream come true, not only for the diner, but also for the owners, a family who fled Cambodia by boat, settled in Honolulu, and trained at the famous Keo's restaurant, waiting for the chance to open up on their own.

*www.explorekauai.com*

Surprisingly pleasant and comfortably air-conditioned, the dining room is as modest as the prices. White linen tablecloths are topped with glass in an attractive compromise between attractiveness and utility. A definite step above formica! Paintings and Thai artifacts, as well as orchids on the tables, lend a touch of color.

But the real attraction at The King and I is the food. For many people, each dish will be an adventure into unknown and exotic tastes. Don't be bashful. The menu is large enough to appeal to a variety of tastes. Spring rolls ($6.25/6) are crisp, light and wonderfully tasty, attractively arranged on manoa lettuce with mint leaf and cucumber, and served with delicious peanut vinegar dipping sauce,

Don't eat too many! It would be a mistake to miss lemon grass soup ($6.50) served piping hot, with wonderfully fragrant clouds of steam. Shrimps with peanut sauce are extremely tender, attractively arranged with shredded cabbage and tomato wedges. Or try the fried rice ($6.95) flavored with tomato, cucumber, and cilantro and garnished with sliced water chestnuts. Don't pass up the Siam Mee Kaob ($5.25), a small mountain of crispy rice noodles, bean sprouts, and scallions, served with a delicately sweet peanut sauce. Sa-teh ($6.95), served with spicy peanut sauce and cucumber dipping sauce, is delicious, whether beef, chicken or the truly amazing fresh mahi mahi ($9.25), crisp and light as a whisper.

You'll love ginger fish ($9.25) made with fresh mahi mahi, fried crisp and served with a mild sauce flavored with ginger and scallions, or try one of the outstanding curries. Yellow curry is served with potatoes and onions; colored with saffron, it would be the easiest to identify as a "curry." Green curry takes its color—and flavor—from fresh basil, as well as coconut, lime leaves, and lemongrass. Red curry is the sweetest, flavored with coconut. Best of all, in our opinion, is a mild, sweet curry flavored with peanut and coconut and chock full of tender chicken. It's not on the menu, but you can ask for it as 'Evil Jungle Prince' ($9.25). Don't miss Siam eggplant ($6.95), pungent and wonderful. More than a dozen vegetarian specials range from $5.95 to $6.95, many flavored with basil and spices grown fresh in Kilauea. For dessert, try Thai tapioca pudding, which will be more soupy perhaps than the lumpy stuff you may remember from school lunches, and flavored with delicious apple-bananas and coconut. Most wines on the small list cost less than $20.

The King and I is a special place, a great choice for those times when you find it hard to look at another ahi or ono. You'll love the change of pace, the distinctive cuisine, and the friendly family atmosphere. And when you get your bill, your royal pocketbook will hardly notice.

Wailua, Waipouli Plaza, 4-901 Kuhio Highway. 822-1642. Lunch 11am-2pm (M-F). Dinner 4:30-9:30 daily. Reservations a day in advance. Non-smoking section. Credit cards. Map 1

# Kintaro

For more than fifteen years, Kintaro has remained Kauai's best Japanese restaurant, a must if you are looking for delicious food in an attractive, comfortable setting. In fact, you will probably see the owner, Mr. Kim, hard at work running the smooth operation begun by his father. You'll also see a tasteful harmony of blues, whites, grays and tans in pleasing proportion. A fountain set in blue tiles and a sushi bar take up one long white wall. Nut-colored wood tables are set with chopsticks in blue and white wrappers, blue and tan tea bowls, and a striking single flower. Ceiling fans and air conditioning make Kintaro comfortably cool, and subdued Japanese music sets a relaxed mood.

What you choose to eat determines where you sit. Cocktails and pu pus are served in a comfortable, attractive lounge, where you can sip a wonderful chi chi, sample elegant sashimi, or munch on crispy fried won tons from the owner's factory next door. In the same spacious room, you can sit at the teppan yaki tables and watch talented chefs chop and flip and make things sizzle. As they will be happy to show you, the raw ingredients are fresh and of the best quality. Teriyaki New York steak ($18.95) or island chicken teriyaki ($14.95) are tender, tasty and juicy.

If you prefer the reasonably-priced dinners on the regular menu, you might be seated in the smaller dining room, where you are served a small salad of pickled cabbage and daikon. Following delicious miso soup, dinner entrees are presented on traditional sectioned wooden platforms and include rice, zaru soba (chilled buckwheat noodles with a seasoned soy-based sauce) and pickled vegetables, along with tea served in a blue and tan pottery teapot. Crispy shrimp tempura with vegetables ($13.95) is light and delicious, particularly the green beans. Teriyaki beef made with slices of NY steak is exceptionally tender ($15.95). Beef sukiyaki in a cast iron pot ($15.95) is dark and dusky with translucent noodles, meat, and vegetables. Teriyaki chicken is a family favorite, with great sauce.

Sashimi is excellent. Ours arrived with six elegantly arranged selections: thin slices of

*Excellent Japanese cuisine & sushi*

*Island sunsets are especially lovely when reflected on eastern shores.*

ahi, translucent slivers of ono, dark strips of pungent smoked salmon, shrimps cooked so perfectly that they seemed to melt as you tasted them. According to our family expert Jeremy, Kintaro makes the best sushi on Kauai, particularly 'California rolls' ($4.50) with fresh crab and avocado, spicy tuna rolls, as well as the 'salmon skin hand roll' ($4.50), with crispy pieces of fish wrapped in a rice and nori cone. Watching the sushi chef's lightening speed is great entertainment.

Children are welcome, as is appropriate for a restaurant named in honor of a legendary Japanese boy hero, and service is polite and, on the whole, unrushed. As our children have grown into young adults, Kintaro has become not just their favorite Japanese restaurant, but their favorite, period!

Wailua, Kuhio Hwy. (Rt. 56). Reservations 822-3341. Credit Cards. Dinner 5:30-9:30 pm. Closed Sundays. Non-smoking section. Map 1

## Kountry Kitchen

For years, and despite changes in ownership, the best spot for breakfast on the island's east coast has been the Kountry Kitchen, which serves terrific food at equally terrific prices. The large menu offers delicious eggs, expertly cooked bacon and sausage, as well as omelette creations, including sour cream, or bacon and tomato ($6.50), or 'vegetable garden' ($7.25). You can also design your own omelette by ordering a combination of separately priced fillings. Kountry Kitchen's omelettes are unique—thin pancakes of egg rolled around fillings almost like a crepe—tender, moist, and delicious. Or try Eggs Margo, a version of Eggs Benedict with turkey instead of ham ($7.50). Our children loved Cheesy Eggs — toasted English muffin with bacon and poached eggs, covered with golden cheese sauce ($6.50), and our babies have all loved the honey and wheat pancake ($4.95). Hash browns are perfectly golden and crisp pancakes of shredded potatoes.

At lunch you can choose sandwiches, salads and hamburgers priced from $6 to $8, including an excellent Chinese chicken salad ($7.25). Go early to breakfast—the line may be out the door by 8 am. For homestyle breakfasts, hot, tasty, and filling, you can't do much better!

Kapaʻa, 1485 Kuhio Hwy. 822-3511. Credit cards. Breakfast 6 am - 9 am. Lunch 11 am - 2: 30 pm daily. Map 1

# La Bamba

Walk into La Bamba and you'll see about a dozen formica tables with vinyl cloths. You'll think you've wandered into a luncheonette, except for the murals on the tan stucco walls. These depict a vaguely southwestern scene, including a boat named, whimsically, 'La Bamba.' Quantity is the main attraction here. If you order a taco salad, for example, it fills the plate, stuffed with beans and chunks of chicken. Overlook the soggy lettuce because you'll have a filling meal for only $7.95. Fly fans encourage the breezes in a room where dining is comfortable if spartan. Parking may be hard to find — the lot next door has only 4 spaces!

If you're on a budget, or have a big appetite, La Bamba is a good choice for generous portions, reasonable prices, and swift service in an informal, friendly atmosphere.

4261 Lihue, Rice St. 245-5972. 11 am - 10 pm daily. Cash only. Map 1

# Margarita's

Perched right on Kuhio Highway in Wailua, Margarita's is hard to miss. The rambling green building houses a bright white dining room with two tiers as well as a wrap-around porch for dining and a bar and lounge. The dining room is spacious and attractive, with green formica-topped tables and rattan armchairs with cheerful red and green cushions. Lots of leafy plants, brass, copper and pottery, as well as interesting black and white photos of old Kauai, decorate the walls. Ceilings are open to the rafters, and fly fans keep the air moving. If you are dining on the terrace, bring some 'Off' and/or ask for a mosquito coil. A friendly donkey from the pasture next door may stroll over to say 'hey.'

The menu is the largest you will find in a Mexican restaurant on Kauai, offering dinners from $9.95-$14.95, with many entree choices available vegetarian style, as well as a wide variety of less expensive a la carte items. Seasoning is not overly spicy, portions are reasonable, and ingredients of good quality. You can order your chicken or beef burrito for about $8.95 and pay $2 extra for beans or for rice, or you can choose the whole package for $12.95. Margarita's ahi burrito ($14 .95) is excellent, with lots of tender fish, avocado, tomatoes, black beans, cilantro and tomatillo sauce.

Margarita's is a good choice for middle-of-the-road, American style Mexican dining in a relaxed and pleasant atmosphere. If you order from the a la carte menu, you will be surprised at how little a dinner can cost!

Wailua, Kuhio Hwy. (Rt. 56). 822-1808. Credit cards. Daily 5 to 10 pm. No Reservations. Non-smoking section. Entertainment. Map 1

## Ma's Family, Inc.

Ma's tiny luncheonette is so far off the beaten path in Lihue that you'd probably never find it if you didn't stumble onto it by chance. For more than 25 years, Ma's family has established a reputation for well-priced and well-cooked breakfasts and lunches, and you'll probably find the dozen tables filled with local people on their way to work in the morning or stopping off for lunch.

The few tourists who happen onto it will love Ma's expertly cooked eggs, delicious pancakes and waffles that one of our teenagers described as "about the best." The menu, which is posted on the wall over the pass-through to the kitchen, also lists some Hawaiian dishes, for example roast kalua pig that shreds perfectly for little ones to pick up with their fingers. Even the toast is excellent. Corned beef hash lovers may find Ma's version too much like a potato pancake, but fried min noodles with eggs and sausages may open your eyes to new possibilities for breakfast.

Service is fast and extremely friendly in the sunny, spartan dining room. Coffee arrives immediately in a large carafe and the food shortly thereafter. If you don't like canned milk in your coffee, ask for a small glass of the fresh stuff. When you leave, you'll be astonished to find how little your meal has cost you. When a hungry family can dine so inexpensively, you feel like popping into the kitchen to give the cook a big hug! And many of our readers do just that!

Lihue, 4277 Halenani St. Cash only. 245-3142. Daily 5 am - 9:30 pm. Weekends 12:30 am to 10 am. Coffee or tea free with breakfast! Map 1

## Masa's

When you walk into Masa's, you may be surprised to find yourself in a rather crowded room. That is, all four tables may be taken, as may be the nine stools by the sushi bar. Masa's is popular for reasonably priced, reasonably prepared sushi. Masa's serves very little besides sushi —a little soup, salad, and sashimi, so don't expect variety, but it's fun to watch the chef chop, wrap, and roll. Kappa maki ($2.75), the un-fish sushi, satisfied our finicky eaters with its peeled cucumber center. Kyoto vegetable roll arrives in a tofu wrapping, a real taste treat, and both salmon skin rolls and spicy ahi rolls ($4.25) are tasty.

Prices are reasonable, so expect to cut a few corners. Ginger seemed a bit on the stale side, and service is slow. The chef and waitress do it all,

*Sandy beaches rim the Eastern shore near Lydgate Park in Wailua.*

and the waitress will tell you frankly how many orders are ahead of you. Take her seriously, and order delicious miso soup ($1.50) to tide you over.  For beer or wine, you may have to stop in at the ABC store across the street beforehand, if Masa's liquor license is still in the planning stage.

With its tiny storefront in downtown Kapaʻa (look carefully or you'll miss it), Masa's is unpretentious and fun.  It's sushi, local style, perhaps not be in the same class as Kintaro, but prices are more reasonable and the atmosphere a stop down.

Kapaʻa, 1384 Kuhio Highway. 821-6933. Lunch 11am - 2pm. Dinner 5:30 - 9:30. Non smoking restaurant. Credit cards. No checks. Map 1

## Mema's Thai & Chinese Cuisine

Can you believe it?  Two excellent Thai restaurants within a half-mile of each other in tiny Wailua!  Mema's and The King & I are more like 'cousins,' operated by two branches of the same Thai family.  There are differences: Mema's features Chinese cuisine as well as Thai; its Thai food is slightly spicier, and the decor is more dramatic.  The dining room looks like a garden, with bamboo, orchids, and leafy green plants to provide a colorful backdrop for statues and paintings from Thailand and intricate woodwork in red and gold.

*delicious Thai cuisine*

What comes to the table is as tasteful and pleasing as the decor.  Spring rolls ($6.95) are wonderfully crisp, attractively served with fresh leafy lettuce and peanut sauce, and can be ordered vegetarian style.  On the Chinese side of the menu, cashew chicken ($8.95) is delicious and chock full of nuts, and lemon chicken ($8.95) is excellent, very crispy and golden with a lightly flavored lemon sauce. Thai dishes can be hot, so be sure to ask your server which ones match best with your taste.  According to the pricing structure, each dish can be prepared with vegetables or tofu for $7.95, with chicken, beef, or pork ($8.95) or with shrimp, fish, or calamari ($9.95).  Try green curry with coconut milk, lemon grass, kaffir lime leaves, eggplant, and fresh basil— truly wonderful and not overly spicy.  On the other hand, red curry looks deceptively placid, garnished with fresh basil and chopped cabbage, but it's a scorcher!  Mahi mahi satay ($9.25) is a delicious version.  Vegetarians have many choices on the menu, and the kitchen will also tailor dishes to specific tastes or philosophies.

While experts may grumble that no authentic Thai peppers blister the dishes at Mema's, the temperature is up a few degrees from The King & I. With reasonable prices, lots of variety on the menu, an attractive dining room, and friendly service, Mema's is a great choice for a pleasant, relaxing evening, and the Thai food is as good as you can find—anywhere! In Wailua Shopping Plaza, 4-361 Kuhio Hwy. 823-0899. Credit cards. Lunch 11 am till 2 pm M-F, and Dinner nightly 5 pm - 9:30 pm.  Map 1

# Norberto's El Cafe

In the heart of Kapaʻa, Norberto's has served first-rate Mexican food on Kauai since 1977.  White stucco walls and woodgrain tables create a setting like a cantina, colorfully decorated with hanging plants, sombreros, and gas lamps.  Trophies won by the girls' softball team, coached by Norberto, sit atop a piano, where guests occasionally contribute to the informal atmosphere with impromptu entertainment.

Over the years, prices have not changed much, and almost everything is very reasonable, including margaritas by the pitcher and a la carte entrees, as well as complete Mexican dinners with soup, vegetable, beans, chips and salsa for $16 or less.  Be sure to ask for the homemade chips made with flour tortillas.  Nachos are generously covered with cheese. When we finished our bean soup, we were asked if we wanted seconds!

The Burrito El Cafe ($9.50) deserves to be called a house specialty— the tortilla generously stuffed with flavorful beef, beans and cheese, baked enchilada style and topped with guacamole and fresh red tomatoes and lettuce. The tostada ($5.50) is a huge colorful salad mounded over a crisp tortilla, and the chili relleno is dipped (not drowned) in egg and gently cooked, so that it comes to your plate light, tender and delicately flavored. An El Cafe specialty, enchiladas made with taro ($4.75) are first rate, the taro leaves, which taste not unlike spinach, providing an island flavor. Almost all dishes can also be ordered vegetarian style.  For the some who like it hot, plenty of homemade salsa is on the table to add to your dishes, and the kitchen will say *"Ole!"* to any challenge!

Service is friendly,  prices are reasonable, and children are treated with tolerance, even when cranky.  When the salsa proved too hot for the short people on one occasion, the fast-thinking waitress brought over a bowl of bean soup. Once the  kids started dipping chips, all you could hear was happy crunching!

Kapaʻa, 4-1373 Kuhio Hwy. 822-3362. 5:30-9:00 pm daily. Closed Sundays. Breakfast 6 am - 11 am except Monday. Smoking in bar only. Children's menu. Credit cards. Map 1

## Okazu Hale

Want to vote on who serves the best saimin on Kauai? Try Okazu Hale—we think it has the freshest noodles, the most fragrant, steaming broth, the best vegetables! Or try the Japanese style noodle soup, which has a richer flavor, and more spice. In this tiny eatery, inside a tiny shopping center across from Ace Hardware in Lihue, you'll find noodles, saimin, sushi, Japanese style 'local food', as well as chicken, fresh island fish, teriyaki and barbecue dishes, and even old-fashioned pot roast. Prices are inexpensive ($6-$9). The decor is spartan, to put it mildly. Fly fans keep the air moving.

It's jammed when the plate lunch crowd arrives, but the saimin is worth the crush. Try the saimin special ($5.95), which comes with shrimp tempura, chicken katsu and vegetables, or you might prefer the large plain version with a side order of vegetables. Or choose from a large variety of fresh made sushi. This is local style Kauai—don't miss it!

*hidden saimin!*

Lihue, 4100 Rice Street. 245-6554. Cash only. Lunch:11-2 pm. Dinner: 5-9 pm. M-Sat. Non-smokers, take your chances! Map 1

## Oki Diner

Your body's still on east coast time and hungry in the middle of the night! Well, Oki Diner is open 22 hours a day, and all day long on weekends. For breakfast, it's a full range of eggs and pancakes. For other times, there are sandwiches, burgers, noodle dishes of all kinds, 'mini meals' like 'Mom's chicken' ($3.99) and 25 'local favorites' like stir fry or beef stew ($5.95-9.95), Hawaiian style ribs and pork, complete with rice and salad. Saimin (from $2.75) is hot and tasty. Take it out to the beach, even though the container (with lid) will cost fifty cents. Don't forget the pies! 'Pumpkin crunch' is a local legend, worth a visit by itself, and available by the slice (it's square!).

Oki Diner may not win any awards for imaginative decor—it's formica utilitarian — but for straightforward meals at honest prices, and at any hour, Oki may just be what you need on Hawaiian time.

Lihue, 3125 Kuhio Hwy (next to McDonald's). 245-5899. Daily menu served 22 hours (closed 3am-5am) and 24 hours weekends. Map 1

## Ono Family Restaurant

Ono Family Restaurant has been a long-time favorite among local people and tourists alike for wholesome, inexpensive family fare, most recently winning a nod from the *New York Times!* Breakfasts and lunches are well-cooked, attractively served, generous and reasonably priced. The dining room is cozy, with polished wooden booths, some with a removable partition to accommodate large families. Antiques harmonize with a homey assortment of square and round tables.

At breakfast, you'll find more than 30 egg creations priced from $3.50, including 17 omelettes! For a new idea, try eggs with fresh ahi, a perfectly cooked filet, or tasty corned beef hash and scrambled eggs ($6.50). Coffee is only $1; pancakes start at $3.25. At lunch, you'll find a wide array of sandwiches, burgers, plate lunches, and salads from $5, as well as Ono's famous Portuguese bean soup.

Service can be slow, but everyone is friendly and cooperative. Wait persons are helpful with things like crackers, straws, extra napkins and extra cups for tastes of grown-up coffee—those etceteras of family dining that don't seem essential until they're missing. People seem ready to help with each other's restless little ones. On one occasion, when we could not find our waitress to get a glass of water that had suddenly become a necessity, an adjacent Daddy passed over an extra. Just outside the door, two old timers shared their donuts with a wandering seven-year-old, patted his head as he chewed, and listened politely to his latest fish story.

4-1292 Kuhio Hwy, Kapa'a. Open daily 7 am- 2 pm. 822-1710. Credit cards. Map 1

## Ono Char Burger (Duane's)

For years, a tiny shack next to the general store at Anahola was famous among local people for delicious hamburgers and fresh fruit smoothies. As tourists heard about the hamburgers, the shack, along with its reputation expanded! Picnic tables appeared under the tree, and the menu grew. Even if the most recent coat of paint doesn't catapult Duane's into a McDonald's time warp, the facade is certainly brighter! Times change: the 'ono burger' has made the *New York Times*, and now management accepts plastic!

Duane has sold the business, but the burgers are still delicious, if somewhat smaller than before. Quarter pounders can be made with various cheeses (even blue cheese) or teriyaki style (from $3.90). Our favorites are the 'local girl' with teriyaki, Swiss cheese and fresh pine-apple ($5.65), and the vegetarian sandwich ($4.95). Children can order 2.5 oz. hamburgers ($2.60) or deep fried chicken strips and fries ($3.40) that will make the rest of the party want to order the adult portion ($6.95). Add sizzling crisp french fries ($1.80 feeds two) and you can wash it down with smoothies and ice cream shakes, floats and freezes ($2.95). Service can be slow, particularly at peak lunchtime. Be patient, and pack up your sandwiches (each half will be separately wrapped) and head for beautiful Anahola Beach just a mile down Aliomanu Road. Save time and phone in your order! Westside, try the Ono Burger branch in Waimea.

Anahola, Rt. 56, next to Whalers Store. 822-9181. Open daily 10 am to 6 pm; Sunday 11 am to 6 pm. Credit cards. Map 1

## A Pacific Cafe

A Safeway shopping center is an unlikely spot for a gourmet restaurant, but A Pacific Cafe, owned by chef Jean Marie Josselin, has achieved fame for blending the culinary traditions of Europe and the Pacific Rim, while emphasizing fresh ingredients from Kauai.

As you enter the air-conditioned dining room, you will see the chefs hard at work behind a tall counter pass-through. That is appropriate, for the kitchen is the centerpiece of this restaurant. You will be delighted with the ingenious, sometimes whimsical, artistry of each dish. For example, sashimi served tempura style ($10.50), the ahi wrapped in seaweed, then deep fried and sliced in elegant, dainty medallions, the fish cool in the center, the wrapping crisp outside. Poached scallop ravioli ($7.75) is wonderful, the won ton shaped noodles delicately flavored and the lime ginger sauce delicious. Even an ordinary dinner salad ($6.50) looks like kaleidoscope of colors.

Familiar entrees appear in arresting fashion. Fresh fish can be almost magical—sizzling hot, meltingly tender, and enhanced with wonderful sauces. Try 'wok-charred' mahi mahi with garlic sesame crust and lime ginger sauce ($25.50), or delicate opah (moonfish). Ahi appears in a huge portion with stir fry vegetables, rivaling even the steamed fresh ono, our favorite island fish. Among the inventive desserts, chocolate lovers will adore the hot chocolate tart, and sorbet aficionados will love fresh lichee. 'Toasted Hawaiian' remains a family favorite, and the macadamia nut tart with coconut ice cream will please anyone nuts about nuts.

The dining room is attractive, with black lacquer chairs surrounding polished wood tables, set with black bamboo placemats and shining crystal. Many plates are whimsical creations by Sophronia Josselin, and they frame the appetizers and entrees like culinary paintings. The only disadvantage in the air-conditioned room is noise. This cafe is really best on a night when it's not busy, if you can find one. When a restaurant on Kauai is featured in *Sunset Magazine*, you should expect it to be jammed.

Chef-owner Jean Marie Josselin splits his time among his other restaurants on Oahu and Maui. Some readers and also local residents have complained about uneven quality in food and service due to staffing changeovers and the loss of his on-site supervision. He's currently considering plans for a new ocean front location across the street. Despite occasional disappointments, our own experiences have been largely excellent. A Pacific Cafe has a loyal following, and everyone seems to agree that it's special, even four Horowitz children who can't seem to agree on much else. They'll all tell you: Don't miss this one!

Wailua, Kauai Village Shopping Center, Kuhio Hwy. 5:30 - 10 pm nightly. Reservations a day (or two) in advance: 822-0013. Credit cards. Non-smoking section. Map 1

## Palm Tree Terrace

You'll find Palm Tree Terrace on a porch in the Coconut Plantation Marketplace—two small porches to be precise, attached to an even smaller room which shelters a small salad bar, soup table, and a large cooler for drinks. Yet on these porches you can enjoy a delicious meal, served attractively and cheerfully, and you'll soon forget the somewhat cramped quarters and think instead of the tasty fresh fish, the generous portions of pasta, the remarkably reasonable prices. The salad bar, though limited in choices, has the vivid colors and textures of freshness—not only lettuce but also broccoli, cucumbers, and tomatoes. Add to that fresh, ripe papaya and you have a great value at a great price—$5.95, which buys not only the salad bar but also soup, like clam chowder, dipped from a large soup pot, or an especially tasty broccoli bisque.

Your entrees will be generous, well prepared, and attractively presented. Fresh island fish is cleanly grilled, moist and flaky, and at $16.95, a real bargain for the thick, juicy ahi steak we sampled. Chicken breast 'sienna' arrives on a bed of pasta and vegetables, very tender and flavored, rather than overpowered, with garlic. If you prefer chicken teriyaki style, you'll love the large leg and thigh (breast upon request) served with a homemade sauce with real zing ($8.95). Wines and beer are reasonably priced. Service has the personal touch that comes when the owner serves the food, and his pride in what comes to the table is shared by the cook, his wife Gloria, who clears the plates pleased to find so little left on them. Another cook moonlights from the Sheraton Princeville.

Palm Tree Terrace may be a porch, but it's a clean porch, with green painted railings, white table cloths, the vinyl variety, and candles on the tables. If the rain comes down, so do the vinyl curtains, but on most nights, you can look up at the stars and plan the next day on the beach!

Wailua, Coconut Plantation Marketplace. 821-1040 Lunch and dinner daily. Credit cards.

## Panda Garden

Next to the Safeway in the Kauai Village Shopping Center, Panda Garden looks clean and attractive. Tables with white cloths covered with shiny glass tops are set with blue and white china, making the white painted dining room look cheerful and bright. Bamboo, a favorite taste treat of the panda, is the main decorative motif. Local people like the place for its reasonable prices and friendly informality.

Most menu choices are priced between $7 and $10. Won ton soup ($6.25) is hot, delicately flavored, and generous with won tons. Spring rolls ($4.95) are crisp and tasty without being greasy, clearly freshly made. Lemon chicken ($7.50) is deep fried to a golden brown and served with a piquant sauce. Moo shi vegetable ($7.95) is another good bet. Portions are generous, the food tasty, and service, though occasionally slow, is very pleasant and polite.

Although Panda Garden has no view, given its shopping center location, the dining room is comfortable and air conditioned, the service pleasant, and the food reasonably-priced and reasonably tasty.

Wailua, Kauai Village Shopping Center, 4-831 Kuhio Hwy. 822-0092. Lunch 11 am - 2 pm except Wednesdays; dinner 4:30 pm - 9 pm daily. Non-smoking section. Map 1

## Papaya's Garden Cafe

One of increasing number of vegetarian eateries on the island, Papaya's is actually a full-service natural foods store. The deli operation offers a wide range of sandwiches and casseroles with the flavors of Mexican, Cuban, Indian, Szechwan, Thai, Greek and Italian cuisines, including tempeh, fish, or chicken burgers, as well as 'garden lasagne' and spanakopita ($4 to $8.95). Fresh ahi sandwich is excellent. You can also enjoy espresso, capuccino, lattes, mochas and teas.

Dine outside at tables on the "patio," more accurately the walkway of the mall. Their umbrellas come in handy when the rain comes down.

Wailua, Kauai Village Shopping Center, Kuhio Hwy. 823-0190. Open 9 am - 8 pm. Closed Sunday. Map 1

## Paradise Seafood & Grill

Paradise Seafood has taken over the space which once housed the popular Fisherman's Galley. Fortunately, the chef continues on, and you can still enjoy the signature dish, fresh island fish and chips. Prices are up, however. Fish and chips made with fresh local fish now costs $16.50 for 4 pieces, and complete fresh fish dinners, including salad or soup, and rice or baked potato, are up to $18.50. The new menu is also much larger. Non-fishy eaters can choose steak ($15.95-$19.95), chicken ($14.95), even prime rib in two sizes ($16.95/12oz or $23.95/24 oz.), or pasta. Fish chowder is tasty and thick, tasting as it did in the old days, though not quite as chunky with the seafood as before. A new dish, lasagne, arrives steaming in a generous casserole with lots of cheese ($13.95).

The rear dining room has improved with remodeling, and looks both clean and welcoming. Walls colored a soft grey are cheered by leafy green plants, and the concrete floor shines with white paint. Woodgrain tables with white wrought iron chairs are generously spaced, so you don't feel crowded. You can also dine outside on the porch, and keep an eye on what's happening at Kauai Community College across the intersection.

At Paradise Grill, fresh island fish 'n chips remains one of our favorite meals. The fresh fish sandwich, served on a soft bun, is also worth a stop. After dinner, or for a mid-afternoon treat, try coffee from the full espresso bar. For other beverages, a full bar is open all day.

On Rt. 50, Kipu. Open daily 11 am- 11pm. 246-4884. Credit cards.

## Pony Island Cantina

Tucked under Safeway's wing in the Kauai Village Shopping Center, Pony Island Cantina is a tiny eaterie with a half-dozen tables. The menu may be Mexican, but the emphasis is on the healthful and fresh, so expect your tacos, tostadas, enchiladas, and burritos to be heaped with organic greens, and accompanied not only with beans but also organic brown rice, as an alternative to the traditional Mexican version.

In addition to a la carte Mexican choices, you'll find full dinners and combination plates ($12.50 to $14.95). This is Kauai, so be sure to try the fresh fish! Delicious 'Tropical Tacos' are stuffed with locally caught ahi (2/$7.75), or you can sample fresh ahi salad ($7.95), or an ahi burrito ($7.95) so stuffed that you won't be able to get your mouth around it! Looking for vegetables? Try the wonderfully inventive 'V-ital tacos' filled with tofu, carrots, and Hawaiian purple sweet potato ($7.75). Or, if you prefer greens, choose Kauai grown lettuce salad with chili lime vinaigrette, a bargain at only $5.95; for an additional $2, you can have meat or chicken or vegetables added. On a limited budget? The 'good times bowl' may be for you, filled with organic rice and beans and served with salsa and fresh homestyle corn bread, at $4.95, a great portion for a great price!

Pony Island Cantina has no liquor license. But you can find beer and wine on ice at Safeway right next door. You probably won't remember the dining room with its seven tables after you leave, for the decor is pretty much the sum of the television, cash register, and drink cooler. But you will remember tasty food and inexpensive prices. Come for the fresh ingredients, the light taste, and fresh island fish.

Wailua, Kauai Village on Rt. 56, next to Safeway. 823-9000. Credit cards. Take out.

*Beautiful torch ginger*

## Rocco's

With its shining double storey windows looking over the central crossroads of Kapa'a town, Rocco's offers reasonably-priced Italian cuisine in a comfortable, informal setting with friendly service. Rocco's menu features chicken, pasta, fish, fresh-baked pizzas, and no fewer than seven variations of Caesar salad, both hot and cold (when Gourmet Magazine praises your Caesar salad dressing, you go with it!). Many entrees come with a cup of soup or a small green salad, which can be served with that memorable Caesar dressing as an 'upgrade.' Minestrone (a la carte $3.75) is filled with vegetables and flavorful broth. Fragrant bread still warm from the oven arrives with the disconcerting reminder that seconds cost $2.25 (though we were not charged for our extra basket). Try home baked pizza from Rocco's brick oven, with wonderful crust, crisp yet soft inside. Rocco's manicotti ($12.95) is generously stuffed with cheese, though we also found a rather distinctive clove of garlic. In fact, garlic dominates most dishes, overwhelming the chicken ($14.95) the eggplant marsala ($14.95), even french onion soup! Best was the sauteed fresh ono which we ordered garlic-free ($17.95)

Service is prompt and generous. The menu does not offer great variety, and garlic is a clear favorite of the chef, but if you are in a hurry for noodles, Rocco's offers fast, reasonably-priced dining.

Central Kapa'a. 822-4422. Open daily for lunch and dinner. Full bar. Non-smoking section. Credit cards. Map 1

## Sukothai Restaurant

Less than a mile away from the two local Thai favorites, King and I and Mema Thai Cuisine, Sukothai tries to find a market niche by offering a larger combination of cuisines: Thai - Chinese - Vietnamese, and, as if that weren't enough of a challenge for the kitchen, Barbecue.

The small dining room is bright and welcoming, decorated in cheerful yellow, with a red carpet and red tablecloths woven with gold and covered with protective glass. Yellow orchids provide the tropical touch, while roomy rattan armchairs and air conditioning make dining pleasant and comfortable. Most dishes cost about $8. Tom Kar, or coconut and lemon grass soup, is wonderful, presented in a lovely earthernware serving bowl ($7.95). Rice pancakes filled with minced chicken, cut in sections and deep fried, are also delicious ($7.50). Vegetable fried rice is colorful with vegetables ($6.95), and cashew chicken is very tasty. Pad Thai, made with rice noodles, is excellent ($8.25). We ran into trouble when we asked to alter a dish by eliminating or reducing one of its listed ingredients (garlic) or to modify the spiciness. Impossible, we were told—sauces are prepared in advance.

Though in our opinion its cuisine is not as distinctive as King & I or Mema's, Sukothai offers a more varied menu, a large undertaking —

and a reason for its success. Prices are reasonable, and so is food quality, and so you won't go wrong if you want to try this one out.

Kapaʻa Shopping Center (near Big Save). 821-1224. Credit cards. Lunch 11 am - 3 pm. Dinner 5 pm - 10 pm daily. Air-conditioned. Map 1

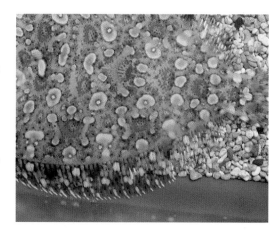

## Tip Top & Sushi Katsu

The name Tip Top conjures up certain 1950's type expectations: a clean room for under $20, a square meal for $5. But you're not really sure that you should believe in this any more than you would in the tooth fairy! It is true, though. Since 1916, Tip Top has served fairly–priced, honest, unpretentious food, more popular with local people than the tourists who manage to find it on a side street of Lihue.

The dining room has comfortable large booths, and on hot summer days, you'll appreciate the air conditioning. The real attraction is the prices. Delicious pancakes with macadamia nuts, bananas, pineapples or raisins cost $4. French toast is only $3.25. Ham and cheese

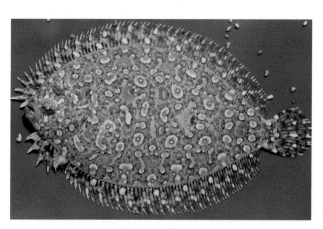

*Political fish— blends in with current conditions!*

*Fragrant plumeria*

omelette or bacon and eggs, accompanied by a scoop of hash browns, are $6, with oxtail soup, the most expensive item on the menu, at $6.50. Meals are well-prepared if unexciting, but homemade pineapple and guava jam is special. Have it on toast, but that's a la carte.

At lunch, try hamburgers ($3.20) and plate lunches (from $5.50). Or visit Sushi Katsu, a small sushi bar (there are only 8 seats) inside Tip Top, and sample California roll ($4), or spicy ahi roll ($5). An enormous bowl of saimin is only $4.75. In the evenings, you can enjoy Sushi Katsu's full Japanese dinners at modest prices.

Tip Top is an island tradition. Breakfasts are hot, fast, and filling—perfect for those mornings when you're on the way to the airport and need every ounce of strength to get those bags through the agriculture inspection without misplacing anything—or anybody!

Lihue, 3173 Akahi St. Credit cards. 245-2333. Breakfast & Lunch 6:30 am- 2 pm. Sushi Katsu serves lunch & also Japanese dinner from 5:30-9:30 pm. Closed Mondays. 246-0176. Map 1

## Tokyo Lobby

Tokyo Lobby's dining room is attractive and comfortable in an informal way. Black lacquer chairs and grey tables make an attractive contrast to the clean white walls, and a jaunty red pagoda roof extends over the sushi bar.

The menu offers a wide variety of Japanese appetizers and entrees, and dinners include an excellent miso soup, tsukemono and rice. Hibachi lemon chicken ($12.95) is first rate, tender, moist and tasty, served with a somewhat spicy salad with coconut dressing. BBQ salmon or fresh island fish ($13.95) is another good choice. Tempura ($10.95) is light, crispy and filled with vegetables still crunchy and colorful as well as either fresh island fish or shrimp ($14.95). You can order tempura in the appetizer portion, which contains 5 pieces ($7.95), enough to sample and still have room to try some sushi, like California roll of crab and avocado wrapped in rice and nori ($4), or salmon skin hand rolls ($4). A special feature: the Tokyo Lobby Love Boat, a lavish display of sushi served in a wooden boat, with soup, salad and rice ($21.50/pp for 2 and more). Service can be slow, particularly when it's full, but Tokyo Lobby is a good bet for well-prepared food in a comfortable, informal setting.

Lihue, Pacific Ocean Plaza, 3501 Rice St. 245-8989. Lunch 11am-2pm Mon-Sat. Dinner 4:30-9:30 pm daily. Non-smoking section. Beer, wine and sake. Credit cards. Map 1

## Wah Kung Chop Suey

If you didn't know where to look for it, you probably would never find Wah Kung, tucked away in the interior of Kinipopo Shopping Village on Kuhio Highway in Wailua. Peek inside the tiny kitchen and watch the cooks hard at work in steam and sizzle. The tiny dining room will probably be crowded with local families who appreciate the large portions and small prices, most around $6. Try saimin ($2.95) or tasty stir fried vegetables ($5.75)! Take-out containers (each costs a quarter) sit ready for action atop twin freezers, which by default provide the focal point of the decor. There's barely enough room left for a few tables, some Chinese decorations, and the handmade signs describing the daily specials. Tables outside on the patio are cooler and more pleasant. You'll probably be in for a wait, but you can explore the mini-mall and browse Goldsmiths Kauai nearby for wonderful island jewelry designs.

Wailua, Kinipopo Shopping Village, Kuhio Hwy. 822-0560 Cash only. Lunch: Tues.-Sat 11 am to 2 pm; Dinner 4:30 pm to 8:30 pm daily.

## Wailua Marina Restaurant

For more than 30 years, the Wailua Marina has been an island favorite for family dining. The large dining room features an enormous mural of an underwater vista complete with stuffed fish and a turtle shell. Weather permitting, ask to sit on the large covered porch decorated with plants and fresh flowers. Cooled by delightful breezes, it looks out over the Wailua River, where boats rock gently in the docks. In the evening, candles light the tables with a golden glow, and the air is soft and fragrant.

A pleasant waitress will probably recommend the fresh fish, which is usually delicious. Fresh ahi stuffed with crab ($16.50) is well seasoned and flavorful. Fresh ono with marina sauce ($15) is also tasty, accompanied with small cups of both teriyaki sauce and drawn butter. Fried chicken ($10) may be more moist than teriyaki chicken, but kids love that teriyaki sauce for dipping, so order some on the side. Most entrees cost less than $16 and include rolls, rice or potato, a vegetable and salad bar. Hot, crispy french fries are considerably better than the somewhat oily fried rice, although even that's not too bad if you flavor it with the kitchen's delicious teriyaki sauce.

To keep prices down, the Marina cuts a few corners, but they're the kind no one really misses if you catch the spirit of the place. The pleasantness of the setting more than compensates for paper napkins and placemats. The salad bar may lack imagination, but you can fill your plate with vegetables. Children can chose from ten dinners for about $3 less than adult prices. The dozen wines are not very exciting, but most cost less than $20. You'll love the homemade pies!

Prices are up, and the cost of the Marina's fresh island fish dinner is now almost even with the Bull Shed's. The Marina is still reasonable, however, and you'll come away with a pleasant memory of lights on the river twinkling as dusk deepens into night.

Wailua River State Park, just south of the bridge on Kuhio Hwy. 822-4311 Lunch: 11am-2 pm & Dinner 5 pm- 9 pm. Early Bird Special 5-6pm. Closed Mondays.

## Waipouli Deli & Restaurant

Does this sound familiar? Your body clock is off. You're fully awake—and starving—3 hours early. You'll never make it till lunch, but you want to spend the morning on the beach and not in some dark, air-conditioned restaurant with poky service!

Well, the Waipouli Deli is for you! Generous portions of tasty food coupled with speedy delivery and unbeatable prices have made the Waipouli Deli a favorite spot on the eastside for local families and increasing numbers of tourists. It looks like formica city, so don't go expecting orchids on the table! But though short on atmosphere, it's got a "breakfast special" deserving of the name. For $2.99, you get an egg cooked the way you like, two slices of bacon, and two pancakes — perfect for hungry children, not to mention adults. Eggs are expertly cooked, side meats not overly fatty, and pancakes light. On the lunch and dinner menus, you'll find bargains in American and Oriental food.

Service is fast, efficient, and very friendly. We were in and out and on our way in less than an hour! If you want to save money and be well fed before the morning slips away from you, this is your place!

Wailua, in the Waipouli Town Center, behind McDonald's. 822-9311 for take-out orders. 7:30 am - 9:30 pm daily. Map 1

## Whaler's Brew Pub

With its dramatic perch on the side of a rocky point, Whaler's Brew Pub has a panoramic ocean view. (Whaler's ad says, 'Come for the view - stay for a brew.') We prefer the view! As for the brew, you can't miss the shining brewery vats right at the entry, across from an enormous aquarium with colorful fish on their own trips.

The scenery is best in daylight, so consider Whaler's for lunch, or an early dinner, especially if the moon is full. The dining room is comfortably informal, arranged in two tiers, with roomy booths along the walls. From tables on the lanai, you can sometimes see whales and more often, a jet approaching Lihue with a new load of eager tourists.

Whaler's offers reasonable prices and generous portions, like excellent seafood chowder ($4.50), piping hot and filled with fish. A large platter of grilled eggplant and cucumber ($7.95) is also tasty, as are oysters or mussels in a sampler plate, including two each of barbecue, teriyaki, and Rockefeller styles. Dinner entrees include fresh fish ($17.95) and NY steak ($17.50), or Whaler's signature twenty-ounce cheeseburger, as well as vegetarian dishes like stir-fry ($15.95). Fresh fish cleanly broiled is the best bet, with the plain sauteed ono and plain grilled ahi much tastier than the version crusted with ground pistachio nuts for $2 more. Vegetable lasagne ($12.95) is unique, the lasagne noodles rolled, stuffed with cheese, spinach, and zucchini, and set on end on the plate. Dinners are attractively served in the comfortable, uncrowded dining room.

*great perch overlooking the ocean*

You'll want to try the home brewed beers, ones with intriguing names as 'Wild Wahine Wheat' ($3) or 'Tropical Guava.' If your beer seems rather light in body, you can choose a bottled 'guest brew.'

Service is friendly, in part because the staff seems to have the enthusiasm of youth rather than the seasoned professionalism of age. Whaler's is a favorite spot for the local wait staff on their off hours, and they have an advantage: they know how to find it at the end of a long winding road through the Marriott's grounds, across bridges and a lagoon. Once upon a time, this restaurant was part of the hotel—the Westin— and in those days you could travel across the lagoon to this cliffside perch on a Venetian launch! Today, it's a pretty drive by car, well worth taking, particularly at mid-day, when you can walk around afterwards, look out at the ocean, and enjoy the breezes. At Whaler's Brew Pub, you'll find well-prepared food, great prices, pleasant service, and an incomparable view. A hard to beat combination!

On grounds of Kauai Marriott, Lihue. Credit cards. Daily lunch & dinner 11 am - 10 pm. Oyster bar till 11 pm. 245-2000. Map 1 www.whalersbrewpub.com

## Vegetarian Ventures

Once upon a time, the best you could do on Kauai for vegetarian food was a salad bar, or in a pinch, some vegetable chow mein. Now that Kauai has entered a health-conscious new age, vegetarian and natural food eateries are opening in almost each major tourist area. *Papaya's Garden Cafe* in the Kauai Village Shopping Center in Kapa'a offers breakfast, lunch, and dinner choices, including Garden Burgers, Tempeh Burgers, grilled fish and chicken teriyaki burgers, vegetarian sandwiches, as well as pasta, lasagna, Greek salads, Oriental flavored rice and stir fry dishes priced from $4 to $8.95. Across the Street is *Ambrose's Natural Foods* for fresh organic produce and foods. Nearby, *Caffe Coco* offers a wide variety of tasty vegetables, vegetarian dishes, including vegan offerings.

*Aloha Kauai Pizza* in Coconut Plantation Marketplace is ready to experiment with cheeseless vegetarian pizzas and sandwiches. In Lihue, try *Kalapaki Beach Hut*'s vegetarian sandwich or salad.

On the north shore in Hanalei's Ching Young Shopping Village, *Hanalei Natural Foods* is vegetarian with a New Age flavor. In addition to packaged foods, you'll find sandwiches and wraps. *Zababaz* specializes in vegetarian take out, while across the street, *Neidie's Salsa & Samba* turns out distinctive vegetable dishes with a Brazilian accent.

In Kilauea, try taro buns at *Roadrunner Cafe* in Kilauea, as well as vegetarian Mexican take-out with homemade tortillas. *Kilauea Farmer's Market* around the corner makes salads and our favorite vegie sandwich on the island. Call ahead (828-1512).

Hungry for fruit? *Banana Joe's* and *Mango Mama's* (Kilauea) *People's Market* (Puhi), and *Pualani's* (Waimea) make fruit smoothies and amazing 'frosties' made from frozen fruits blended smooth.

On the west side, *Hanapepe Cafe* serves vegetarian salads and sandwiches, as well as, occasionally, dinners. At *Wranglers* in Waimea, try great vegetarian sandwiches, pizzas, vegie wraps, & salads.

Pizzerias are also catering to the health food crowd. *Pizza Hanalei* will make pizza with 'tofurella' cheese upon request, and a 'veggie special' pizza on whole wheat as well as white crust. In Kilauea, try *Pau Hana Pizza* for a whole variety of vegetable pizzas with excellent crust. *Brick Oven Pizza* in Hanapepe makes some of the best traditional cheese or 'vegetable' pizza you'll ever find —anywhere! In Koloa, try *Pizzetta's* cheeseless vegetable pizza (742-8841).

Salad bars are coming back! Try them at *Duke's Canoe Club* in Lihue ($9.95), *Brennecke's Beach Broiler* in Poipu ($4.95-$8.50), *The Green Garden* in Hanapepe (sometimes! $5/lunch; $7/dinner), and *Wranglers* in Waimea ($6.95). *Chuck's Steak House* in Hanalei ($8.50/dinner). In Wailua, *The Flying Lobster* ($11/dinner), *The Bull Shed* ($6.95), *Wailua Marina*, *Palm Tree Terrace* ($6.95), and *Pizza Hut*.

Some of our favorite vegetarian meals on Kauai are the vegetable curries, stir fries, and spring rolls at both *Mema* and *King & I*, Taro enchiladas at *Norberto's El Cafe,* the V-ital burrito at *Pony Island Cantina*, vegetarian sandwich at *Kilauea Farmer's Marke*t, and vegetable lasagne at *Cafe Portofino.*

## Cheap Eats & 'Local Grinds'

It still seems odd to see a McDonald's golden arch on this remote island paradise, but in both Lihue and Kapa'a (and inside Wal-Mart!) you can close you eyes as you bite down on a Big Mac and feel like you've never left home! Burger King and Taco Bell keep you in touch with mainstreet, USA; Pizza Hut delivers, and Subways are sprouting all over the island! Some things haven't changed, though. Webvan is still unknown.

Some local restaurants offer swift and tasty alternatives to the national chains for just a small amount more. In Lihue, *Barbecue Inn* (245-2921) has one of the largest, most reasonably-priced lunch and dinner menus on Kauai, and it's air-conditioned! Or try wonderful saimin at *Hamura's* or *Okazu Hale* (245-6554) across from Ace Hardware on Rice St. *Tip Top* (245-2333) is a Kauai tradition for breakfast, also lunch.

In Kapa'a, *Ono Family Restaurant* offers a bargain-priced children's hamburger platter. Best in the Coconut Plantation Marketplace, in Mikey's judgment, is *Aloha Kauai Pizza* with crispy crust and tasty sauce; Jeremy prefers *Fish Hut's* outstanding fresh fish sandwich – his favorite: ahi teriyaki with fresh pineapple (822-1712). *Palm Tree Terrace* (821-1040) cooks up great, inexpensive hot lunches. Try *Wah Kung* (822-0560) in Kinipopo Shopping Village for tasty Chinese food. A favorite family take-out spot on the eastern shore is *Ono Char Burger* (formerly Duane's) in Anahola (822-9181). While service can be pokey, the burgers, french fries, onion rings, and fried chicken will seem worth the wait! Take your order to nearby Anahola Bay and eat on the beach. Near Kalapaki Beach, try *Kalapaki Beach Hut* (246-6330) and decide for yourself whether Steve makes better burgers than Ono Burger in Anahola. Steve's fish sandwich is great, especially if he has fresh ono in his kitchen!

In Kilauea on the north shore, near the Kong Lung Store, *Kilauea Bakery & Pau Hana Pizza* (828-2020) features fragrant breads, rolls, cookies and fresh baked pizza. Great deli sandwiches can be found at *Kilauea Farmer's Market* next door (828-1512), and, at *Roadrunner Cafe & Bakery* (828-8226), tamales, burras, tostadas, enchiladas, sandwiches, salads, and terrific fresh fish tacos.

In Hanalei, try *Hanalei Gourmet* (826-2524) for sandwiches on fresh baked breads and rolls, packed as a picnic lunch. At *Hanalei Wake Up Cafe* (826-5551), sample home-cooked, inexpensive breakfasts and lunches daily and dinners Fri. and Sat. *Subways* turns out sandwiches from inside Big Save, while across the street, *Bubba Burgers* fries up burgers within a reasonably short wait, and *Neidie's* makes wonderful Mexican lunches with a Brazilian accent. At *Pizza Hanalei* (826-9494) the homemade crust is crispy and the cheese and toppings generous. Next door at *Hanalei Health & Natural Foods (826-6990)* you'll find delicious vegetarian sandwiches, and try small plates and wraps at *Zababaz*.

The inexpensive (around $4) 'plate lunch' with' local grinds,' is a Kauai tradition. Try one at Kukui Grove's *Joni-Hana*, at the lunch counters at the *Big Save Markets*, or the *Dairy Queen* in Lihue, where you can get miso soup and a salad with an entree like boiled akule fish that, according to one reader, "has to be tasted to be appreciated." *Kauai Chop Suey* offers a "special plate" ($6.45) which is almost enough to feed two. *Garden Isle Barbecue & Chinese* in Lihue has great plate lunches and saimin to go. On the South shore, don't miss *Taqueria Nortenos* (742-7222) at Kukuiula. *Pizzetta* in Koloa (742-8881) offers free delivery of excellent pizza, as well as inexpensive pastas and calzones. A few miles down the road in Kalaheo you'll find great burgers and chicken at *Camp House Grill,* fabulous pizza and sandwiches at *Brick Oven* (335-8561). *Kalaheo Coffee & Cafe* (322-5868) makes great sandwiches and coffee drinks, while down the road in Ele'ele, try *Grinds* (335-6027) for take-out sandwiches and plate lunches. It may not look like much on the outside, but you're in for a surprise! In Waimea, stop in at *Wrangler's* (338-1218).

## Some Useful Hawaiian Words

*aloha – (a LOW ha) hello,
    good-bye, love,
    kindness, friendship*
*hale – (HAH lee) house*
*haole – (HOW lee) foreigner
    white man*
*heiau – (HEY ow) ancient
    Hawaiian temple*
*hui– (HOO' ee) club or group*
*kahuna– (ka HOO and) an
    elder, wise person*
*kalua– (ka LOO a) to roast
    underground*
*kai – the sea*
*kama'aina – (ka ma EYE and)
    a native*
*kane – (KA neh) man*
*kapu – (KA poo) forbidden,
    keep out*
*keiki – (KAY kee) child*
*kona– (KOH na) leeward side
    of the island*

*lani – (LAH nee) heavens, sky*
*lomilomi – (low me low me)
    massage*
*mahalo – (ma HA lo)
    thank you*
*makai – (ma KAI) ocean side*
*mauka– (MOW ka) towards
    the mountains*
*menehune– Kauai's
    legendary little
    people'' & builders*
*nani – (NA nee) beautiful*
*ohana – (o HA na) family*
*'ono – delicious*
*pali – (PA lee) cliff, precipice*
*paniolo – (pa nee O lo)
    cowboy*
*pau– (pow) finished, done*
*puka – (POO ka) hole*
*wahine – (wa HEE neh)
    woman,wife*
*wikiwiki – hurry up*

*Learn more about Hawaiian language and culture from 'Aunty D' at www.geocities.com/TheTropics/Shores/6794/*

*View from Bali Hai Restaurant*

# North Shore Restaurants
## ʹfavor...eatsʹ

Perched on the ocean bluff, some restaurants in PRINCEVILLE have unforgettable ocean views! From **Bali Hai Restaurant**, you can watch the sun set over Hanalei Bay, and the view from the restaurants at the Princeville Hotel, **La Cascata** and **Cafe Hanalei**, is equally breathtaking. Try **Cafe Hanalei's** breakfast buffet, excellent lunches, or sunset dinners, or come for tea or sunset cocktails at **The Living Room,** the hotel lounge overlooking the bay. The hotel's Italian specialty restaurant, **La Cascata,** combines excellent food with an amazing view. Come early, enjoy the sunset, and bring your camera.

In nearby HANALEI, **Postcards Cafe** takes healthful foods into a whole new dimension. You'll love the pastas and fresh island fish! At **Neidie's Salsa & Samba,** tasty Mexican lunches and dinners have a Brazilian flair and unbelievable prices. A local spot for fresh island fish is the **Hanalei Dolphin,** for both dinner and lunch. **Zelo's Beach House** has reasonably priced breakfasts, lunches, (salads, sandwiches, burgers), and dinners. Try **Sushi & Blues** for fish dinners and excellent sushi.

For inexpensive lunches, try **Bubba Burgers** for hamburgers, and the **Hanalei Gourmet** next door for deli sandwiches. **Old Hanalei Coffee Company** serves sandwiches on fresh-baked breads, and vegetarians can select from salads and sandwiches at **Hanalei Natural Foods** across the street. **Princeville Golf Course Restaurant** has excellent salads and sandwiches in a relaxed setting overlooking the golf course. Pizza lovers can try **Pizza Hanalei's** homemade whole wheat crust. After lunch, try shave ice at **Wishing Well** in the silver trailer near Kayak Kauai.

In nearby Kilauea, **Pau Hana Pizza** serves home-baked pizza with imaginative and delicious flavorings. **Kilauea Farmer's Market** makes first-rate deli sandwiches and vegetarian delights. Just down the street, **Roadrunner Cafe & Bakery** serves delicious breads, rolls, pastries and Mexican treats.

## Bali Hai

Imagine dining as the sunset paints the sky all gold and orange above the magnificent angles of the dark and mysterious mountains, turning the ocean almost purple in Hanalei Bay. Sip a cocktail while the cool evening breeze, fragrant with tropical flowers, touches your skin like silk. At the Bali Hai Restaurant, you can find the Kauai of your imagination, the dream of an island paradise that haunts you in the dead of winter.

The dining experience could not be more relaxing, the food brought at a leisurely pace by polite waiters and served at large, elegantly appointed tables, on china painted in colors of the sea. Open to the air on three sides, the dining room's tall ceilings and two-tiered arrangement of tables make the room spacious and, even when full, remarkably quiet. Tables are angled and set to put each chair in the best position, while a wonderful salt water pool meanders through tropical gardens one level below, so that you can look out at the flowers and palm trees and listen to the sound of waterfalls. As we lingered over coffee to watch a sudden shower fill the air with shining drops, we felt more at peace than when we arrived.

For years, and through many changes in management, Bali Hai has struggled to find a cuisine to equal its view. In its newest incarnation, the menu and chef seems to have found the right niche with an imaginative, yet practical, Pacific Rim cuisine. For example, fresh fish entrees ($25) come in five styles: "Taste of Kauai Rich Forest" (pan seared with shiitake mushroom sauce), "Rock Jumping Fisherman" (Thai style, with coconut sauce), "Black Pot Pulehu" (oriental style), "Bali Hai Sunset" (sauteed with papaya ginger glaze), or "Tropical Breeze" (grilled with fruit salsa). We still prefer the fresh fish plainly grilled, though we enjoyed having

*View from the Bali Hai Restaurant*

these sauces served on the side for a quick dip. Most of the dozen entrees are expensive, like the tasty Lamb chops ($26.50), and are accompanied only by vegetable and 'starch of the day.' Appetizers will drive up the dinner price, though they are appealing, like blackened seared ahi with cabbage and wasabi cream, or crab cakes ($12.75) served with two scoops of mashed Hawaiian sweet potatoes and carrot-cucumber vinaigrette. Both topped 'Hanalei Bay Salad' ($6.50), which was pretty much overwhelmed by its 'hearty combination' of chopped vegetables and dressing. You might prefer to request a plain dinner salad.

Come for lunch and enjoy the view in sunlit splendor! Sandwiches appear with french fries, fruit or cottage cheese, with the turkey club especially generous, or try a fresh looking salad.

Bali Hai has a wonderfully romantic ambiance and unmatched view. Before dinner, head towards the cliff along the sidewalk between the tennis courts. From path's end, you can look down at Hanalei Bay, sparkling with beads of light and turning deep purple as the sun descends. A sailboat cuts silently across the water, the sails filling with the breezes which brush your face and fill your head with the fragrance of evening flowers. The dark craggy edges of the cliffs blend into soft purples and deep blues as the gold and orange sun sinks slowly towards the water, shining more brightly with each second, until flattened into a disk that shrinks to nothing before your eyes. A golden glow remains, burnishing the clouds, polishing the water, then slowly fades to a darkening dusk.

Princeville, Hanalei Bay Resort. Reservations: 826-6522. Credit cards. Smoking section. Breakfast 7 am -11 am. Lunch 11:30 am - 2 pm. Dinner 5:30 -9:30 pm. Children's menu. Enter Princeville at the main gate, take third left onto Liholiho Rd., turn right onto Hono'iki Rd. Map 2

## Bubba Burgers

Bubba's began life on Kauai on main street, Kapaʻa, with the philosophy that a decent hamburger should cost no less than a can of dog food! This idea, and the burger (2.5 oz. of 88% fat-free fresh-ground Kauai beef) caught on, and now Bubba's in Hanalei is equally jammed! Children will like the "frings" (a portion of fries topped with a couple of onion rings), and the burgers are, to quote the teenage connoisseurs, "O.K. — sorta in-between McDonald's and Burger King." It's fast food, sorta cooked to order, and generally predictable. The indoor dining room in the Hanalei branch has a handful of tables; the picnic tables outside lack something when it's raining, and can be hot when it's not. Bubba's in Kapa`a offers free e-mail.

Kapa'a and Hanalei 823-0069. 10:30 am - 6 pm daily. Kapaʻa location closed Sundays. Cash only. Map 1 & 3.

## Cafe Hanalei, Princeville Resort Hotel

You could not imagine a more spectacular spot for breakfast than Cafe Hanalei, with its panoramic view of a bay that in any weather has the romantic beauty of a fairy tale. Even in the rain, you can watch the mountains peek out from veils of mist like shy princesses. Or watch as the sun's sorcery transforms the landscape from smoky greys into blazing colors—vivid greens and golds, brilliant blues, and on the mountains rising majestically above the bay, the shining silver ribbons of waterfalls. In this land of enchantment, each moment reveals a new mystery, and under the spell of such beauty, you could enjoy breakfast with only a chair!

The breakfast buffet will draw you indoors, a generous display of fruits, juices, and fresh baked pastries, blintzes with sour cream, even an omelette bar where your eggs will be whipped into a colorful and tasty creation right before your eyes. While expensive ($22), the breakfast buffet combines an incomparable setting with delicious food and friendly, polite service. Where else could you find such radiance in the rain?

At dinner, the setting sun kindles the sky to flame in orange and turquoise behind the darkening cliffs. Visit the lounge, appropriately called the 'Living Room' first, and enjoy a cocktail while you relax on one of the plush couches in the elegant room, with marble fireplaces and tall shelves filled with books. But who can stay inside at sunset? Outside, the terrace is enclosed by waist high panels of glass, so that you can enjoy the spectacular panorama of Hanalei Bay without a railing to obstruct your view. Boats

*View from the terrace, Princeville Hotel*

glide silently; the only sound is the soft music of the waves. Mountains are shrouded in clouds, and the sky turns to gold as the sun slips slowly into the sea, and colors deepen the reflections in tall glass windowpanes.

As Hanalei Bay recedes into the velvet darkness and the first stars appear, walk downstairs to Cafe Hanalei, where tall windows mirror dozens of dancing candle flames. Tables generously spaced are beautifully laid with damask cloths, elegant china and sparkling crystal and silver.

All this romance is expensive. A dozen entrees, priced above $25, reflect the flavors of the Pacific Rim. Try fresh island mahi mahi steamed with ginger and scallions and served in an oriental steamer basket with vegetables ($28.95), or opakapaka presented like a stir fry, with shiitake mushrooms and Hawaiian sweet potatoes ($28.95). Don't miss appetizers like spinach salad with fresh shrimp and lobster ($14.95), or crispy crab cake ($12). You could almost make a meal of two. Leave room for desserts — pineapple macadamia nut crunch with vanilla ice cream, or a superb lilikoi mousse cake with almond rainbow stripes ($5.95).

At Cafe Hanalei, the presentation is attractive, the service friendly, and under the supervision of Rosemary Caldwell, professional. The best part of a wonderful dining experience remains the setting, which is spectacular enough to make dinner unforgettable. Walk around the hotel afterwards, take the elevator down to the beach and listen to the music of the waves and the melodies in the evening breezes.

Princeville, in The Princeville Hotel. Reservations 826-9644. 6:30 am - 9 pm daily. Sunday Brunch ($31.95) & Friday nite seafood buffet ($41). Children's buffet prices are calculated by age. Credit cards. Enter Princeville's main gate and stay on this road for until it ends at the hotel.

## Chuck's Steak House

People who live on Kauai seem to like Chuck's in Hanalei even though (or perhaps, even because) it looks more like a mainland restaurant than a tropical island hideaway.  When you walk through the door, you could be in Chuck's in West Haven, Connecticut, one of nearly fifty Chuck's which have opened nationwide over the last 25 years.

Prices are reasonable and menu choices extensive.  More than 25 entrees range in price from $16.95 (chicken) to $25.95 (14 oz. prime rib), including children's dinners (teriyaki chicken, hamburger or barbecued ribs) at $8.  Dinners include rice, warm Hanalei taro buns, and the salad bar ($8.95 by itself). Request pacing the dinner, or your entree may arrive when you've barely finished your salad. Wines are fairly priced.

Over the years, we have found dinners at Chuck's to be reliably well-prepared.  New York steak (12 oz. for $25.95) is excellent, tender and juicy with great flavor and no gristle, prepared with teriyaki sauce upon request.  Fresh fish ($19.95) is cleanly sauteed, moist and tasty.

Families might enjoy Chuck's for lunch.  Hamburgers ($5.95) are a third of a pound and delicious.  Our prime rib sandwich was tasty, moist, and served with a sauce that made it come alive.  Club sandwiches are very good, and tuna salad with white meat tuna is first rate.

Lunches and dinners at Chuck's will be reasonably priced and reasonably good.  On the other hand, you don't get anything special either, in food or ambiance.  Chuck's offers no views of Hanalei's magnificent mountains or valleys to paint a memory for dark winter evenings back home.  Its reputation among local people may have something to do with that.  Unlike many of us, who dream of vacationing on Kauai, perhaps they dream of vacationing in West Haven, Connecticut!

Princeville Center, Rt. 56. 826-6211. Non-smoking section.  Credit cards. Hawaiian music. Lunch: 11:30 am- 2:30 pm (M-F). Dinner 6 pm- 10:00 pm daily.  Seniors/children's menus.

## Hanalei Dolphin

For years, the Dolphin has had the reputation of serving the finest fresh fish on the north shore.  Now, however, Dolphin has strong competition in the fish department from Postcards Cafe and Cafe Hanalei, and the drawbacks of its dining experience seem more pronounced.  The menu hasn't changed much over the years, and neither has the no-reservations policy, which can start your meal off with an irritating wait. The fresh fish dinners are expensive, and although service is often friendly, at times it can be harried, as the small restaurant is almost always crowded. If you choose a weeknight and arrive before 7 pm, you have your best shot at a quick seating. If there's a line, you can order wine and appetizers on the porch, and watch painter Mark Daniels at work in his tiny studio. He's great with kids, letting them try a brush stroke or two.

In the softly lit dining room, shutters are raised to let in evening breezes, and lanterns glow pleasantly on polished table tops. The menu features locally caught fresh fish. Depending on the season, you may find opah or moonfish, mon chung, as well the familiar ahi and ono. Two and sometimes three chefs alternate during the week, and so the cooking inevitably varies—sometimes excellent, sometimes needing more (or less!) doneness. On our last visit,  the mahi mahi ($23 for an 8 oz. filet) was moist, tender, and flaky—cleanly broiled, with no taste of the grill. Moonfish, a thick steak, was also right on target. The ahi teriyaki ($26 for an 8 oz. portion) is one of the most delicious fish dinners on Kauai—juicy, tender, and full of spark. Non-fishy eaters can try teriyaki "Hawaiian" chicken ($16.50). Choose rice or hot, crispy steak fries.

Some entrees are priced in a regular as well as a smaller, "menehune" portion at about a 40% discount, and include fresh hot bread as well as Dolphin's signature 'Family Style Salad,' a huge bowl of lettuce, cherry tomatoes, bean sprouts, and choice of oil and vinegar, or creamy garlic or Russian dressings (and you can request seconds). For $14,  you can have a "light dinner" of broccoli casserole or seafood chowder, served with salad, rice or french fries, and bread. Seafood chowder (also  a la carte for $5), is creamy, steamy, full of fish, scallops, clams and potatoes.

The wine list offers good choices  in the $25-$35 range, like Kendall Jackson chardonnay. We were sad to discover that an old friend on the list — the bottle of Chateau Lafitte Rothschild, which had survived Hurricane 'Iwa in 1982 even when the roof did not — hadn't made it through Iniki and was no longer available for $200. Suddenly, we felt older.

You can try Dolphin's fresh fish for lunch— an ono or ahi sandwich , as well as steak burgers, or chicken and vegetable sandwiches. Dine at picnic tables next to the Hanalei River.  And you can stop in at the Dolphin's fish market tucked around the back of the restaurant and take your local catch home to cook.

The Dolphin has been a local favorite for years. The riverside setting can be pleasant, though if mosquitoes tend to pick on you, bring Off and ask for a mosquito coil, for there are no screens.  The fish is usually delicious, though warn the waiter that any overcooked fish will be thrown back, if not into the ocean, at least onto his tray!

Hanalei, on Rt. 560, just past Princeville and the one-lane bridge over the river. No reservations. 11 am-10 pm. 826-6113 Non-smoking. Children's dinners: chicken, steak, or shrimp.

## The Hanalei Gourmet

For years, on our way to the beach at Hanalei, we have wished for a first rate deli where we could buy sandwiches for picnics on the sand. The Hanalei Gourmet in the old Hanalei schoolhouse features home-baked breads and pastries, deli meats and salads, fine cheeses, soups, and a selection of gourmet foods and fine wines. Insulated backpacks are available for picnics. Order a sandwich ($6- $8) at the deli counter (or phone ahead), or take a table in the 'classroom' next door, converted into an attractive cafe *cum* bar for those who would prefer to avoid the sand altogether! In this 'tropical bar,' you'll find a large surprisingly large assortment of entrees ranging in price from $8 to $15. Many cost less than $10, and include pastas, salads, as well as chicken, fish, and steak. Try the 1/3 pound hamburger ($5.95) or fresh ahi sandwich ($8.95).

Hanalei Center. 826-2524. Credit cards. Open 8 am to 10 pm daily. Custom picnic baskets. Live entertainment at dinner. Map 2

## Kilauea Bakery & Pau Hana Pizza

Some of the most imaginative pizzas on Kauai are created at Kilauea Bakery, whose small storefront displays crusty golden breads, cookies, macadamia nut sticky buns, as well as pizza by the slice at the counter. Don't leave without a bag of bread sticks — so popular that they are now distributed all over the island. When you arrive, you may find a pizza of goat cheese, sun dried tomatoes, and eggplant. Or perhaps one made with feta cheese, olives, zucchini, fresh mushrooms, and tomato slices. The crust, either white or whole wheat, will be very thin and crisp, and you'll find six different cheeses, including 'tofurella.'

About a dozen tables surround the counter, and outside, patio tables with umbrellas protect you from the sun as well as the sudden showers that can threaten to dampen your lunch. Service is friendly. You can order a salad of local organically grown lettuces, and sample organically grown coffee drip brewed with filtered water in unbleached filter paper.

Kilauea, Kong Lung Center, on the Lighthouse Road. 828-2020. Open 6:30 am to 9 pm daily except Sundays. Pizza 11 am to 9 pm. Cash only.

## La Cascata, Princeville Resort Hotel

A sunset dinner at La Cascata can be one of your most memorable island experiences. Even arriving at the Princeville Hotel is unforgettable. You drive up around a spectacular fountain, and then walk into an enormous lobby, where all along the western wall, giant windows which appear seamless reveal the spectacular colors of the cliffs beyond Hanalei Bay. In this wonderful spot is a beautiful lounge, called 'The Living Room,' where you can stop off for a glass of wine or a cocktail (or in the afternoons, enjoy afternoon tea and scones). Comfortable sofas invite you to relax and look out over Hanalei Bay, glistening in the sunlight as the colors deepen to rich gold and orange. Lovely melodies played by musicians add to the witchery of the moment.

Walk down one level below the Living Room, and you will find La Cascata, with an equally dramatic and panoramic view of Hanalei Bay. At sunset, you can watch the sky break in brilliant gold and orange waves across the mountains. Bring your camera! Window screens slide open, and you may just capture that unforgettable moment, those matchless colors. The sunset views are more spectacular than the understated decor of the dining room itself, where the soft golden terra cotta color of the walls blends with the quarry tile on the floors to create an informal, comfortable ambiance. Tables widely spaced for privacy are set among arches painted with ivy to resemble an antique Tuscan garden, with picturesque looking chips in the plaster and water stains which are, we suspect, authentic souvenirs of Iniki. Murals provide scenes of Italian landscapes. Candle lamps cast flickering golden light on the tables, dressed with white linen, decorated with tropical flowers in cut glass vases and elegant china, and surrounded with comfortable upholstered armchairs. A singer and guitarist provide pleasant, relaxing  melodies.

Foccacio and rolls arrive with a wonderfully soft extra virgin olive oil, along with balsamic vinegar and a 'salsa' of fresh tomatoes and basil. This will put you in the best frame of mind to consider the menu, which changes monthly as the chef experiments. Because there is no longer a separate kitchen for la Cascata, one chef and one kitchen serve both La Cascata and Cafe Hanalei, so you can order from either menu at either dining room at comparable prices. Try a light and delicately flavored fish soup, or perhaps a salad of arugula, pear, and gorgonzola cheese with walnut vinaigrette ($8.95). Thin crust pizza with fontina, romano cheese, yellow and red tomatoes and fresh basil ($12) is another outstanding choice. At least four fresh pastas are available each day (from $19.95). Cannelloni of roasted duck with wilted greens is delicious, the light, thin

*At sunset, an outrigger canoe glides silently across Hanalei Bay*

crepes filled with slices of duck and fresh tasting vegetables, the sauce light rather than thick ($8.50 or $14). You'll find at least two fresh island fish, perhaps roasted herb red snapper on citrus risotto with stewed tomatoes, zucchini and eggplant ($28) or fresh ahi, beautifully presented on a bed of potato and spinach gnocci ($28.95). A prix fixe dinner ($43.95) includes 3 courses, coffee, cappuccino or espresso.

Service is polite, pleasant, and professional; every effort is made to be attentive to your needs. Do noodles leave your children cold? They may order a cheeseburger or grilled cheese sandwich from the children's menu in Cafe Hanalei. Not sure about a wine selection? You may be offered a taste before choosing from the extensive, and expensive, list.

At La Cascata, the food is not exceptional. But the setting truly is, and taken together, it can make for a magical evening. When planning your dinner, try to set the time for sunset, when the dining experience is gilded with spectacular colors, particularly in summer when the angle of the sun allows it to sink right into the sea before your eyes. After dinner, stroll around the hotel, and take the elevator down to the beach and watch moonlight sparkle on the waves.

In the Princeville Hotel. 826-9644. Reservations recommended. Dinner nightly 6 - 9:30 pm. Non-smoking section. Credit cards. Enter Princeville at main gate and follow this road to the end. Map 2

## Lighthouse Bistro Restaurant

Now that Casa di Amici has moved to Poipu, some of the former staff have taken over the space and opened Lighthouse Bistro in its old location in rural Kilauea, amid sugar cane fields and papaya groves, on the back streets of a former sugar plantation town which still seems closer to Kauai's past than its present. New owner and chef Michael Moore continues the Italian cuisine he helped to develop at Casa di Amici, maintaining the same focus on local ingredients and the informal setting. The grey and white dining room is attractive, with sliding glass doors that open to evening breezes. In the candlelight, the tables, colorful with red ginger blossoms, look romantic, and the spare decor has its own charm.

Like Casa di Amici, Lighthouse Bistro offers pasta, fresh island fish, chicken, and steak. Dinners include soup or salad, an attractive plate of lettuce, tomato, cucumber with home made dressing, like a fruity papaya dijon or a blue cheese chunky with cheese. Seafood bisque is creamy rather than thick, perfectly flavored, and generous with fish and shrimp. A loaf of fresh baked whole wheat bread arrives promptly, and entrees are served with rice and lightly sauteed vegetables at reasonable prices. The wine list is extensive, with many choices under $25. Lighthouse Bistro is rapidly earning a loyal local following, and it's well worth a stop!

Kilauea, Kong Lung Center, on the Lighthouse Road. 11:30 - 2:30 pm and 6-9 pm daily. Children's menu. 828-1555. Credit cards. Map 2

## Neidie's Salsa & Samba

On a back porch in Hanalei, with only a tiny sign out front, you will find a slight young woman, with a long dark braid, cooking in a tiny kitchen just across a counter from a half dozen tables. Don't be fooled by appearances. Neidie makes magic in there, deftly blending Brazilian spices with Kauai's flavorful fresh vegetables and fruits.

You may have to wait for one of the tables, as there are only ten and they are usually full. The reasons is a combination of great food and great prices. Home-made chips and delicious fresh salsa start the meal, but save room for Neidie's delicious Mexican and Brazilian cooking. She weaves Kauai's bountiful fresh fruits, vegetables, and fish into recipes from her homeland. Fresh island fish is cleanly grilled and tasty, with a delicious coconut milk sauce, served on a large platter with Brazilian rice and vegetable—at only $14.95, one of the best bargains on Kauai! Or try a vegetarian pancake with fresh island pumpkin, tropical squash and

*Hanalei Valley's fields of taro*

whatever vegetables have tempted Neidie at the market. (Demand for Neidie's pumpkin pancake has shifted a neighboring farmer into hyperdrive to keep her supplied! ) Service may be on the slow side but for the right reason— Neidie cooks everything to order. Spicing is subtle rather than flashy, so if it's not hot enough for your taste, you can add as many chilies as you want. Prices are amazing considering the generous size of the portions.

For delicious, carefully spiced and imaginative Brazilian dishes served with a pleasant, personal touch, don't miss Neidie's. She loves to cook and takes great pride in her fledgling business, so be sure to stop at the counter and say "hi" to the girl with the long black braid neatly tied.

Hanalei Village. 826-1851. Credit cards. 11am - 3pm; 5 - 9pm daily.

## Postcards Cafe

As you round the last bend in the winding road into Hanalei, you'll see Postcards Cafe in the old green Hanalei Museum. Despite its modest exterior, Postcards surprises you with a carefully crafted dining experience, an interesting, thoughtful cuisine served in a comfortably informal atmosphere. You enter Postcards from a small porch. Inside, you'll find a surprisingly spacious dining room with open beamed ceilings and soft lighting that makes everything look at once clean and relaxing. Vintage

*Catching a wave at Hanalei*

Hawaiian postcards appear under glass table tops and in collages on the walls, along with black and white photographs of old Hanalei, even old-time ukuleles. Dinner is cafe-style informal, the tables without linens, and the plantation style windows, with the modern addition of screens, sliding open for evening breezes, or closed for occasional showers. The cuisine is exceptional, both in concept and execution, and everything is generous and fresh, prepared without meat, poultry, or chemicals. Taro fritters ($9) make a wonderful appetizer, the small patties deep-fried and served with a tangy home-made mango chutney. In salmon rockets ($10), tender slices of salmon are rolled in layers of lumpia and nori and quick fried. Summer rolls ($9) are delicious, as is soup.

The dinner menu is small, only seven entrees featuring local, organically grown vegetables, or fresh island fish. Least expensive are pasta primavera or a Chinese vegetable dish with roasted tofu and a tamari ginger sauce ($15). Fresh ono was cleanly cooked, moist, flavorful and flaky, and although we sampled all four sauces on the menu and enjoyed each unique flavor, particularly the coconut, we preferred the fish cleanly grilled. Of the three pasta choices, two vegetarian, we liked 'Seafood Sorrento,' a combination of shrimp with medallions of all four fresh fish on the menu. It was delicious, gently seasoned in a sauce of mushrooms, tomatoes, bell peppers, and as requested, only light on garlic ($22). The portion was so generous that our son raved about the leftovers the next day! Children can choose pasta or quesadilla ($8). If you can't decide, the kitchen is ready to prepare your request, or you can opt for a beautiful local salad, filling a whole plate, for $8 ($5 for smaller size).

Desserts are elegant. Passion fruit mousse arrives in a lovely colored tumbler, and chocolate cake is amazingly light for its dense chocolate flavor. The wine list is small, though well-selected, and includes some delicious organic wines, or you can try organic smoothies and juices ($5), or organic Kona coffee ($3). Waitpersons are friendly, following the example of the owners who circulate among the guests, stopping to chat and give sound vacation advice to diners whom they treat as guests. Postcards Cafe is a must stop on the north shore for excellent, imaginative cuisine served in an attractive, comfortably informal dining room. If you aren't a vegetarian, Postcards might even change your mind!

Hanalei. 8 am-11 am and 6-9 pm daily. 826-1191. Reservations in advance. Credit cards. Smoke-free.

## Princeville Restaurant

With a spectacular panoramic setting amid mountains, rolling fairways, and ocean, the clubhouse restaurant at the Prince Course is a great spot for a surprisingly inexpensive lunch or breakfast. The entry is all glass, and through enormous windows you can see all the way to the horizon as you walk downstairs, past the glass enclosed health club, to the dining room. The menu is small, offering fewer than a dozen sandwiches and salads priced around $9, but portions are generous and the choices well-prepared. The vegetarian sandwich ($8.75) is stuffed with carrots, lettuce and sprouts, and accompanied by first-rate, crispy french fries. Tangy Chinese chicken salad ($9.50) is full of crunchy vegetables and a tender grilled chicken breast. Ask for homemade papaya seed dressing. Fresh ahi salad is tasty and generous, the fish moist and tender ($8.95). A full bar is available, or choose smoothies and juice mixes ($4.50).

At the Princeville Restaurant, the view is incredible, the servers pleasant, and the portions generous. For the price, it's hard to find a more reasonable slice of ocean on seven grain bread!

Just east of Princeville on Rt. 56. 826-5050. Breakfast and lunch daily. Monday night Japanese sushi and buffet (5:30 - 8:30 pm). Credit cards. Air-conditioned. Non-smoking area. Map 2

## Roadrunner Cafe & Bakery

Under new ownership, Roadrunner Bakery & Cafe turns out excellent Mexican food as well as pastries, pies, cookies, and breads, including wonderful taro buns made with Hanalei grown taro. (Jeremy loves to poke a hole in the top and fill it with honey from the jar on the counter.) Our favorites are 'coconut rolls,' a spiral Danish pastry filled with coconut and baked toasty brown. Order in advance, or come early!

A small dining area adjacent to the bakery features Mexican tacos, tamales, enchiladas, tostadas, and some of the tastiest fresh island fish tacos on Kauai ($8.95/2)! Vegan tacos and vegetarian burras will tempt you, wrapped in tortillas fresh from the bakery, with deft spicing and local ingredients, like purple cabbage and Kilauea eggplant. The white painted dining area is decorated with murals, or your can take your burras out to nearby Kalihiwai Beach. If you like freshly prepared Mexican food with good quality ingredients, Roadrunner is for you!

Kilauea, 2430 Oka St., off Kilauea Rd. Call ahead for take-out. 828-TACO. 7 am - 8:30 pm M-F; until 9 pm on Sat. 8 am - 1 pm Sundays.

## Sushi & Blues

Looking for tasty sushi spiced with a little entertainment? On the second floor of Hanalei's shopping center, you'll find rolls of all kinds, as well as first-rate dinners in generous portions. While cost is high, so is quality, and you'll find some funky local-flavor twists to the rolls. Saki? Choose from dry, white, gold, and silver. The dining room, decorated in music poster art, feels spacious with open ceilings. Two nights a week, enjoy jazz, or come another night and dance. Check schedule in advance.

Hanalei, Ching Young Village. 828-1435. Call for Reservations (6 or more) & entertainment updates. Credit cards.

## Tahiti Nui

Local people have enjoyed Tahiti Nui for years, ever since Louise Marston opened the doors and created its special character as a place where tourists could meet old timers and hear fascinating stories about the island over generous drinks in the bar. Even Tahiti Nui's famous 'family style luau' was not your typical Hawaiian extravaganza, but more like a local talent show, with Louise, her family and large circle of musician friends, providing the entertainment — occasionally even guests! Some evenings, Louise herself would stroll through the dining room singing 'Hanalei Moon' in her own inimitable style, spreading aloha from table to table, and guests would catch themselves grinning at perfect strangers across the room.

But Tahiti Nui never quite stayed the same from visit to visit. We'd pass Tahiti Nui on our way to the beach and note the changes— these had a reassuring rhythm of their own. Lunch would be advertised one day, disappear the next. Chef gone surfing? Probably. (But you expected that one day he would be back!) One time, we would be served complimentary bowls of soup ('Time to make a fresh kettle!') and another time, a salad of leaves you could count. But never, in all our imaginings, did we expect to arrive one day and see a Thai restaurant (Sukothai from Kapa'a) doing business in Tahiti Nui's dining room! We caught that change just as we were going to press with our 15th edition.

Well, once again, we've had to hold the presses to catch up with Tahiti Nui! Gone is Sukothai — Louise is back! Her new menu is intended to offer the best meal for the best price. Fresh island ahi, teriyaki chicken, pasta with vegetables, scampi, steak, and calamari are all priced a dollar or two below the competition, and are served with a salad, rice, and french bread. With $12.95 at the low end (pasta with vegetables) and nothing costing more than $20, Louise offers a real bargain. For about $8, kids can choose hamburger and fries, chicken, fish or pasta. For lunch, Louise has salads, including our favorite fresh ahi salad, and sandwiches, even kalua pig ($5.95-$8.95). We'll catch up with Louise's doings in our next edition, and you can check our web site for updates.

Like an old friend, Tahiti Nui has grown and changed over the years. The friendliness has remained, and serendipity is– always– on the menu!

Hanalei village. 826-6277 for reservations (recommended). Breakfast 7am; Lunch 11am - 2 pm; Dinner 5:30 -10 pm. Luau: Wed. Credit cards.

## Winds of Beamreach

For more than ten years, Beamreach has served some of the north shore's best steak dinners. The menu features pastas, chicken, vegetable dishes ($14.95-$22.95), as well as steaks — an 8 oz. filet mignon ($22.95), and a NY steak ($20.95 for 10 oz. or $23.95 for 13 oz.). Inquire about the restaurant's special discount arrangements with neighboring condominiums. Sunset special menu includes hamburger (8 oz. for $10.95) and fresh fish ($15.95) from 5:30 to 6:30pm.

Dinner begins with white and taro buns and includes soup or salad. Our fresh ono filet was steamed in a Ti leaf; we asked for the sauce served on the side and our reward was a delicious fish, very moist, flaky and tender ($21.95). The Kansas steaks, however, are what make Beamreach special: truly elegant pieces of beef – tasty, juicy, and very tender. Service is efficient and pleasant, with friendly attention to children, and the wine list, though limited, has excellent choices in the mid-$20 range.

Tucked away in Princeville's Pali Ke Kua condominium, the restaurant is pleasant in an understated way, with comfortable chairs and polished wood tables lit cozily with candles, arranged in a two-tiered dining room decorated with original Hawaiian paintings. Regrettably there is no view— the only water you can see is in the apartment swimming pool. But come early for a walk. Cross the parking lot to Pali Ke Kua and enjoy spectacular summertime sunsets before dinner!

In Princeville. Dinner nightly from 5:30 pm. 826-6143 for reservations. Credit cards. Non smoking section.

## Zelo's Beach House

Once upon a time, the old Shell House was a favorite spot for drinking with a little dining. Iniki destroyed all that. Now on the site, Zelo's Beach House has erected snazzy new quarters for dining with a little drinking. The dining room is comfortable, the ceiling open to the rafters, and glass doors open to the outside. The effect is cool California. The dining room shines in cheerful white, with blond wood tables, and behind the counter, Zelo's trademark, a copper espresso machine.

Zelo's has become the in-spot in Hanalei for well-prepared meals at reasonable prices, with most breakfast choices around $8; most lunch items around $6-$9; and most dinner choices around $15 - $20. The lunch menu features Zelo's specialty fish chowder ($3.95/$5.95) thick, creamy and tasty. Hamburgers (from $5.25) are excellent, served on a sesame seed bun with fries, and other choices include wraps, salads, fish tacos, fish 'n chips, and sandwiches. Lunch salads and sandwiches, particularly fresh ahi, are excellent, as are seafood fajitas and fish tacos. Dinners range from pasta ($15) to fresh island fish ($22.95) and include a small salad, vegetable, bread, and rice or baked potato. Entrees are competently prepared, and the truly hungry can order the 'all-you-can-eat' spaghetti for $9.95. Zelo's has a full bar as well as an espresso machine. Of particular note: 'mocha frosted,' a delicious chocolate espresso shake with coffee ice cream ($3.95), and 'Grasshopper Pie,' with mint chocolate chip ice cream in an oreo crust ($4.95).

Service is sometimes friendly and efficient, sometimes not. Given the reasonable prices, it's often crowded. Expect to wait on line if you come at peak mealtimes, so be early if you plan to take the kids!

Hanalei. 826-9700. Open from 7:30 am daily. Entertainment some evenings. Happy hour 3:30-5:30. Non-smoking restaurant. Credit cards. http://mmv.com/zelos. Map 2.

*Thousands of sugar cane tassels wave in the breeze near Koloa. Sugar plantations are closing, however, and tourism is now Kauai's main industry.*

## 'favor..eats'

In Poipu, **Brennecke's Beach Broiler,** with a view of Poipu Beach, remains a local favorite for the best in fresh island fish, with a great salad bar. For a spectacular oceanfront setting, particularly at sunset, try **Beach House Restaurant** near Spouting Horn. **Roy's Poipu Bar & Grill** features the signature Euro/Asian cuisine of Roy Yamaguchi, while next door at **Keoki's,** families and hearty eaters can enjoy generous steak and seafood dinners at reasonable prices. **Piatti** at Plantation Gardens serves Italian cuisine in a romantic garden setting. At **House of Seafood,** you'll find more varieties of fresh fish than at any other restaurant, and at **Casa di Amici,** reasonably priced pastas and dinner selections.

Wherever you dine, be sure to stroll through the beautiful **Hyatt Regency Hotel** afterwards, a treat which can be yours for the modest cost of the tip for the valet who parks your car! Enjoy Hawaiian melodies at the Seaview Lounge overlooking the gardens and ocean, or stop in at Stevenson's Library for an after dinner drink or game of billiards, or simply stroll the hotel's lovely grounds.

On a budget? try Mexican take-out from **Taqueria Nortenos,** Kukui'ula Center, on the road to Poipu. In Poipu Shopping Village, visit **Pataya** for inexpensive and tasty Thai food.

But don't stay in Poipu! Take a short drive to Kalaheo for wonderful, reasonably priced restaurants — **Brick Oven Pizza,** a family favorite for the island's best pizza, or just down the road, **Camp House Grill** for outstanding hamburgers and milk shakes made in a genuine milk shake machine. **Pomodoro,** an intimate, family-owned Italian restaurant, offers food and service you'd expect at much higher prices, and try **Kalaheo Steak House** for steaks, fresh fish, prime rib—one of the best dollar values on Kauai!

# The Beach House Restaurant

A longtime favorite of both residents and visitors, the Beach House once perched on a sea wall only inches from the waves, a great spot to watch the sun set into the ocean and enjoy dinner in a relaxed and casual setting.  In fact, the tables were so close to the waves that when Hurricane 'Iwa struck Kauai in 1982,  the entire restaurant was swept out to sea— leaving only the concrete slab to mark the spot where so many evenings had passed so pleasantly.  Even though rebuilt at a more respectful distance from the waves, Beach House was again destroyed ten years later by Hurricane 'Iniki, and then re-opened once more in the same location, clearly in hopes that the third time is the charm!

For the past few years, Jean Marie Josselin, owner of the popular Pacific Cafe in Kapa'a, has operated Beach House very successfully.  However, just before the new millennium, the building was bought, the lease was lost, and this changeable restaurant changed hands yet again, this time to experienced Maui restauranteurs who wanted a toehold on Kauai's sands. Many of the staff are staying on, including executive chef Linda Yamada who helped to develop the elegant Pacific Rim cuisine which became the restaurant's signature.  In actuality, Jean Marie spent very little time here, and so his departure may have very little effect.

The dining room has certainly benefitted from a facelift! The two tiered room with sweeping ocean views is now more elegantly detailed, with lovely art and table dressings.  Dinner begins with  a basket of oven-fresh breads, and on the appetizer menu, you'll find intriguing choices.  Beach House crab cake is delicious, attractively presented with tomato compote and curry oil ($7.25).  Grilled artichoke is served with potato corn fritters ($7.95) perfect in texture.  Best, in our opinion, is Hoisin beef wontons, served with a delicious Asian guacamole and tasty sweet and sour glaze ($8.95).  A salad of greens from nearby Omao appears with a light sesame and orange vinaigrette ($5.50) Entrees, particularly fresh island fish, are delicious, like grilled fresh ono, both flaky and tender, served with mushroom linguini ($24.95).  The menu also features steak, salmon, and rack of lamb, as well as chicken and seafood, with entree prices more than $20, although two could make a light meal of several appetizers.

The setting is truly lovely. Tables are well-separated, and sliding glass doors open to the evening air and to

*spectacular sunset dining & elegant cuisine!*

spectacular views of surfers catching waves as the sun sets into the shimmering sea. It's lovely even after dark, as the last light of sunset fades, and you can linger over coffee and watch the waves begin to glisten with moonlight. At Beach House, romance is clearly on the menu!

Poipu, on Spouting Horn Road. 742-1424. Reservations recommended, a day in advance. Request a window table, but be prepared to wait for it. Credit cards. Non-smoking section. Dinner 5:30 - 10 pm nightly. Map 3

## Brennecke's Beach Broiler

For more than fifteen years, Brennecke's has been the front runner when it comes to the best reasonably-priced fresh fish dinners on Kauai. It also offers a varied menu, a first-rate salad bar, friendly service, and a memorable dining experience for the whole family.

In this second-storey restaurant across the street from Poipu Beach Park, you'll find the atmosphere informal, so you'll feel comfortable no matter what you're wearing. But the informal ambiance is the result of the meticulous attention to detail which enhances every aspect of the dining experience. The decor, for example, looks very plain — a porch in soft grey and white tones — but everything is spanking clean, the paint shiny and fresh looking, the chairs and grey formica tables immaculate, the flowers in the window boxes bright and cheerful. It's the kind of porch where your child could retrieve a piece of bread from the floor and put it in his mouth and you wouldn't have to look the other way.

The food receives equal attention to detail. Clam chowder ($3.95) is creamy rather than thick, generous with clams, and delicately seasoned. Teriyaki chicken stix ($7.50) are medium rare, tasty, and sizzling hot. In the newest appetizer, tiger eye sushi, fresh ahi is wrapped in rice and nori and quick fried, so that the fish is cool while the wrapper is hot. Dinner entrees include beef, pasta, poultry, even prime rib in three sizes, as well as a host of sandwich baskets and munchies, but fresh island fish is the reason to come to Brennecke's. Your fish, no matter which fin you choose, will be perfectly cooked, crisp on the outside, meltingly moist and delicious inside. The secret to Brennecke's flawless broiling is the grill, designed by owner Bob French and fueled by charcoal of kiawe wood. It burns extremely hot and clean, sealing in juices quickly, leaving no aftertaste.

Even the old standbys, ahi and ono and mahi mahi, are cooked so perfectly that they seem extraordinary. But at Brennecke's you should try out new fins! Opakapaka, or snapper, could not be juicier or tastier. Grouper, or white sea bass, is also sensational, with a texture somewhat like lobster, garnished with homemade tartar sauce. If onaga is on the menu, try it, for Brennecke's prepares it beautifully ($21.95).

*15 years of the best fresh island fish!*

Dinners include rice or herb pasta, sauteed fresh vegetables, and a visit to a first-rate salad bar— fresh, colorful, ripe, and appetizing. Instead of rice, try Brennecke's pasta with your entree, or as a side order ($3.95). Not hungry enough for a full dinner? Brennecke's offers more than a dozen reasonably-priced options, including a huge platter of nachos ($7.95), burgers ($8.50) including a vegetarian variant, as well as several sandwich baskets, like an excellent chicken sandwich, cleanly grilled and served on a soft bun. Vegetarians will enjoy kiawe broiled seasonal vegetables ($16.25), or a delicious fresh fish sandwich ($10.50). Or stick with the salad bar ($8.50/multi-trip or $4.95/single visit) and add a cup of seafood chowder ($2.95).

The wine list is small and fairly priced, with a Kendall Jackson chardonnay at $23.95. The 'under-12's' have a great menu, with pizza ($7.95), spaghetti or burger/fries ($3.95), fish & rice ($5.95) or soup & salad ($3.95). They can have chocolate milk ($1.25) or a grown-up looking fruit punch ($1.50). Kid's burgers, chicken, and fish are very successful, judging from the enthusiasm of six youngsters seated nearby. You can order coffee in a special Brennecke's souvenir cup.

For the best in fresh fish, beautifully broiled and attractively served, it's hard to find a better spot than Brennecke's. The staff is friendly and professional, the dining comfortable and open to evening breezes. It may be noisy when full, but it's busy for all the right reasons. Since 1983, Brennecke's has been one of the most popular restaurants on the south shore. Be sure to phone ahead for a reservation if you don't want to stand in line, and you might check the fresh fish on the menu and reserve a portion of your favorite fin in advance!

Poipu, on Ho'one Rd. 742-7588 for the daily fish report & reservations (necessary). Credit cards. 11 am - 10 pm daily. wwwbrenneckes.com for those wonderful tee-shirts, Nukomoi surf wear, and the surf report!

## Brick Oven Pizza

Ask just about any Kauai resident where to find the best pizza, and you'll probably hear, 'Brick Oven.' We agree! This family-owned operation in Kalaheo has been one of our most popular stops. And we're not alone, for tourists, as well as local families, have made Brick Oven a favorite for years. The cheerful dining room has red–checked tablecloths and murals of pizza serendipity — a pizza shaped like the island of Kauai, for example, with "Garlic Grotto," "Mushroom Valley," "Grand Pizza Canyon," and "Port Anchovy." Friendliness is in the air.

*the best pizza on Kauai!*

But good as all this is, the pizza is even better, as fine as you'll discover anywhere. The homemade dough—either white or whole wheat—is delicious, crunchy without being dry and with a fluted crust like a pie, shiny with garlic butter. The sauce, in the words of the teenage judges, has "awesome spice, cooked just right." There is lots of cheese, the Italian sausage is made right in the kitchen, and tomatoes are red, juicy and fresh. Portions are generous and quality unbeatable. A family size (15 inch) starts at $18.35, but you may be tempted to try one of the outrageous special creations described on the menu, like the 'super.' Or consider a delicious sandwich on fresh baked roll, or a salad ($3 to $6). You can wash it all down with ice cold beer ($4.75 for 1/2 pitcher) or soda ($3.15/ pitcher). A nice touch - the ice comes in the glasses, not in the pitcher. Kids will love to watch the dough spin into pizza during that hard, hungry time of waiting, especially at peak hours when it's jammed.

At Brick Oven, you'll find a smile and pleasant word for short persons no matter how cranky. When one child spilled coke, our waitress not only wiped her dry but brought her a new glass filled to the very brim! Each child can ask for a ball of pizza dough, which feels so good in the hands that it usually manages to stay out of the hair—all the way home.

Kalaheo, on Rt. 50. 11 am - 10 pm. Closed Mondays. Smoke-free. Credit cards. 332-8561.  Map 4

## Camp House Grill

Who would think to look for one of Kauai's best hamburgers in the tiny town of Kalaheo (already sufficiently blessed, one would think, with

the island's best pizza)? It's worth the drive to the 'original' Camp House to try a hamburger, 1/3 pound of ground chuck, served in a basket with a pile of some of the hottest, crispiest french fries you have ever tasted, and amazingly priced at $3.95. New Camp House Grills have opened in Wailua and Hanapepe, but there's something special about this one.

If you were able to find Kalaheo, a tiny blip on the line of Rt. 50 going west from Poipu, you would probably decide Camp House Grill looks too much like a greasy spoon, and drive right on by — that is, until you glanced at the parking lot — which is packed — or peeked in at the dining room — which is full. Once you're inside, you'll be pleasantly surprised by the crisp, clean decor: the woodgrain formica tables well-spaced, the blue window frames a nice contrast with whitewashed walls, and even the green plants looking healthy and well-fed. A cheerful waitress will seat you with a smile, no matter how much sand you bring in from the beach, or whether everyone in your party has managed to come up with an even number of shoes.

Though you cut some corners for such reasonable prices, paper placemats and napkins — even paper cups — are a small price to pay for such tasty food and pleasant service. And the placemats with a drawing of a sugar plantation 'camp house' give hungry kids an opportunity to color, crayons courtesy of management. Another generous touch: sodas are served in a "bottomless cup" for $1.50, and the drinks are served immediately and refilled cheerfully. Better yet, try a milk shake ($3) which you can see (and hear) being made fresh at the gleaming silver fountain machine. No soft ice cream made pasty with thickener, Camp House Grill's shake has the genuine texture of ice cream mixed with milk. Camp House Grill makes kids feel welcome. Ten-and-unders can eat a "mene-hune special" cheeseburger or hot dog for only $2.75, while bigger little people can choose quarter pound burgers, fish, hot dogs, and four types of chicken breast sandwiches from $4.95.

Everything is cooked to order, so you might have to wait a bit, but it will all seem worth while once you start eating. Waimea Burger ($4.95), a barbecue cheeseburger, is perfectly cooked medium–rare with tangy sauce and great cheese. In a Hanapepe Burger, broiled pineapple and teriyaki sauce make an ideal complement to the beef, Swiss cheese, lettuce, and tomato. Deep fried chicken ($7.95) comes to you hot, golden brown, and moist inside, a sure crowd-pleaser, more so than the barbecue 'Huli' chicken ($7.95/half) which is on the spicy side. To cool it all off, you can have draft beer, available by the glass, or pitcher for $4.95. Note:

there is a different chef on the dinner shift, so consistency varies. Steak, ribs, or chicken dinners include soup or salad, potato or rice from $7.95.
Camp House Grill is cheerful and sincere. What you see is what you get—and then some extras, including wonderful home-baked pies — in many flavors! A deer head and a stuffed rooster look out through the window at what is passing by on Rt. 50. Don't let that be you!

Kalaheo, on Rt. 50. 332-9755 for take-out orders. No non-smoking

section, but tables by a breezy window serve the purpose. Daily 6:30 am- 9 pm. Breakfast special till 8 am. Map 3

# Casa di Amici

Casa di Amici has moved to Poipu from Kilauea, where chef-owner Randall Yates had acquired a loyal local clientele. Now a property owner, not simply a tenant, he has refurbished a space that was once called Cantina Flamingo, and before that the Aquarium, so named for the enormous aquarium which divided dining from bar, whose fish population rose and fell with the restaurant's fortunes. The aquarium is still there, the fish are thriving, and Casa di Amici has updated the dining room to make it both more spacious and intimate. Tables are well-separated and set with shining candle lamps, and sliding glass doors open to evening breezes.

Many of the entrees that were popular at the Kilauea location are still on Casa di Amici's Poipu menu, including house specialities like 'Tournedos Rossini,' with medallions of beef, and pate de foie gras and fluted mushroom caps ($24). Most choices are priced in full or 'light' portions, and include veal and poultry, fresh fish, a wide range of pastas, and some vegetable dishes. Prices range from $17 for chicken or eggplant casserole, to $27 for fennel crusted lamb loin. The chef enjoys experimenting with flavors, and although sometimes you might wish that he had a lighter touch with garlic, on the whole his combinations of spices and sauces add zest and interest to his creations.

Of the variety of appetizers on the menu, the onion soup ($6) is rich and flavorful, topped with toasted bread and melted cheese. Salad of local greens is heaped with lettuces, perfectly flavored with a sesame ginger vinaigrette ($8).  Lasagne fills a large bowl,  layered with grilled eggplant and zucchini, ground sirloin, and spicy sausage ($19).  Fresh ahi ($23 for the 9 oz. portion) was cleanly grilled and tender, served on linguini with a sauce flavored with dill and 'scent of lobster' (as well as, though not advertised on the menu, a generous scent of garlic). The sauce was so intense that we were relieved to have asked for it on the side.

Everyone is friendly, as is appropriate in a restaurant which calls itself Casa di Amici, from the hostess to the valets who ask you how you enjoyed your dinner and remind you to drive safely.  This helps make to make dining at Casa di Amici an enjoyable experience, where you can enjoy your dinner with a good bottle of wine in the $20 range.  Of the more expensive choices, a 1995 Swanson merlot was fairly priced at $40 (compared with $55 at Roy's).  If you choose not to give $4 to the valet (on Kauai!) simply turn around at the small lot and go back the way you came in, and try your luck at finding a spot on the street.

Poipu, 2301 Nalo Rd.  Reservations necessary 742-1555. Dinner nightly. Credit cards.

## Dondero's, Hyatt Regency Hotel

Decorated in vibrant green and white, Dondero's is an elegant restaurant, designed to capture the more leisurely pace of the 1920's before jet-set timetables pushed life into permanent fast-forward. Dondero's dining room is attractively arranged on two levels, with tables comfortably spaced for privacy.  Gracefully twining ivy vines painted on the walls complement the pattern of jade green and white tiles, some designed with seashells, so that the room seems poised on the edge of a seaside garden, with large windows and french doors opening to the terrace. During summer months, the colors of the setting sun make terrace dining beautiful.  Tables set with china and silver are softly lit by crystal lamps with pleated shades, a golden glow in shades of darkness.

More than a dozen a la carte entrees range in price from $24 to $28 (Cioppino), as well as pastas from $16.50.  As some appetizers and entrees are generous enough for two, you may choose to share, and your waiter may even serve them in individual portions.  For appetizers, try porcini mushroom crepes, with fontina and parmesan cream sauce ($8.75), and balance this substantial dish with a shared salad of island greens and portobello mushrooms, tomatoes, goat cheese and lemon vinaigrette ($7.25). Or try salad of fresh spinach, lettuce and sundried tomatoes and peppers ($8). Fresh fish, a local swordfish, is perfectly cooked ($27.50), moist and tender. We also chose a dinner portion of a dish on the appetizer menu, homemade triangle pasta with shrimp, asparagus, tomatoes, shiitake mushrooms, lemon butter sauce ($11.50/$23 dinner portion). Chicken breast stuffed with mushrooms, rice and spinach was tasty though somewhat dry. The Hyatt wine list is expensive, with most of the more the fifty selections priced above $30, including a 'Captain's List' with *Wine Spectator* ratings, so you might consider one of the 14 vintage wines available by the glass. You'll love the desserts—chocolate mousse, outstanding tiramisu, and strawberry flambeau with vanilla ice cream.

At Dondero's, prices are expensive— even if you share an entree and appetizer as we did, the cost per person will be at least $30— but the hotel comes with the meal! Consider your dinner as a single course in your entire evening. For an aperitif, walk around the lovely hotel and listen to Hawaiian music in the Seaview Lounge. After dinner, stroll the beautifully lit gardens and enjoy the breezes of the evening.

Poipu, Hyatt Regency Hotel. Reservations a must: 742-6260. Credit cards. Non-smoking section. Free valet parking. Children's menu. Map 3

## House of Seafood

For more than ten years, House of Seafood in the Poipu Kai Resort has specialized in a variety of fresh fish imaginatively prepared, as the owner is on excellent terms with local fishermen — a big advantage in winter months when the surf can get very rough for the fishing boats.

These fresh fish filets will not be simply grilled and sprinkled with paprika, but presented in imaginative preparations, like fresh sea bass cooked in parchment, fresh mahi mahi sauteed with macadamia nuts, fresh snappers of every hue, even shark! Try sauteed fresh mahi mahi served with orange and cashew sauce, or the more pungent fresh ehu. Sea bass may be served with a delicious combination of teriyaki, orange, and miso sauce on a bed of soft noodles, or sometimes with a curry sauce that is too strong for its delicate flavor. If you're not sure you'll like the sauce on your fish, ask to have it served on the side, and request the chef's special tartar sauce with fresh pineapple.

Entrees (about $25) are accompanied by fresh rolls, vegetables, and delicious herbed wild rice. If you add soup, salad, or appetizers, the cost per person goes up rather quickly. The dinner salad ($4.50) is an attractive mix of leaf lettuces, enoki mushrooms, water cress and tomatoes, with fanciful dressings like 'passion fruit vinaigrette' or 'guava-basil,' a tropical alternative to 'thousand island.' Chowder with taro leaves ($4.50) is generous with fresh fish and clams. Vegetables are fresh, carefully

cooked and attractively served.
Service is polite and friendly, and you get the feeling that the staffers genuinely enjoy their jobs.

You can spend a lovely evening in the comfortable, quiet dining room. Tables are well-spaced for privacy, many near a window, and are attractively set with white cloths and shining silver and glassware. Wines are well-selected though above $30. Children can choose from

*Nature's disposable container*

hamburger, fresh fish and grilled cheese, served with rice or french fries, vegetable, dessert and drink ($7.50-$9.50).

You may spend more than you would at other seafood restaurants, but in exchange you get a wider variety of fresh fish and an imaginative range of preparations. You also get a quiet dining experience, especially pleasant if you come on a night with a moon. The dining room is open to the night air, and from the darkened room lit by the soft light of candles, you can watch the last light of evening fade, the pattern of darkness changing with each moment. As stars twinkle through thin filmy clouds, the full moon glows in the deep blue sky, while soft breezes rustle through the hibiscus leaves and crickets sing themselves to sleep.

Poipu, in Poipu Kai Resort. 742-6433. Reservations suggested. Credit Cards. Dinner nightly 5:30 pm - 9:30 pm. Non-smoking section. Map 3

## Kalaheo Coffee Company

When you walk into this tiny eaterie on the main street of Kalaheo, you notice the fragrance. Sample specialty coffees grown on Kauai while you wait for your sandwich! At the first rate deli, you'll find sandwiches, salads, and cold and hot plates prepared with high quality ingredients. Try a ham and avocado sandwich with fresh vegetables on whole grain bread. Don't miss the grilled vegetable sandwich (eggplant, zucchini, and lettuce and tomato) memorable for its unique spice and flavors. On the children's menu, you'll find grilled cheese or PBJ ($3.50).

For a beach picnic, call ahead to save waiting time, for a lot of local people like the place too. You can also buy Kauai coffee to take home.

Kalaheo, Rt. 50 at the traffic light.  6 am - 4 pm (M-F); 6:30 to 4 pm (Sat.); 7 am - 2 pm (Sun.) 332-5858 or 800-255-0137 www.kalaheo.com

## Kalaheo Steak House

For more than five years, the Kalaheo Steak House has been serving some of the best, most reasonably-priced steaks on Kauai. The cozy, knotty-pine interior is both pleasant and informal, with comfortable booths along the wall and roomy tables set with fresh flowers and candles.

The restaurant prides itself on the finest of ingredients. Steaks are top-grade Midwestern beef. Bread is baked each day at the bakery across the street. Even the dinner salad is exceptionally attractive, served on a lovely glass plate with ripe tomatoes, white beans and red onions. Choose between a delicious papaya seed dressing, or as a special treat for cheese lovers, a blue cheese dressing made with the genuine article crumbled in a delicious vinaigrette and topped with fresh ground pepper.

The menu offers steaks, seafood, and poultry dinners which include rice or baked potato as well as salad. Our waitress recommended the New York steak ($18.95) and the fresh island opah (10 oz. for $19.95), and we were pleased with both. The generous portion of opah was flaky and tender, though you might have the butter sauce served on the side, unless you love garlic. When the steak arrived too well done to be 'medium rare,' the replacement was even larger, perfectly cooked, and accompanied by a second baked potato–well worth the wait! Prime rib ($18/12 oz. or $24/24 oz.), was both tender and tasty. Entrees are cooked with little salt, a nice feature. Service is friendly and efficient, and prices are extremely reasonable, with teriyaki chicken ($13.95) at the low end of the entrees. You can also choose a 'refillable salad plate' ($6.95).

Kalaheo Steak House offers one of the best values on Kauai, as two can dine in style for less than $50, including one of the 14 nicely selected wines on the almost unbelievably reasonable wine list. An excellent alternative to higher-priced Poipu restaurants, it's well worth the drive!

Kalaheo, 4444 Papalini Road. 332-9780. Credit Cards. A smoke-free restaurant. Dinner nightly 6 pm - 10 pm. No reservations. Map 3

*On Kauai, poinsettia bloom along the road, and glisten in rain showers.*

## Keoki's Paradise

At Keoki's you might feel as if you've wandered onto the set of
Gilligan's island.  Tables arranged on several levels surround a wandering
stream, where taro grows among lava rocks, and a frog or two rest among
the lily pads.  Tropical plants grow everywhere, and the night is filled
with the sound of crickets.  Wooden tables are roomy and rattan chairs
comfortably upholstered.  Ask to be seated outside, where dining is cooled
by evening breezes and you can watch the light of evening fade and the
sky turn luminous with shining stars.  Should a passing shower threaten to
douse the table, waiters will quickly set up the awnings!

One of the most successful restaurants on the south shore, Keoki's
offers reasonable prices as well as an atmosphere of South Pacific chic.  In
busy times, lines of hungry diners begin to form at about 7 pm, so even
with a reservation, don't be surprised to see company when you arrive!

To the right of the entrance is a bar and lounge, where you can eat pu
pus, nachos, burgers, Mexican specialties from $6.95, and local style
plates like BBQ chicken at $9.95.  Come early and  sit at one of the half
dozen tables near the bar and you can put together an inexpensive dinner.
Keoki's main dining room features a reasonably-priced, extensive menu

*Heliconia Parrot's Beak*

offering fresh fish, chicken, steak as well as a huge 28 oz. portion of prime rib ($23.95) aptly named 'the Flintstone Cut' and available only "while it lasts." Entrees include salad, rice, and fresh bread. Many cost about $12, though you can spend less for a burger ($8.95) — without fries, of course! Children's full dinners are reasonable, $4.50 for a hamburger or $5.95 for chicken.

For appetizers, try 'summer rolls,' ($6.95), a sushi roll with crab, vegetables and avocado with a spicy Thai dipping sauce that is also delicious with fish entrees, so be sure to ask for some extra on the side. Some may find the fish chowder ($3.95) overly thick and salty. Dinners include homemade bran muffins and salad, a sharply seasoned Caesar salad with too much cheese, too many croutons, and the limpness of bulk preparation. You might try asking for romaine lettuce, oil and vinegar!

Fresh fish ($19.95-$23.95) can be ordered in 5 preparations, including 'simply healthy,' cleanly grilled with no butter or oil and served simply with pineapple salsa. This is the preparation of choice, as we have found the sauces and marinades to be of varying quality, like the strongly flavored wine and caper sauce which overwhelmed the fresh ono and should have been left on the side (or in the kitchen!). Fresh–baked opakapaka, on the other hand, was moist, generous, and fragrant with basil which complemented its flavor. Prime rib is moist and tender though a bit bland, although its appearance, at 28 oz., was a show stopper. You might prefer teriyaki sirloin ($15.95) or Bali chicken, served with light lemon shoyu sauce. You can also order a half-pound cheeseburger ($8.95). Entrees are accompanied by an adequate herb rice and vegetables, or you can have baked potato ($2.50), though only one of our order arrived in time for dinner! The small wine list offers a nice selection of California wines mostly in the $20 range. Try hula pie ($4.95)—oreo crust with macadamia nut ice cream and chocolate sauce.

Keoki's attracts a large clientele because of reasonable prices and generous portions. Service is friendly, though geared to the masses, so you may have to stand up to catch your waitperson's attention. Be prepared to enjoy what comes your way rather than trying to customize your order or change the way the kitchen prepares it. Don't expect the kitchen to excel in subtle seasoning, and stick to simple dishes. You really can't go wrong with all that prime rib! And you can enjoy live music Thursday and Friday nights, and Sunday afternoons.

Poipu Shopping Village. 742-7534 Reservations a must. Credit cards. Cafe menu from 11 am;  Dinner 5:30-10 pm nightly. Taco bar 4:30-midnight. Children's menu $4.50 - $5.95.

## Naniwa

Naniwa, the Japanese restaurant in the Sheraton Poipu Resort, won't whisk you away to an exotic world.  The cuisine might be Japanese, but the restaurant was designed for western clientele, so you won't have to remove your shoes upon entering, and you won't be sitting on the floor.

Naniwa's dining room is spare, with wood tones and black harmonizing into a relaxing atmosphere for well prepared entrees, which can be ordered either a la carte ($16-$20) or as complete dinners including rice, Japanese pickled vegetables and a delicately flavored miso soup ($23-$27). Beautiful sushi is prepared by the chef at net speed, though the table-side dining which was a picturesque feature of Naniwa before 'Iniki struck and destroyed the hotel, is gone now, only a memory.  Today's menu features chicken, seafood, striploin, tempura and noodle entrees.

The dining room is comfortable, though you may find it noisier than you'd like because, though attractive, it is rather small and can feel crowded.  You will eat on paper place mats with disposable chopsticks, and though the restaurant overlooks a lovely garden and lagoon, most windows do not open to evening breezes.  The wine list is small and so undistinguished that Japanese beer may be your best bet.

Sherator Kauai Resort, Poipu.  5:30-9:30 pm.  742-1661.  Credit cards.

## Pattaya Thai Cuisine

At Pattaya, everything looks clean, from the shiny wood tables to the gleaming tile floor.  It looks more like a dining room outdoors, bordered with leafy green plants, than an outdoor restaurant. The owner, Mr. Mee, will greet you pleasantly and help you order some of Pattaya's delicious Thai cuisine. Vegetarian spring rolls ($6.95) arrive crispy and hot. Ginger-coconut soup ($8.95) is delicately flavored and light, generous with chicken and the kaffir lime leaves which make the dish special. 'Evil Jungle Prince,' a coconut flavored curry dish served with chicken or fish, is filled with vegetables ($9.95). Eggplant with tofu appears in a tangy and flavorful brown sauce, and delicious curries cost only $9.95. Vegetables are carefully cooked and attractively served, and the sticky rice ($2.25) is first rate. Try a bowl of brown rice ($1.95) with some peanut sweet and sour sauce!

An offshoot of the very successful Mema's Thai Cuisine in Wailua, Pattaya offers a very pleasant evening at a very reasonable price.

Poipu, Poipu Shopping Village. 742-8818. Credit cards. Lunch: 11:30 am - 2:30 pm. (M-Sat). Dinner: 5 pm - 9:30 pm nightly.

## Piatti at Plantation Gardens

For more than 20 years, the lovely Moir Gardens have provided an especially romantic setting for a restaurant—a beautiful old plantation home, where you can dine outside on a veranda cooled by evening breezes fragrant with tropical flowers, and see water lilies glow in moonlit ponds like night-blooming stars.

Piatti is the newest resident of the old plantation home and by far the most elegant. China and crystal sparkle in candlelight on crisp linen

cloths. At the same time, the decor is understated, so that the gardens, lit with subtlety and flair, draw the eye outside to a landscape brushed with shades of darkness. The dining room glows softly yellow and pink in the evening, like a plumeria blossom. At Piatti, romance is on the menu!

*Water lilies bloom at night in Moir Gardens.*

The newest link in a chain of successful west coast Italian restaurants, Piatti brings to Kauai an Italian cuisine with a touch of nouvelle California, and incorporates island flavors. Fresh vegetables abound, sauces are light, pasta fresh, spicing judicious. Herbs, spices, greens, even eggplant, are grown in the restaurant's gardens. Crusty bread still warm from Piatti's brick pizza oven arrives immediately, along with a dish of signature garlic and basil olive oil pesto which your server will invert, with a flourish, onto a serving plate. Purists might prefer the extra virgin olive oil as a more subdued complement to Piatti's foccacio baked with fresh mushrooms. The wine list offers the best as well as some of the lesser known California vintners; for connoisseurs, there's a reserve list.

You'll find home-baked pizzas and fresh pastas from $12.95, more than a dozen salads and antipasti from $6, and entrees ranging from lamb, veal, beef, pork, to chicken and seafood ($14.95 - $27.95). Vegetarians will enjoy the variety of fresh vegetables (from $3.50) which can be ordered as a platter ($11.95). Appetizers are inventive, for example 'porcupine shrimp' wrapped in crispy, thin fried noodles, crunchy and very tender ($9.95). 'Mista salad' of fresh island greens is generous as well as crisply fresh ($8.95), or try Caesar salad, which can be ordered in a single serving ($5.95). White bean soup is tasty ($4.95).

Entrees are artfully arranged and on the whole well-prepared. Many feature Kauai specialties. Fresh island snapper is both flaky and tasty, though if you prefer the pure taste of fish, you might order the sauce served on the side ($23.95). Fresh ahi is moist and tasty. The cuisine emphasizes island tastes, like poi potatoes, or homemade pappardelle pasta with shrimp and home-grown arugula ($18.95).

If you are looking for a romantic dinner, Piatti is a good choice. The setting, almost more than the menu, is the centerpiece of the meal. Dine on the veranda, or if you prefer a more informal experience, on the porch near the bar, where you can see the gardens glimmering in candle light.

In Kiahuna Resort, Poipu. 742-2216. Request veranda. Credit cards. 5 pm- 10 pm daily. Lounge from 3 pm. Take-out orders, FAX 742-2216.

## Poipu Bay Clubhouse,

With its comfortable air-conditioned dining room and spectacular views, Poipu Bay Golf Course Clubhouse Restaurant has gone through several transformations trying to define its relationship with the Hyatt Hotel. At one time it was a Chinese restaurant with a huge tank holding jet set lobsters. At another time, it presented a terrific soup, sandwich, and salad bar for self-serve, speedy lunches. Now, the Clubhouse restaurant has finally been absorbed into the Hyatt Resort and offers the Hyatt cuisine and hotel prices. You can still look out over the rolling green fairways of the Poipu Bay Golf Course, studded with palm trees. You can still see sand dunes and the ocean waves smashing against the rocky cliffs in bursts of brilliant spray. But gone is one of the best food values on Kauai, the soup-salad-sandwich bar. Now you'll pay high prices and, if the dining room is crowded, wait a long time for rather pedestrian food, especially irritating if you want to get to the beach!

The lunch menu offers a variety of sandwiches, including a half-pound hamburger served plain ($6.50) or with sauteed fresh mushrooms melted cheddar cheese. ($7.50). The fresh fish sandwich ($9.50) is tasty if on the small side, and you have to request teriyaki sauce and pay extra for the pineapple ($1.50) that gives it flair.

Servers are pleasant, tables are spacious and comfortable, and you can't beat the view. But it's just not the same, when, in place of the sandwich and salad bar, you have two billiard tables and a video game!

Poipu, adjacent to Hyatt Regency Hotel. 742-1515. Breakfast 7 am - 11 am. Lunch 11 am - 5:30. Credit cards. Non-smoking section. Map 4

## Pomodoro

Once upon a time, two hardworking brothers from Italy arrived on Kauai via New York City, where one found a wife, and opened the island's first Italian restaurant. Over the years, as Casa Italiana grew into a successful restaurant, they imported the island's first pasta machine from Italy. As time went by, other restaurants, including the specialty restaurants in the big hotels, began to order their pasta, and so they sold Casa Italiana and became full-time purveyors of fine noodle creations.

But long hours with eggs and flour were just not as interesting as working with people. A true New Yorker, Gerry missed all those midnight hours in the restaurant, the seven-day workweeks, the temperamental customers and frazzled servers. So the family sold the pasta company and opened Pomodoro Restaurant, and Gerry is once more in her element, bustling from table to table keeping her diners happy.

*great pasta in a friendly setting!*

Pomodoro is both attractive and small, with only ten tables, all of which may be occupied when you arrive. The main dining room, filled with leafy green plants, is clean, comfortable, and informal; a second room accommodates small parties. Everything is prepared to order, and prices are reasonable, with pastas from $9.50, and the most expensive dishes, the veal specialties, at $17.95. If you add a salad or soup, both of which are a la carte, the price goes up by about $4. Children can eat spaghetti for $5.95 or ravioli for $6.95, as well as small portions of selected entrees.

What comes to the table is fresh, light, and tasty. Dinner begins with homemade foccacio served with extra virgin olive oil and balsamic vinegar instead of butter, a sign of the healthful times. Salad of mixed greens ($3.25) looks beautiful with purple and green spinach as well as various fresh organic lettuces. Minestrone ($3.50) arrives in a large bowl generous with noodles, beans, and still crunchy vegetables. Pomodoro's sauces are light and flavorful without being overpowering, for example in pasta primavera, where the vegetable broth perfectly complements the fresh zucchini, carrots, tomatoes, green onions. Traditional pastas are more robust, like delicious manicotti, thin crepes generously stuffed with cheeses, or cannelloni, stuffed with meat and spinach ($13.95). Or try ravioli ($9.95) filled with ground beef or ricotta cheese, and even served with tasty meatballs ($11.50), or a delicious lasagne ($13.95). There's no fresh fish on the regular menu, but you'll find first rate meatless choices like chicken cacciatore ($16.95), a skinless breast, and eggplant parmiagiana, an enormous platter ($16.95). Children can choose spaghetti ($5.95) or ravioli ($6.95). You'll find a full bar (try an excellent chi chi) as well as a variety of wines with some excellent choices in the mid $20 range.

At Pomodoro, two can enjoy a first rate dinner for a remarkably small price, about $40. For excellent Italian cuisine and service at modest prices, Pomodoro is well worth the short drive from Poipu to Kalaheo.

Kalaheo, Rainbow Shopping Center. 332-5945. Children's menu (under 12). Credit cards. Dinner nightly. Non-smoking section. Map 3

## Roy's Poipu Bar & Grill

Roy's is 'dining theater' at its best! From the time you arrive (and you'll probably have to wait, even with a reservation), you're part of a performance. No matter where you stand, you'll feel like you're in the action, as waiters whoosh by, leaning like skiers into the turns in the pathways between tables, steaming plates in hand, perhaps even an inverted chair. Given Roy's long, narrow layout (it occupies converted souvenir stores along one arm of the Kiahuna Shopping Center), each step, each turn counts, as servers maneuver through an obstacle course of patrons and supply stations. You wonder if there should be a traffic light—or at least a stop sign!

The kitchen takes up a long slice of the restaurant, or it could be equally accurate to say that the dining room takes up a long slice of the kitchen. For at Roy's, the cookery is the main act, and the kitchen is center stage, just behind a wall of glass from the nearest tables. So the best seats in the house are only inches away from the gleaming chrome and tile workspace, where chefs and servers hustle and bustle as if performing in a silent movie starring Charlie Chaplin. Watch one chef weigh pizza dough on a small scale, spin it expertly into a crust and pop it into the tiled oven, while another adorns plates with colorful greens and vegetables, and a third flames pasta dishes in seeming defiance of fire safety rules. In a constant stream, servers enter the in-door, scoot along a narrow pathway picking up plates, and emerge from the out-door, while the executive chef surveys it all, smilingly serene, in his baseball cap.

At Roy's, the pace is fast bordering on frenetic, and the amazing thing is that with all this volume and activity, what emerges from the kitchen is, for the most part, carefully crafted and delicious. Since most entrees can be ordered in appetizer portions for about half the price, you should sample as many dishes as possible. Try potstickers flavored with lobster and miso sauce ($5.95), or delicious ravioli of shiitake mushrooms and spinach served in a creamy sauce of sun-dried tomatoes and riccotta cheese ($6.95). Spring rolls ($5.50) are light and crispy; 'Hibachi salmon' ($8.25) is about as tender and moist as fish can be, and blackened ahi ($8.95) perfectly seasoned. Don't miss Roy's pizza ($5.95-$6.95), the crust both chewy and soft, though you'll be hard pressed to choose from options like grilled eggplant and tomato, roast duck, and grilled chicken.

For entrees, crispy Thai chicken is served with sticky rice, green beans, and almonds in a light spicy sauce, at $15.95 the least expensive entree. You'll sometimes find as many as seven varieties of fresh island fish ($23-$25) in memorable preparations, like baked fresh salmon served with a delicious balsamic and cabernet sauce, or fresh sesame crusted ono. Vegetarians have few options besides salad, however— not even a dairy-free pasta or pizza.

*imaginative Pacific Rim cuisine*

To keep prices reasonable, Roy's is organized for volume. The staff is highly trained and the tasks diversified: one waiter takes your order, another serves bread and water, and food is delivered by runners. This system works well for the most part but is not fool-proof, as some parts of our order arrived late, one never appeared at all, and sometimes dishes come so fast that there is no time to appreciate the presentation. The kitchen was out of five items by 8:30, and custom ordering, we were told, requires prior consent of the chef!

The first Roy's opened in 1988 on Oahu, and now has ten branches in Hawaii, Guam, Tokyo, and even Pebble Beach, California. All feature the same Pacific Rim cuisine, the same system, even the same wines, as Roy has arranged with some of California's finest vintners to bottle a 'Roy's' label. While one page of the menu contains selections generic to all Roy's, for example, another details the Kauai chef's creations.

*Dinner time! Geckos feast on insects trapped in tropical flowers. They also bring good luck, and very important, eat mosquitoes.*

If you were to imagine the finest in dining, you might envision your table as a peaceful island, where discrete waitpersons present each course unobtrusively, and the only sound you hear is the delicate tinkle of silverware and china. Well, not at Roy's! You won't find a quiet table in the house, and you are never alone, for the plan, in the words of our waiter, is to 'attack the table' with a barrage of attention — serving and clearing, offering fresh baked rolls or ice-water, sweeping away crumbs from the granite-topped table or just asking how you are enjoying your meal. It's interactive dining! You're part of the performance, and everyone on the staff seems to be enjoying the show. And this almost electric energy, as well the truly delicious food, makes Roy's a unique dining experience on Kauai.

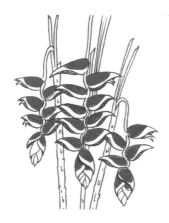

Poipu Shopping Village. 742-5000. Reserve well in advance. Nightly 5:30 pm - 9:30 pm. Non-smoking section. Credit cards. Map 3

## Shells

The main restaurant of the Sheraton Kauai Resort Hotel, Shells offers sweeping views of Poipu Beach and a spacious dining room with a relaxed ambiance. The room is lovely, with large comfortable tables, widely separated for privacy. Tall ceilings keeps temperatures cool, and entertainment by Hawaiian musicians makes dining very pleasant.

The emphasis is Pacific Rim, with a la carte entrees ranging from grilled vegetable pasta ($15) to rack of lamb ($25.95). Appetizers quickly increase your dinner cost, but you can visit the extensive salad bar for only $4.95 ($9.95 by itself). The open air setting, however, had attracted some unwelcome insects to the fruit! Dinners are of good quality but uneven. Rack of lamb is well-trimmed and tender, accompanied by garlic mashed potatoes and colorful vegetables, but our ahi was not cooked to order, and had to be sent back for revision, an unfortunately lengthy process ($22.50).

On the other hand, Shells has a spectacular ocean view and a special friendly feeling. Many of the servers (about 80% of the hotel's entire staff) have returned from the Sheraton staff of pre-Hurricane Iniki days and create an indefinable but unmistakable spirit of aloha. On certain nights, Shells's offers theme buffets, and families have a great deal– one '12 & under' dines free with each adult.

Sherator Kauai Resort, Poipu. Open daily, 7-11:30 am, 11:30-2 pm; 5:30-9:30 pm. 742-1661. Credit cards. Map 3

## Taqueria Nortenos

When you drive by the Kukui'ula Center in Poipu, you often see a jammed parking lot and a small cluster of people on the sidewalk. This congestion is due to Taqueria Nortenos, which serves some of the best, most sensibly priced Mexican food on Kauai.

You'll have to wait on the take-out line by the tiny kitchen, (For those in a rush, there's an 'express window') and while you're being driven crazy by the wonderful aromas, you can calculate the price of your selections.  The menu offers meat or vegetarian burritos, tacos, and tostadas at modest prices ($3-$4) with fillings and toppings priced separately ($.45 each).  You can skip the sour cream and not pay for it! Beans, rice, and sauce come free, and inexpensive extras like tomatoes or onions will be cooked right inside your burrito or taco.  Nachos are generous with cheese and plenty of everything, both fresh corn and flour chips.  Guacamole is chunky with avocados.  Your beef burrito will be filled with huge chunks of tender and tasty shredded beef, and covered with cheese, in a portion so large you will be hard pressed to clean your plastic plate ($6).  Spices are mild, with plenty of hot sauce available.

Poipu,  Kukui'ula shopping center.  11 am – 10 pm.  Closed Wednesdays 742-7222.  Map 3

## Tidepools, Hyatt Regency Hotel

Nestled at the bottom of the cliff in the center of the lovely Hyatt Regency Hotel, Tidepools combines an elegant ambiance with expertly prepared dinners, particularly fresh island fish.  To get to Tidepools, you walk down from the hotel lobby, a spectacular marble perch built into the cliff and overlooking the sea.  At the bottom, clustered near the edge of the hotel's wandering waterways, is the restaurant, a 'village' of connected Polynesian style huts.  The dining room is comfortable, spacious, and attractive.  Parquet tables with cloths of Hawaiian tapa design are well spaced for privacy (there's not a bad table in this restaurant). Candle lamps glow golden in the evening light, reflected in dark blue glassware.

Tidepools' cuisine features steak and seafood flavored with contemporary versions of Hawaiian recipes and local spices and ingredients.  On the appetizer menu, Kauai barbecued ribs are served with lilikoi glaze ($7.50), and vegetable lumpia, a Portuguese favorite, arrives with plum dipping sauce ($7.50).  Try seared spicy ahi served with three-lentil salad and papaya relish dressing ($9.75)—it's outstanding.  Entrees include meat, chicken, even Maine lobster ($36) and fresh island fish, which can be steamed, sauteed, grilled or even blackened.  Try Hawaiian opah (moon fish) or onaga, our favorite snapper ($26).  We like the unique flavor of the fish, and so usually order all sauces served on the side. Those who don't care for the finny set can choose from lamb, chicken, prime rib and steak, and vegetarians can choose an attractive array called 'vegetarian cupboard' ($18.50) or vegetable stir fry ($17.50) as well as salads.  Filet mignon ($27.50) is excellent, crisp on the outside, moist and

*Tidepools Restaurant, Hyatt Regency Resort Hotel*

tender inside. Children have a great menu — chicken nuggets ($7.50), grilled cheese ($5.50), fish, pasta, prime rib, or hot dog, with fries.

At Tidepools, portions are reasonably generous, presentation attractive, service polite and unhurried. Prices are high, but the hotel comes with the meal! Be sure to explore the lovely grounds, walk along the ocean and find one of the hammocks, lie back, listen to the sound of the waves, and look up into the bowl of stars.

Poipu, Hyatt Regency Hotel. Dinner nightly. Reserve a day in advance. 742-6260. Valet parking. Non-smoking area. Credit cards. Map 3

## Tomkats Grill

In a covered veranda at the rear of Koloa's historic Kawamoto Building, Tomkats offers informal, open-air dining at reasonable prices. About a dozen tables with cushioned rattan chairs cluster on the plank floor, and just beyond the railing is a small quiet garden, fringed with red ginger, and a small fishpond, where goldfish tuned in to 'Hawaiian time,' swim slowly enough to entrance the twelve-and-under set. Fly fans encourage breezes, and even in a sudden shower, this sheltered spot is peaceful, the rain beating a muffled tatoo on the tin roof.

Tomkats courts families, as the supply of high chairs and booster seats indicates, and features a special "kittens" menu with hamburger or grilled cheese ($3.00). The all-day menu offers a wide range of sand-

wiches, burgers, salads (from $6.50) and dinner entrees (from $8.50/rotisserie chicken). Sandwiches are carefully prepared, and attractively served in baskets piled high with french fries. The Turkey club on rye ($6.50), with avocado as an extra ($1.25) was first rate, as was the large Cobb Salad ($6.50). Portions are generous, service is friendly, and the hours make Tomkats a convenient stop after the beach, when some of your party may be hissing with hunger!

Central Koloa. 742-8887. 11 am -10 pm daily. Credit cards. Take-out available. A full bar is adjacent, though not intrusive. Map 3

## Espresso Kauai

**Eastern Shore:** At *Border's Espresso* (246-0862), you can sip tasty coffees, teas, or Chai tea freezes and discuss the latest books at what is fast becoming *the* spot on Kauai! Nearby in Lihue, *Island Java* (245-6503) serves the only non-fat lattes we found, as well as teas, ice cream and shakes, on an outdoor terrace with a view of Kalapaki Beach. You can try the other branch in downtown Kapa'a. In Wailua, *Papaya's Gourmet Food Market* (833-0190) near Safeway in Kauai Village Shopping Center combines coffees with vegetarian deli treats, salads, and sandwiches, on a self-serve patio.

**North Shore**: In the Princeville Shopping Center, try *Hale O' Java* (826-7255). In Hanalei, *Old Hanalei Coffee Company* (826-6717) serves delicious coffees and sandwiches, as does *Zelo's Beach House* (826-9700). *Postcards Cafe* (826-1191) features organic coffees. In Kilauea, sample coffees and pastries at *Kilauea Bakery* (828-2020), organic to the filter paper! At *Roadrunner Cafe* (828-8226), be sure to try taro buns or a coconut roll.

**South & Western Shore:** *Hanapepe Cafe & Espresso* (335-5011), main street in Hanapepe, has sensational coffees, vegetarian salads, sandwiches, pastas. Lunch daily, Dinner served on weekends in a pleasant setting. *Kalaheo Coffee Co. & Cafe* (332-5858), Kalaheo, serves coffees, pastries, breakfast & lunch, and sells whole bean and ground coffees. Westside, try *Waimea Coffee Cafe*.

*Sunflowers in Waimea fields*

# Westside Restaurants

*'favor...eats'*

In Hanapepe, **Hanapepe Cafe & Espresso** serves wonderful
vegetarian dishes, as well sandwiches and coffee drinks. Nearby, the
**Green Garden Restaurant** is a Kauai tradition for 'island style food'
reflecting the multi-ethnic heritage of the island—Chinese, Japanese,
Filipino, Portuguese, and American— and for lilikoi chiffon pie. After
lunch (or before) visit beautiful Salt Pond Beach Park, one of our favorite
family beaches. **Camp House Grill & Cantina** serves Mexican lunches
and dinners, as well as its signature hamburgers and real milk shakes. In
Eleele, visit **Toi's Thai Kitchen** for inexpensive, and delicious, Thai food.

Visiting Koke'e or the westside beaches? Stop in at **Wrangler's
Steakhouse** for excellent hamburgers, sandwiches, pizzas with homemade
crust, and a salad bar. Don't miss the fresh fruit 'frostee' at **Pualani's
Fruit Stand** on your way to (or from) Kekaha's lovely beaches.

## Camp House Grill & Cantina

You'll still see traces of the old Sinaloa Taqueria —walls painted like a technicolor Mexican jungle, with a leopard prowling through Mayan ruins, even a parrot flying across a painted ceiling. You'll still find the pumpkin colored bar, where you can watch sporting events on tv or, on a quiet day, the shadows slide silently across the tiled bar. Not much happens along Rt. 50 in Hanapepe, even when you're not looking!

Camp House Grill & Cantina merges the old Sinaloa's Mexican flair with the tried and true, homestyle burger and fries menu that has made the original Camp House so successful in Kalaheo. Try a first-rate fresh fish sandwich ($5.95), both cleanly grilled and very tasty (add a side of grilled pineapple!), or fresh fish tacos ($3.95). Camp House hamburgers (from $3.95 for 1/3 pound) are also delicious. Prices are reasonable, with dinners between $10.95 and $13.95, and a 'bottomless cup' of soda, lemonade, or iced tea only $1.50. Ten-and-unders can eat for $3.95, and the giant milk shake ($3) which we had ordered to share arrived in two glasses. Everyone seems eager to please, and the dining experience is pleasant.

Hanapepe, Rt. 50.  335-5656.  Credit Cards.  11 am - 4 pm and 5 pm - 9 pm daily.  Map 4

## The Green Garden

There has been a Green Garden Restaurant for about as long as Kauai has been called the Garden Island. Owned and operated by the same family since 1948, its reputation is based on generous portions and inexpensive prices, and the menu features American, Japanese, and Chinese dinners, many priced around $5. Even at lunch, meals include several courses as well as a beverage. Service is fast and very friendly in a large dining room, filled with plants and flowers. Aloha is in the air!

You certainly get full value for your money. Where else could you find a hamburger platter with fries, a salad, dessert, and iced tea for under $4? At $5.50, fresh fish or shrimp tempura is another bargain. Club sandwiches cost about $4, and grilled cheese for kids is only $1.95. It may not win culinary awards, but remember: this price includes salad, lots of fries and a drink! Occasionally, a salad bar offers an assortment of fruits, vegetables, and great dressings for the amazing price of $5 at lunch and $7 at dinner. (To be sure it's 'on,' call ahead and ask!). Combine it with soup, priced in three sizes; a 'medium' ($2.80) is actually large!

The Green Garden's pies would stand out at any price, and we recommend them all— chocolate cream pie is a child's favorite treat, and coconut cream pie has a light flaky crust filled with marvelously light egg custard topped with toasted coconut. Lilikoi chiffon pie, for which Green Garden is justly famous, has a light texture and a taste of passion fruit that will arouse your taste buds.

With dinner prices about $1 higher than at lunch, The Green Garden is ideal for large families on small budgets, or anyone who wants a square meal and a fair deal.

Hanapepe, on Rt. 50. Reservations suggested for dinner. 335-5422. 9 am - 2 pm and 5 pm - 9 pm. (Opens 8 am Saturdays and 7:30 am Sundays). Closed Tuesdays. Credit cards. Map 4

## Hanapepe Cafe & Espresso

The sign to Hanapepe announces 'Kauai's Biggest Little Town,' and Hanapepe Cafe & Espresso is a major attraction for its vegetarian cuisine with an island flair. You'll find scones flavored with passion fruit, as well as a changing menu reflecting what's up with the chef and what's fresh at the local farmer's market. In the tiny restaurant, which has only a half-dozen tables, paintings by local artists brighten the clean white walls with color, and leafy plants, along with fresh flowers on white formica tables, provide the green and growing look. Dominating the dining area is the

gleaming tiled counter, a remake of the 1940's curved lunch counter of the Igawa Drugstore, and now the home of Larry's espresso bar.

You don' have to be a vegetarian to enjoy this menu. A garden burger made from oats, carrots, cottage and mozzarella cheese is served on a cracked wheat roll with bright red local tomatoes, lettuce and a tasty spinach spread. Accompanied by an excellent potato salad, it's well priced at $6.75. Vegetable fritatta ($7.75) is stuffed with red and green peppers, zucchini, squash, mushrooms, mozzarella and topped with local tomatoes. Pasta of the day ($6.75) features fresh local vegetables with a light, delicious creamy tomato sauce. 'Healthnut' sandwich ($5.25) was spread with homemade humus and served open faced so that we could assemble it ourselves, selecting just the right proportion of tomatoes, lettuce, sunflower sprouts, cucumbers and onions. Dinner is served only certain nights during the week, and they can vary, so call ahead. The dining room turns Cinderella-like into a lovely black and white cafe, with soft lighting and  music. Entrees from $16.75 (vegan lasagne or pasta with fresh mushrooms and tomatoes) to $18.50 (Eggplant parmesan), as well as salads, soups and appetizers ($5-$10).

While your meal is being cooked, browse 'Uncle Eddie's' selection of hand-crafted angels, dressed in the latest Kauai shells and fashions.  In one of the more interesting touches for a Ladies Room, we found a plant growing in a fixture usually reserved for men! Afterwards, you can stroll the main street—it won't take you very long. You can try out the swinging bridge and sample some taro chips made at the Taro-Ka 'factory,' just around the corner. You'll love those chips!

Hanapepe, 3830 Hanapepe Road. 335-5011. Breakfast/Lunch: 8 am - 2 pm Tues. - Sat. Dinner (call). Smoke-free. Credit cards. Map 4

## Toi's Thai Kitchen

You can't get more underground that Toi's Thai Kitchen! It's original home was a carport semi-attached to a bar called 'Traveler's Den' in sleepy Kekaha, with a half dozen formica dinette sets, some with card table chairs.  Now you'll find Toi's in a shopping center in almost-as-sleepy Eleele, or you'll try to find it, huddled under the arm of Big Save. Painted cinderblock walls are decorated by white lace curtains and plants, while fresh anthuriums brighten up the dozen formica tables. What comes out of the kitchen is much more special! Toi's has developed a loyal clientele who have spread the word, attracting newcomers who can't believe their eyes when they arrive—and are smiling when they leave.

We came in for lunch one afternoon, hungry and sandy from the beach. We loved Toi's saimin with its Thai accent—fresh white flat noodles float in a gently spiced broth colorful with vegetables, several varieties of bean sprouts ($5.95 for vegetarian) and because the fishermen had been lucky, fresh and delicious ono ($7.95)  Rich and flavorful tofu soup ($7.95) was also terrific.  The rest of the group ordered crispy spring rolls served with fresh lettuce, mint leaves, and a zesty peanut sauce ($6.95). The hot yellow curry pleased Jeremy, our spice enthusiast. Everyone loved Thai fried rice ($7.95), so colorful and tasty that it was devoured to the last grain. Those who prefer American food can try hot, crisp french fries ($1.50/$3), sandwiches, or burgers (about $5).

Dinners include green papaya salad, dessert, and brown, jasmine, or sticky rice. Try Pad Thai ($7.95), the tender chicken and fresh Thai noodles sweetened with coconut milk and fresh basil. Fresh eggplant sauteed with tofu and huge fresh mushrooms offers a marvelous contrast, both pungent and spicy ($7.95). Be sure to try Toi's Temptation, a sweet curry made with your choice of chicken, beef, pork, or fish simmered in coconut milk and flavored with lemon grass, lemon and basil leaves, and served with either potatoes or pineapples.

With prices so reasonable and food quality first rate, Toi's Thai Kitchen makes great family fun!

Eleele Shopping Center, Rt. 50. 335-3111. Lunch 10:30-2:30 pm. Dinner 5:30-9:30 pm daily. Closed Tuesdays & Sunday for lunch.

## Waimea Brew Pub

Waimea Brew Pub serves a modest lunch and dinner menu in the living room and on the porch of a restored planation house in Waimea. You can order sandwiches, burgers (a third pounder for $6.75) at lunch, or steak ($16.95), fish ($15.95) and chicken ($13.95). Try saimin ($5.95) flavored with curry, and garnished with a chicken brochette. The fresh

fish on the sandwich seemed a bit small for the bun, though attractively served in a basket with fries and spicy peanut cole slaw. Children can choose a hot dog, PBJ or grilled cheese for $3.50. As for home brew, four beers are typically on tap, two ales, a porter, a stout, and a wheat .

The comfortable old planation house has wonderful wide verandas which would make an elegant dining setting (as once they did, in the days before Iniki). The present restaurant occupies only a small part of the house, however, and shares that part with the bar, which is a smoking area. Dining on the patio outside can be quite pleasant, but at mid-day, the awnings provide only partial shade.

Just west of Waimea Town, 9400 Kaumuali`i Hwy. 11 am-9 pm daily. 338-9733 www.wbcbrew.com

## Wrangler's Steakhouse

Wranglers' dining room retains the outlines of its historic building, where you expect to see Matt Dillon stroll in at any moment. Ceilings are open to the rafters, fly fans keep the air moving, large windows bring in light. Tables are roomy and well separated, arranged on two levels for quiet and privacy, and there's a veranda for open air dining. The decor retains its plantation flavor— saddles and tools from the Hawaiian cowboys, the paniolos. On the lower level, you can order calzones and wraps ($4-$5), and home-baked pizza with light, crispy crust and wonderful sauce (from $9).

With most lunches, Wrangler's now offers a salad bar, with a variety of fresh greens, tasty pasta salad, and even home made chips and salsa. (Soup and salad bar alone: $7.95) The menu offers 'Mexican Lunches' and plate lunches featuring local specialties like fresh island fish or the chef's 'cook-off' winning Portuguese Bean soup. The 'Wrangler Burger' is one of the best on Kauai, a juicy half-pounder on a sesame seed roll, with lettuce and tomato, served with lots of fresh, crispy, piping hot steak fries — the real thing ($7.95). The fresh fish sandwich—ours came with ono—is also first rate. Dinner prices are equally reasonable.

Service is very friendly, and those too restless to sit while food is prepared can explore Wrangler's shop, which features lovely items from local artists, including Hawaiian quilts, dolls, and stuffed animals. Deborah Tuzon of Waimea weaves placemats and jewelry of lauhala, and Caz, on the staff, creates wonderful sunflower barrettes and headbands of colorful woven plaid paniolo cloth. You can also find local 'Black Mountain' coffee grown by Dennis Okihara. If you're on your way to Koke'e or to Polihale, you'd be hard pressed to find a better spot than Wranglers. Waimea is a historic town. Right across the street from Wrangler's is the Waimea Hawaiian Church, circa 1820, where Hawaiian language service is held at 8:30 am.

Downtown Waimea, on Rt. 50. 10:30 am - 9 pm daily. 328-1218 Closed Sundays. Credit cards. Non-smoking section. Map 4

# Index

# Kauai Underground Guide 'Campaign for Kids'

A portion of the sales price of each book benefits these outstanding non-profit agencies helping Kauai's children:

* **The YWCA Family Violence Shelter** needs money for books, toys, clothes, writing materials and art supplies, paper and paint, puzzles and learning games. "We have almost no money in our regular budget for the special needs of individual children. That's why Lenore's project is so important." —Director, Nancy Peterson.    3904 Elua St., Lihue HI 96766

* **Friends of the Children's Advocacy Center** helps young victims of abuse and neglect. "Sometimes it's money for summer camp to get a child out of an abusive situation; sometimes it's books, or school supplies. Such small things, though they seem trivial, can have a huge impact on a child's life." —Director, Sara Silverman. 4473 Pahee St.-M. Lihue HI 96766

* **Hale 'Opio** (808-245-2873) helps children referred by the Family Court. "We need help for after- school tutoring, and special learning programs in art, Hawaiian culture, and photography. Our kids thrive when they can learn!" —Director, Mary Lou Barela. 2959 Umi St., Lihue HI 96766

* **Kauai Baby Book Club** (808-246-4570) provides literacy packages including children's books, to each child born on Kauai. Also supported by the Kauai Borders Books, the program tries to 'encourage a lifelong commitment to reading, particularly in families with young parents.'— Director, Mary Daubert.      P.O. Box 772, Kalaheo HI 96714

* **Ambassadors of Aloha** provides scholarship aid for children gifted in the arts. 'Our children need our help to develop their special talents, and to be able to benefit from opportunities beyond the island.' —Founder, Mayor Maryanne Kusaka.      PO Box 1127, Lihue HI 96766

Tax-deductible contributions can be sent directly to these fine agencies.

*www.explorekauai.com*

## Order Form

| Name |
| --- |
| Address |
| City           State           zip code |
| e-mail address |

$12.95 includes a CD of beautiful Hawaiian music by Keali'i Reichel. A portion of the proceeds will be donated to the organizations helping Kauai's children, listed at left.

_____ Number of copies @ $12.95

_____ Shipping ($1.50/bookrate or $3/priority) free with orders of 2 or more copies

_____ Total enclosed by check or money order

**Papaloa Press**
362 Selby Lane
Atherton CA 94027
(650) 369-9994
(650) 364-3252 FAX
papaloa@pacbell.net

*Mahalo!*

*Lenore*

*Keep Up-to-Date on Kauai! For the latest updates, visit our web site*

**www.explorekauai.com**

# Papaloa Press &
# Punahele Productions

present

# KEALI'I
# REICHEL

*Hawaii's foremost entertainer*

An exclusive Kauai Underground Guide
CD Sampler of songs from his hit albums!

## MELELANA
*Keali'i's brand new hit album!*

## KAWAIPUNAHELE
*The top selling album of Hawaiian music!*

## E Ō MAI
*Keali'i's acclaimed
3rd album*

## LEI HALI'A
*Keali'i's 1995
award-winning album*

Hoku Award Winner
> Best New Artist, Best Album of the Year,
> Best Male Vocalist, Most Popular Hawaiian Artist,
> Favorite Entertainer of the Year

To order these albums contact Tropicaldisc.com 888-220-5757

*www.worldsound.com/keali*